Arms Control and National Security

An Introduction

Published by the Arms Control Association

Washington, D.C.

The Arms Control Association

The Arms Control Association is a nonpartisan national membership organization dedicated to promoting public understanding of effective policies and programs in arms control and disarmament. The Association's staff and board of directors include a number of former senior policy makers and negotiators. Drawing on this expertise, the Association analyzes arms control proposals, negotiations, and agreements. Through its press and publication programs and its monthly journal, *Arms Control Today*, the Association provides the media, the Congress, and the interested public with authoritative information on issues of current interest.

The Association's publications are designed to serve as resources for the debate over the value of specific arms control agreements. These publications highlight the vital contribution arms control agreements make to our security. The Association hopes they enable citizens to participate more effectively in this critical area of public policy.

Copyright © 1989 The Arms Control Association

Library of Congress Cataloging-in-Publication Data

Arms control and national security.

    Bibliography.
    Includes index.
    1. Nuclear arms control—History. 2. Security,
International—History. 3. United States—Foreign
relations—Soviet Union. 4. Soviet Union—Foreign
relations—United States. I. Arms Control Association
(Washington, D.C.)
JX1974.7.A6726   1989   327.1'74'09   89-83835
ISBN 0-934766-02-9

Contents

Part I: The Goals and History of Arms Control

Part II: The Arms Control Agenda

Appendices

Preface

The Arms Control Association became increasingly aware in recent years of the need for a comprehensive survey of the role of arms control in US security. The existing literature tended to be either too general or too specialized for the reader seeking a concise but serious summary of specific arms control goals, proposals, and issues. To fill this gap, the Arms Control Association has prepared *Arms Control and National Security: An Introduction*. This book offers the student and concerned citizen an overview of the current arms control scene and the more knowledgeable practitioner a convenient reference for specific arms control topics.

The Arms Control Association is uniquely qualified for this ambitious task. The Association's senior staff members have been involved in policy or negotiating roles in essentially every arms control agreement since President Eisenhower initiated negotiations on the Comprehensive Test Ban in 1958. The staff follows all current arms control negotiations and policy debates on a day by day basis as part of its program to support the media and the Association's monthly journal, *Arms Control Today*. The Association has also been deeply involved in the efforts to preserve the ABM Treaty and the SALT II Treaty and to support the INF Treaty and progress toward a START agreement. In these endeavors, the Association draws on the expertise of its Chairman, Ambassador Gerard C. Smith, and its distinguished Board of Directors, which includes several individuals who played central roles in past arms control negotiations.

Arms Control and National Security covers events up to the beginning of the Bush administration. The book sets the stage for the policy debates and decisions President Bush will have to face in the coming years. The remarkable improvement in US-Soviet relations promises to make the next few years a period of great opportunity for substantial progress in nearly every area of arms control. Agreements for deep reductions in the strategic nuclear arsenals of the superpowers and for massive reductions in the conventional forces deployed in Europe now appear within the grasp of the Bush administration. The outcome, however, is by no means certain and will be influenced by past positions and policies.

Part I of this book provides a conceptual and historical overview of arms control and its role in US national security policy. Part II is devoted to current topics on the arms control agenda, including the major negotiations on strategic offensive and defensive weapons, nuclear testing, nuclear proliferation, and other military threats posed by conventional, chemical, and biological weapons. Special topics such as the verification of arms control agreements and the compliance record with existing agreements are also covered. If read as a whole, the book will provide a thorough introduction to the study of arms control. Each of the chapters also stands alone and allows the reader to use the book as a continuing basic reference on subjects of particular interest.

The book represents a group effort by the Association's entire staff. The preparation of the text drew on the combined expertise and efforts of Deputy Director Jack Mendelsohn, Assistant Director James P. Rubin, Senior Analysts Matthew Bunn, Michèle Flournoy, and Jesse James, Research Analyst Thomas Halverson, and a number of talented junior analysts and research interns. Associate Director Robert Travis Scott, with the assistance of Robert Guldin, Cathie Lorenz, and Richard Tisinger, did the final editing and layout and assembled the graphics for the book.

Arms Control and National Security was made possible by grants from the following organizations: Patrick and Anna M. Cudahy Fund; The William and Mary Greve Foundation; The George Gund Foundation; The John D. and Catherine T. MacArthur Foundation; The Prospect Hill Foundation; Public Welfare Foundation; The Florence and John Schumann Foundation; and The Town Creek Foundation. The Association greatly appreciates their generous support.

Since its creation in 1971, the Arms Control Association has been dedicated to public education on arms control. In order to ensure progress in this critical area of US security, public support has been and will continue to be an important factor. It is the purpose of this book to provide the necessary factual background to the public, whose support is most effective when it is well-informed and conscious of the lessons of the past.

Spurgeon M. Keeny, Jr.
President and Executive Director

PART I:

The Goals and History of Arms Control

Viktor Karpov and Max Kampelman, heads of the Soviet and US delegations during the Reagan administration, shake hands as they begin the Nuclear and Space Arms Talks in Geneva.

1

The Goals of Arms Control

On August 6, 1945, a single atomic bomb reduced the Japanese city of Hiroshima to smoldering rubble. It is estimated that over 100,000 Japanese were killed by the bomb and tens of thousands more injured. On August 14, 1945, five days after a second atomic bomb destroyed the city of Nagasaki, Japan surrendered and brought World War II to an end. With this grim forewarning of what the future might hold, the nuclear age began.

Today, the nuclear arsenals of the United States and the Soviet Union hold some 50,000 nuclear weapons. Most of these weapons have greater explosive power than the atomic bomb that destroyed Hiroshima, and many have explosive power 100 times as great. The use of even a fraction of these weapons in a nuclear war between the United States and the Soviet Union would result in hundreds of millions of deaths and would destroy both countries and their allies as functioning societies. An all-out nuclear exchange would be a catastrophe unprecedented in human history and would have worldwide consequences of unpredictable magnitude. Against this back-

Soviet General Secretary Mikhail Gorbachev and former President Reagan sign the INF Treaty in December 1987.

ground, former President Ronald Reagan and Soviet leader Mikhail Gorbachev agreed, at Geneva in 1985 at their first summit meeting, that "a nuclear war cannot be won and must never be fought." (See Effects of Nuclear Weapons, page 8.)

The history of the nuclear age has been dominated by the adversarial relationship between the United States and the Soviet Union. Divided by deep political differences and ingrained mutual distrust, the two nuclear superpowers have sought to assure their own security through the strength of their own nuclear forces. The resulting perceived need to match or surpass the forces of the other side and to exploit the potential of rapidly evolving new technologies has led to a persistent quantitative and qualitative buildup of nuclear forces over the past 40 years.

The United States and the Soviet Union have each sought to deter the other from attacking through their own ability to destroy the attacker in retaliation. At great expense, both sides have structured their strategic forces to assure their ability to retaliate with devastating force even after a massive surprise attack. These strategic forces have created a state of "mutual deter-

rence," which is widely credited with having maintained an uneasy peace between the superpowers since World War II. Mutual deterrence is based on the grim fact of life in the nuclear age that the United States and the Soviet Union find themselves in a position of "mutual assured destruction." Early critics of strategic deterrence were quick to label this strategic relationship with the acronym "MAD," but so far no one has produced a credible alternative.

In 1983 President Reagan called on the US scientific community to provide a technical solution to the threat of nuclear weapons in the form of an impregnable shield that would make nuclear weapons "impotent and obsolete." Such a shield would permit the transition from an offensive to a defensive strategy. However, after five years of research in the Strategic Defense Initiative, few knowledgeable scientists or responsible officials believe such a defense can be achieved against a determined and sophisticated adversary. The Reagan administration ended with its strategic policy still firmly based on mutual deterrence.

With the acceptance of mutual deterrence and the relaxation of US-Soviet tensions, the chance of nuclear war today is probably very small. The consequences of nuclear war are so catastrophic, however, that even a remote chance of such a conflict when viewed over an extended period of time is a matter of gravest concern.

Paths to Nuclear War

In seeking ways to reduce the risk of nuclear war, it is important to examine how a nuclear war might actually begin. Although the risk of any single path to nuclear war is probably very small today, collectively the risk from all paths over an extended period could be significant. Arms control agreements as well as unilateral actions can help reduce the possibility that any of these paths will ever be followed.

An all-out surprise attack during a period of low tension was once a major concern in US strategic thinking. To be successful, such a "bolt from the blue" attack would have to inflict a high level of damage on enemy strategic forces in a "disarming strike" that would prevent retaliation and force capitulation. The large numbers of survivable US and Soviet strategic forces, capable of retaliating after absorbing a surprise attack, make such a "bolt from the blue" attack appear extremely unlikely.

Escalation of a major US-Soviet political or military crisis presents a more credible path to nuclear war. In a state of extreme tension either side might conclude that nuclear war was inevitable and that getting in the first nuclear blow, a "preemptive strike," would be far better than receiving it, since the retaliatory response would be substantially blunted. This conclusion would be most credible if either side believed that a major portion of its own nuclear forces were vulnerable to attack and that the other side's forces were also seriously vulnerable to attack. In this situation, the choice might appear to be either to use nuclear forces first to possible advantage or lose them to the other side's anticipated attack.

A more likely path to nuclear war lies in a confrontation between the superpowers or their allies that leads to military combat with conventional weapons. If not promptly contained, such a conflict could rapidly "escalate" to the use of nuclear weapons if either side believed this was necessary to avoid defeat. Although at present all parties appear extremely anxious to avoid such perilous confrontations, one can imagine dangerous developments, such as massive uprisings in Eastern Europe, in which the outcome cannot be confidently predicted. Current US military doctrine calls for the "first use" of nuclear weapons in the European theater if a Soviet conventional attack cannot be contained by conventional means. Most observers believe that even the limited use of nuclear weapons in a direct confrontation between the United States and the Soviet Union would probably escalate into a general nuclear war because there would be strong pressures on both sides to preempt with a disarming strategic strike as soon as nuclear weapons were used on the battlefield.

Nuclear war could result from the accidental or unauthorized use of nuclear weapons. Despite extensive technical efforts to prevent such a dreadful mistake, operational failures or faulty intelligence—from computer or human errors—could conceivably lead one superpower to conclude it was under nuclear attack and cause it to launch its own nuclear forces. Despite elaborate procedures to maintain control of nuclear weapons at the top of government, unauthorized use might still occur. This would be a particular danger in time of extreme crisis or during a conventional battle, where military field commanders might be delegated the independent capability to launch nuclear weapons. Through a misunderstanding or in the heat of battle, local commanders might fire their weapons without an order from central authorities.

The "proliferation" of nuclear weapons to additional states adds another path to nuclear war arising from regional conflicts beyond the control of the superpowers. With nuclear capabilities, Third World countries might use nuclear weapons to destroy adversaries or to stave off defeat in a conventional conflict. In either case, such a conflict could escalate to involve the superpowers if their basic interests appeared threatened.

A so-called "catalytic" nuclear war might conceivably result from the actions of third parties. One superpower might mistake a small attack by a third country, or even a single weapon detonated in a major city by a terrorist group, for an attack by the other superpower. In a time of high tension between the superpowers, such an attack might conceivably unleash a series of actions leading to general nuclear war.

The likelihood is very small that mankind will follow any of the many variants of these paths to its own destruction, but the collective risk represented by these paths represents the greatest threat to the future of humanity. The reduction of this risk to the lowest possible level is a goal shared by the nuclear superpowers, their allies, and the world at large.

The Effects of Nuclear Weapons

Nuclear weapons have totally changed the nature of war. The bomb that destroyed Hiroshima was 10,000 times as powerful as a "conventional" high-explosive weapon of the same size. Yet some of today's thermonuclear weapons pack as much as a thousand times the explosive power of the Hiroshima bomb. Man has learned to unleash the power that fuels the stars and to destroy a city with a single weapon.

The energy of a nuclear bomb is released in a tiny fraction of a second in the form of high energy particles (neutrons and fission fragments) and radiation (X-rays). A fireball of superheated air is created, expanding faster than the speed of sound, enveloping the surrounding area in fire and crushing objects with a powerful blast wave. The blast wave from a one-megaton weapon (that is, one with the explosive power of a million tons of TNT) would smash ordinary brick buildings nearly five miles away from the detonation. At that distance, winds of over a hundred miles an hour would surge through the debris, turning much of it into lethal flying shrapnel.

The thermal radiation from a one-megaton bomb would start mass fires in an area of over a hundred square miles. On a clear day, exposed skin would be severely burned at a distance of eight miles. In a city, the thousands of fires sparked by the initial flash could coalesce into a gigantic "firestorm," burning for hours and incinerating everything within its perimeter. Such a firestorm obliterated much of Hiroshima. For those within the firestorm, the chances of survival would be slight even within well-constructed shelters. The fires would create clouds of toxic fumes and consume much of the available oxygen, general temperature levels could rise well above boiling, and hurricane-force winds sweeping inward toward the fire would prevent escape.

A nuclear detonation also creates deadly prompt radiation in the form of X-rays and neutrons. For large-yield weapons, this radiation would not be a major source of fatalities because lethal thermal and blast effects would extend farther out from the point of detonation than lethal prompt radiation. The most serious radiation effects would come later from the radioactive "fallout" from bombs detonated on or near the ground.

A one-megaton blast at ground level would raise as much as a million tons of dust and debris, creating an enormous radioactive cloud. During the next few hours and days, this radioactive material would fall slowly back to the earth, possibly in a thick black rain. This deadly "fallout" would contaminate thousands of square miles downwind from the blast with lethal levels of radiation. Although the radiation would decay over time, radiation levels would remain lethal for weeks, preventing those in shelters from coming out for food and water. The area could not be safely reoccupied for many months, and significant radioactivity would remain for many years. An air-burst weapon would also produce delayed radioactivity, but in this case more of it would travel into the upper regions of the atmosphere and slowly fall to earth worldwide over a period of weeks and years, producing lower levels of long-lived radioactivity.

Depending on the dose, the effects of radiation can range from dizziness to death. Moderate doses

of radiation impair the immune system, creating a condition similar to AIDS and leaving the victim vulnerable to diseases that would be uncontrolled after an attack. Severe doses of radiation lead to massive, irreversible cell damage and death. Over the long term, the unseen damage that radiation causes to genetic material can drastically increase the risk of cancer and birth defects. These hidden genetic effects would be present for generations.

The levels of radioactivity from individual fallout patterns are additive. Consequently, in a general nuclear war, involving thousands of weapons, a large fraction of the United States, the Soviet Union, and their allies and neighbors would be covered with lethal levels of radioactivity. With most of the country devastated or highly radioactive, there would be nowhere for survivors to go for help.

The use of even a small fraction of the thousands of weapons held by the two super-powers today could leave most of the cities of the northern hemisphere ravaged by blast and fire. The devastation of the fragile network of society would add further to the disaster and suffering. Most medical facilities would be destroyed, as would the fuel supplies necessary to keep transportation moving and people supplied with food. Not only would medical attention be unavailable but survivors would likely face widespread epidemics and famine as secondary effects.

There are many other secondary effects that are still not well understood. In recent years, studies have indicated that a large-scale nuclear war that burned most urban areas might also lead to a catastrophic "nuclear winter," with severe, but largely unpredictable, effects on the ecology of the entire globe. Similarly, a major nuclear war might destroy the ozone layer that protects life from ultraviolet radiation. The likelihood and severity of these secondary effects are still highly uncertain. The fact that these effects have only recently been recognized suggests that there may well be other very serious effects of a large-scale nuclear war that have not yet been identified.

But what is known with certainty is enough: one nuclear weapon can destroy a city, and each of the superpowers possesses some 25,000 nuclear weapons, of which roughly half are capable of striking the territory of the other superpower. An all-out war involving these weapons would clearly be "the greatest catastrophe in history by many orders of magnitude," in the words of General David Jones, former chairman of the Joint Chiefs of Staff.

Hiroshima destruction.

9

Arms Control

Arms control seeks to reduce the risk of war by limiting or reducing the threat from potential adversaries rather than relying solely on unilateral military responses to perceived or anticipated changes in the military threat. Arms control is not in conflict with, or a substitute for, military preparedness, but seeks to complement it by providing increased security at lower and less dangerous levels.

Ideally, one might hope to eliminate the threat of nuclear war by agreeing to ban nuclear weapons entirely. The ultimate goal of a nuclear-free world has had much support since the end of World War II. Most recently, Reagan and Gorbachev independently proclaimed this goal, which had been advocated 25 years earlier by President John Kennedy and General Secretary Nikita Khrushchev.

In a nuclear-disarmed world, however, even a small number of illegal nuclear weapons could provide an enormous military advantage. Confirming that all nuclear weapons have been dismantled and no new ones fabricated would appear to be a nearly impossible task. Consequently, so long as nations continue to have deep-seated differences, to entertain territorial ambitions, and to seek military advantage over their adversaries, complete nuclear disarmament will remain a distant goal. Until there have been fundamental changes in international relations, the best that can be done is to reduce to the lowest possible level the chances that nuclear weapons will ever be used.

The concept of arms control today encompasses a wide range of existing agreements and concrete proposals designed to constrain and manage the nuclear and general military confrontation. Through such agreements, nations can pursue a number of important goals that improve their security interests without waiting to resolve the ultimate question of whether, or on what time schedule, nuclear weapons will be eliminated. These immediate goals include: increased stability and predictability in the overall military relationship by limitations and reductions in the level of nuclear confrontation; enhanced military stability in times of crisis; prevention of the spread of nuclear weapons to additional nations; improvement in the political environment; decreases in the potential consequences of nuclear war; and reductions in the cost of military preparedness.

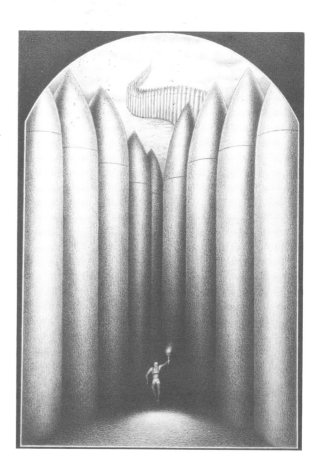

Military Stability and Predictability

Limiting and reducing the level of the nuclear confrontation between the superpowers is a central goal of arms control. Such quantitative constraints lower the risks of nuclear war by stabilizing the military relationship and greatly improving the predictability of the future threat. The experience of the past 40 years has demonstrated that the nuclear military competition in itself contributes significantly to the political tension between the two sides.

In the absence of arms control agreements, the United States and Soviet Union have both built weapons in part to maintain what they perceive to be a favorable military balance with their principal adversary. Whenever an increase in threatening Soviet weapons has been observed, military and political pressures for an increase in US weapons have inevitably grown. The same dynamic has operated within the Soviet Union. This "action-reaction" cycle has been a major factor in the continuing arms race.

Uncertainties about the future also stimulate the cycle of action and reaction. Because new weapons take many years to build, each side must plan not only against today's threat but against tomorrow's as well. Given the mistrust of the other side's intentions, each superpower has tended to assume the worst about the military capabilities and future plans of the other side. Such "worst-case analyses" create pressure to build ever larger or more sophisticated military forces, contributing to the arms competition.

Arms control can greatly reduce these real and imagined pressures to build new forces. When both sides agree to limit or reduce specific military forces in a verifiable manner, the predictability of the military relationship can be dramatically improved. Agreements can constrain the evolving threat each side must plan its military forces to meet. Improved predictability contributes directly to the longer term stability of the military relationship since both sides can have greater confidence that there will not be sudden military developments that will drastically undermine their security. As a result, pressures to build up new forces can be significantly decreased.

Past agreements have done a great deal to improve the predictability of the US-Soviet relationship. The Antiballistic Missile (ABM) Treaty of 1972, which effectively limits the testing and development of ballistic missile defenses, has so far prevented the deployment of nationwide ballistic missile defensive systems. Because of the adversarial nature of the US-Soviet relationship, such defensive systems would not only stimulate an arms race in space-based weapons, but would also increase pressures to deploy more and better offensive systems to overcome these defenses. Agreements through the Strategic Arms Limitation Talks, known as SALT I and SALT II, limited the number of missile launchers each side could build. Rather than having to project the largest number of missiles the other country could build in 10 years, the military could plan on the basis of the limits set in the agreement, thereby decreasing the requirement for future forces.

The Strategic Arms Reduction Talks (START) treaty which is now being negotiated would take this process a step further and create agreed ceilings at a significantly reduced level. This agreement would commit the sides to a verifiable program of phased reductions and reverse the strategic nuclear buildup that has dominated the US-Soviet strategic relationship since World War II. The agreed reductions would not only decrease the perceived threat but would improve the predictability of the resulting relationship.

The complete elimination of specific categories of nuclear activities is a particularly effective way of enhancing the predictability of future developments and creating greater arms race stability. Such bans increase the ability of the parties to foresee the evolution of an adversary's forces in a more restricted context and greatly reduce pressures to pursue matching or reactive military programs. The Intermediate-range Nuclear Forces (INF) Treaty, for example, has eliminated the entire class of intermediate-range missiles which were perceived as being particularly threatening by both the Soviet Union and the NATO allies of the United States.

In sum, the more confidence the major powers have that their adversaries are not seeking to develop new quantitative or qualitative military threats, the less pressure there will be to maintain or increase the pace of military competition. If pursued prudently with due concern for national security interests, such a stable military environment encourages the reduction of political tensions that might otherwise increase the possibility of military confrontations and the risk of war.

Crisis Stability

Reducing the risk of nuclear war in a crisis or military confrontation involving the superpowers is a central objective of arms control, as it is also of unilateral national security policy. A nuclear war could result from a major crisis or military conflict involving the two superpowers. Such a confrontation might begin as a conventional war in Europe or Asia or as a war between allies of the two superpowers in the Third World. There is general agreement that this scenario is far more likely than a calculated surprise or "bolt from the blue" attack that once preoccupied many military strategists.

The world has come closest to the brink in those rare cases when crises between the superpowers have led to direct confrontation, as in the Cuban missile crisis of 1962. (See Chapter 2.) So far, political leaders on both sides have recognized that a nuclear conflict is totally unacceptable and have drawn back from the brink. Nevertheless, a future crisis that might somehow lead to the direct engagement of US and Soviet conventional military forces would pose the terrible risk that the fighting would escalate to nuclear war.

The less incentive each side has to launch a nuclear strike in such a crisis, the less likely it will be that large-scale nuclear war will break out. Real or perceived vulnerability of nuclear forces might create such an incentive to strike. In a severe crisis, in which political leaders concluded that nuclear war was very likely, there could be tremendous pressure to launch a nuclear "first strike" if political leaders thought the damage to their own country would be reduced by attacking and destroying as much as possible of the other side's forces before they could be launched. The pressures would be greatest, and the danger of nuclear war worst, if both sides' nuclear forces were vulnerable to attack. Then each side might believe it was threatened by an imminent preemptive attack by the other side and hope that its own preemptive attack would be successful. In this case, it might decide to strike first before its own weapons were destroyed, in the hope of preventing, or at least blunting, the other side's retaliation. In the tension of such a crisis, even if it were recognized that both sides would probably be destroyed as viable societies, firing first may seem preferable to firing second or not at all. In short, the pressure to "use them or lose them" would create a hair-trigger situation.

Fortunately, a substantial fraction of the nuclear forces of both superpowers are essentially invulnerable to attack. The leaders of both sides know that, even if an attack could destroy a large number of the other side's forces in a first blow, the surviving forces could carry out a devastating retaliation. The inability to escape this state of mutual deterrence minimizes any rational incentive to preempt in a crisis. If mutual deterrence persists even in crises, the strategic relationship is referred to as "stable." Anything that undermines mutual deterrence is referred to as "destabilizing."

To improve crisis stability, the superpowers can agree to reduce reliance on particularly dangerous weapons, such as those that are both vulnerable to attack and capable of attacking other missiles. Land-based missiles in fixed silos, for example, are becoming increasingly vulnerable to attack as missile accuracy improves, and those armed with multiple warheads (so-

Treaty Negotiation and Ratification

Arms control treaties are solemn covenants between sovereign states relating to their most basic security concerns. Even if they share a common objective, the parties may have very different views as to what is equitable and appropriate in framing such a contract. Representatives negotiate, often for protracted periods, to determine if there is common ground for agreement and, if there is, how to record it.

Before an arms control negotiation begins, the US government develops the overall policies governing the negotiations and its opening position at the highest level within the executive branch. The executive agencies involved in arms control policy formulation are the State Department, the Arms Control and Disarmament Agency, the Department of Defense, the Joint Chiefs of Staff, the Central Intelligence Agency, sometimes the Department of Energy, and the President, operating through his National Security Adviser. In the past, there have often been protracted discussions among senior officials in these agencies in the process of developing the US position. In the end, only the President can resolve differences among his

principal advisers, and it is he who approves the instructions to the US negotiator.

The actual process of treaty negotiation is conducted by delegations which usually meet in a neutral city such as Geneva, Switzerland, Vienna, Austria, or Helsinki, Finland. The chief negotiator and his delegation play an extremely important role despite the fact they are operating under instructions and usually have little discretionary authority. Since the positions of the parties are often far apart, the chief negotiator must persuade the other side of the merit and seriousness of his government's position while seeking to determine what compromises might accomplish his objectives in a manner acceptable to both sides. A good negotiator can develop a constructive relationship with his opposite number and identify problem solving options for consideration by policy officials in Washington.

A chief negotiator and his delegation also have the complex and painstaking task of developing and reaching agreement on the specific technical language of the treaty. For example, the INF Treaty with associated protocols and appendices was 236 pages long.

called multiple independently targetable reentry vehicles, or MIRVs) could each theoretically destroy several missiles on the other side, giving an advantage to the side that strikes first.

For this reason, the SALT I and SALT II agreements allowed within specified limits replacement of vulnerable land-based missiles by relatively invulnerable submarine-launched weapons, and the START treaty now being negotiated would cut in half the number of heavy SS-18 intercontinental ballistic missiles (ICBMs), the most accurate and threatening missiles in the Soviet arsenal. Similarly, the ABM Treaty banned the construction of nationwide missile defenses since such a defense would work better against a ragged and disorganized retaliation than against an all-out first strike, giving an advantage to whoever strikes the first blow in a crisis.

Over the long term, the United States and the Soviet Union have both sought to improve the survivability of their strategic forces and now appear to be moving toward adopting even more survivable systems. Arms control can play a vital role in this continuing process by ensuring that systems that are survivable today will still be survivable tomorrow.

Arms control can also reduce the risk of conventional war escalating to nuclear war by lowering overall reliance on nuclear weapons for other than basic deterrence. With many thousands of nuclear weapons available, the military forces and strategies of both the United States and the Soviet Union have become heavily dependent on employing nuclear weapons in case of an actual military confrontation. From long-range missiles to short-range artillery, nuclear weapons have spread throughout military forces, greatly increasing the number of different situations in which such weapons might plausibly be used. Moreover, with so many nuclear weapons available, military doctrines and plans designed to

High-level envoys, such as the secretary of state, may also become involved in major negotiations to resolve final differences.

When a major arms control treaty is completed, it is signed by the US President and his Soviet counterpart. Less important agreements may be signed by the secretary of state and his counterpart. The signed treaty is then submitted to the US Senate in accordance with the Constitution, which obligates the President to make treaties "by and with the advice and consent of the Senate . . . provided two-thirds of the Senators present concur. . . ." The Senate has the option of approving the treaty as presented, approving it with conditions which may or may not require renegotiation, rejecting the treaty and returning it to the President, or simply withholding approval.

The Senate Foreign Relations Committee has initial responsibility for the consideration of treaties. If, after conducting hearings, the Committee approves, the treaty is reported out to the full Senate. In recent years, the Senate Armed Services Committee and the Senate Intelligence Committee have also held extensive hearings on the respective military implications and verification issues of proposed arms control agreements. Although they do not have a formal constitutional role in the treaty process, the House Foreign Affairs and Armed Services Committees have also conducted parallel hearings on important arms control treaties. If the Senate ratifies a treaty without conditions or amendments requiring renegotiation, the President signs the ratification documents which are exchanged with the other party to the treaty. Only then does the treaty enter into force and become binding under international and domestic law.

Under international law, even if a treaty is not ratified promptly, the parties to the treaty are obligated after signature not to undercut its intent until such time as they indicate that they do not intend to ratify it. Thus, both the United States and the Soviet Union continue to abide by the Threshold Test Ban Treaty, which was signed in 1974, even though it has not been ratified.

The task of achieving Senate consent to a treaty has become so demanding a process that some less important and short-term agreements have been treated as "executive agreements." These executive agreements need only simple majorities in the Senate and the House of Representatives. The SALT I Interim Agreement on Strategic Offensive Arms, for example, was an executive agreement. Whether the Executive will prefer—or the Senate will accept—this procedure in the future on an important agreement remains to be seen.

attempt to fight a war with such weapons have become ever more sophisticated. By scaling back the number of nuclear weapons, particularly those likely to be on the front lines during future crises, arms control can help to reduce reliance on nuclear "war-fighting" strategies, and thereby make it less likely that nuclear weapons would be used in future military engagements.

Arms control can play a similar role in reducing the risk of conventional war by limiting each side's capability to launch surprise offensive attacks. This might be done by limiting offense-oriented forces such as tanks, by pulling back forces capable of offensive action from the front lines, or by confidence-building measures that could provide greater warning of a conventional attack. As the risk of conventional war is diminished, so too would be the prospect that such a war between the superpowers would escalate to nuclear war. Some very limited measures of this kind have already been agreed upon. The current talks on Conventional Armed Forces in Europe (CFE) are intended to go further in scaling back the European military confrontation.

Preventing Proliferation

In the future, the greatest risks of initiating nuclear war may lie not with the actions of the superpowers and their allies, but with other countries that gain access to nuclear weapons and other high-technology armaments. One of the highest priority objectives of arms control is to stop or reverse the spread, or "proliferation," of nuclear weapons to additional nations beyond the five that have a demonstrated capability (the United States, the Soviet Union, the United Kingdom, France, and China). This effort is complicated by the fact that a few nations (Israel, India, Pakistan, South Africa) have probably secretly developed the ability to produce nuclear weapons and may have already produced some nuclear weapons.

The more nations that possess nuclear weapons, the greater the chance that a future conflict somewhere in the world could lead to their use. Regional nuclear war could escalate to involve the superpowers. There is even the possibility that a rogue nuclear nation might make nuclear weapons available to terrorists or attempt to spark a "catalytic" nuclear war between the superpowers. The nations of the world clearly share a common interest in preventing the spread of nuclear weapons to countries that have unstable governments or could easily become engaged in regional military conflicts. In an attempt to contain this threat, the Nonproliferation Treaty (NPT) and a complex of other agreements and arrangements have been negotiated.

Other high-technology armaments are also spreading as the international arms market includes ever more sophisticated weapons. In recent years, new negotiations and arrangements have begun to try to stem the spread of chemical weapons. The use of chemical and biological weapons in warfare is banned by the Geneva Protocol of 1925, and the production and stockpiling of biological weapons were banned by the Biological Warfare Convention of 1972. The United Nations Disarmament Conference in Geneva is trying to negotiate a global ban on possession of chemical weapons. Similarly, increased attention is being given to the prevention of the proliferation of ballistic missiles, which could be used to deliver weapons of mass destruction without warning against adversaries. Initially, these efforts have included formal and informal understandings among potential missile technology suppliers.

Arms control can also play a role in improving regional security. For example, the nations of Latin America in 1967 agreed in the Treaty of Tlatelolco to make all of Latin America a nuclear-free zone. Many ceasefire agreements in regional wars—such as the Arab-Israeli ceasefire in 1973—include measures to pull back threatening military forces, or other arms control measures.

Improving Political Relations

Political tensions between countries clearly contribute to the development of crises and the risk of war. In general, a successful arms control regime builds confidence between adversaries and contributes to the reduction of political tensions and distrust. Over the years, progress in arms control has been a central element in improved relations between the United States and the Soviet Union; and at the same time the relaxation of tensions has generally improved the climate for arms control as well. The US-Soviet relationship improved dramatically from the days of President Reagan's speech labelling the Soviet Union as the "evil empire" to the Moscow summit of 1988 when Reagan and Gorbachev walked arm in arm through Moscow's Red Square. It is difficult to know to what extent this change resulted from the successful negotiation of an INF Treaty or made that treaty possible.

There is little question, however, that the completion of the INF Treaty, with the actual destruction of hundreds of missiles under the watchful eyes of inspectors on each side, and a prospective agreement of more far-reaching reductions in strategic arsenals, will help to decrease tensions over the next several years, perhaps creating a new "glasnost" in US-Soviet military relations.

Reducing the Consequences

The reduction of the potential destructiveness of nuclear war is a long-range goal of arms control. At present, however, the nuclear arsenals of the United States and the Soviet Union are so large and the heavily urbanized societies of the world so vulnerable, that even reductions far deeper than those contemplated under a START Treaty would not prevent global devastation from an all-out nuclear war.

In the longer term, extremely drastic cuts in nuclear forces could reduce the number of likely direct casualties in the event of a nuclear war and would certainly reduce the global impact of such a conflict. But so long as there are even hundreds of deliverable nuclear weapons, each tens of times more powerful than the one that destroyed Hiroshima, a nuclear war would remain an unprecedented catastrophe for humanity.

Reducing the Cost

In addition to improving security, arms control can help reduce the economic burden of military forces. Throughout the world, but particularly in the United States and the Soviet Union, staggering sums are allocated to military budgets, diverting resources from other important national priorities. Both the United States and the Soviet Union now face budgetary problems that are forcing them to rethink the size and composition of their military forces. This has clearly been a major consideration in Gorbachev's intense interest in arms control. His concern was underscored by his announcement in December 1988 of unilateral cutbacks in the size of the Soviet army.

Nuclear arms control agreements have already saved many billions of dollars, particularly by avoiding military competitions that might otherwise have taken place. Former Secretary of Defense Harold Brown has estimated that the ultimate cost of the kind of continuous competition between offensive missiles and defensive weapons that could develop were it not for the ABM Treaty and the SALT agreements could reach over $100 billion a year. Specifically, the ABM Treaty has so far prevented the deployment of nationwide strategic defensive systems, which according to former Secretaries of Defense

Harold Brown and James Schlesinger could ultimately cost as much as a trillion dollars. Moreover, by reducing existing forces, a START Treaty could save many billions of dollars over present expenditures for strategic systems.

Even far-reaching nuclear arms control agreements will not result in radical reductions in the military budget, since less than 20 percent of the US military budget is allocated to strategic forces. Indeed, in the short term, some of the savings from nuclear arms control would likely be invested in modernization of conventional forces rather than in the civilian economy.

If major progress can also be made in negotiations to reduce conventional forces, much larger savings could result. In the longer term, a successful arms control regime coupled with improved US-Soviet relations and reduced worldwide tensions should result in truly deep cuts in US and Soviet military budgets. While attention has focused on the potential for reduction in the military budgets of the superpowers and their allies, the reallocation of resources from military to other pressing societal priorities is particularly needed in many areas of the developing world.

Prospects for the Future

Arms control will continue to be a central element in US security policy for the foreseeable future. Actual progress will be realized in incremental steps in the form of specific proposals that contribute in varying degrees to the various goals that have been outlined. Although the general policy objectives discussed in this chapter will continue to find wide support, the arms control debate will focus on the detailed merits and problems of these specific proposals.

To help the reader understand and participate in the debates on these specific proposals, the Arms Control Association has prepared for background and reference this broad survey of the arms control process as it has evolved since the beginning of the nuclear age at the end of World War II. The survey sets the stage for and describes the status of all arms control negotiations and proposals at the end of the Reagan administration. These are the negotiations and issues that will challenge President George Bush and his administration.

Photos identified on page 173.

2

The US-Soviet Nuclear Competition: Truman to Johnson 1945 - 1969

The inescapable reality of the nuclear age is that nuclear war would lead to the almost certain total destruction of the warring nations as operating societies. The prospect of such an unprecedented holocaust distinguishes a war between the nuclear superpowers from previous major conflicts where the prize of victory might have appeared to compensate for the possible loss of life and treaure or even the consequences of defeat. Today, world leaders appear to agree that there would be no victors in a nuclear war.

Despite the growing recognition that there must never be a nuclear war, the adversarial relationship between the two superpowers led them to build ever larger and more sophisticated nuclear arsenals. At the same time, the United States and the Soviet Union have demonstrated a mutual interest in restraining their military and political rivalry to avoid the outbreak of hostilities. Thus, every US president since World War II, while committed to a robust defense policy, has sought in some way to manage this relentless competition through arms control. What follows is a brief history of the military and political competition that has made arms control so important and yet so difficult.

Birth of the Bomb

The discovery of nuclear fission in the late 1930s revealed the possibility of a nuclear chain reaction that would release the enormous energy locked within the atom. Physicists in several countries quickly realized this energy could be used for nuclear reactors for peaceful purposes, or, potentially, for bombs thousands of times more destructive than any that had been developed before.

Spurred by the fear that Nazi Germany would be the first to build such a bomb, physicists rushed to convince the governments of Britain and the United States to begin an atomic bomb project. Their efforts culminated in a 1939 letter from Albert Einstein to President Franklin Roosevelt warning of the danger. By 1942, a crash program, code-named the Manhattan District, was underway to build an atomic bomb. Working at a feverish pace under the pressures of war, and pulling together many of the great scientists of the age, the program succeeded in designing, building, and testing an atomic bomb within three years. On July 16, 1945, the world's first nuclear explosion, the atomic test called Trinity, was conducted at Alamogordo, New Mexico.

Believing that it was the only alternative to an invasion of Japan that would likely have cost more than a million American and Japanese lives, President Harry Truman decided to use the bomb to end the war. On August 6, 1945, a US B-29 bomber named *Enola Gay* destroyed the Japanese city of Hiroshima with a single atomic bomb carrying the equivalent explosive power of 12,500 tons (12.5 kilotons) of high explosives. On August 9, a second bomb devasted the city of Nagasaki. Some 100,000 to 300,000 Japanese died from the immediate and long-term effects of the bombs. On August 14, the Japanese surrendered. The Second World War was over, and the nuclear age had begun.

End of a War, Beginning of an Age

The Trinity atomic test marked the beginning of the nuclear age. Shown at left is the Trinity device; the photograph above was taken during the first tenth second of the Trinity explosion on July 16, 1945. Soon after, the United States dropped two nuclear bombs on Japan to end World War II.

US Nuclear Monopoly: The Truman Administration 1945-1952

Harry S. Truman

"The atomic bomb is the most terrible and devastating weapon that man has ever contrived. Because atomic energy is capable of destroying civilization, it must be controlled by international authority."

The First Nuclear Weapons

The United States and the Soviet Union maintained an uneasy alliance during World War II. At the end of the war, the United States withdrew its forces from Europe and demobilized its troops, while the Soviet Union retained an immense military establishment and set about installing puppet regimes in Eastern Europe. Pro-Soviet Communist political parties emerged as potent forces in Western Europe, and it was feared that Greece, Turkey, Iran, and West Berlin might be absorbed into the Soviet sphere. Against this background, there was a growing consensus in the United States that the Soviet Union represented a clear and immediate threat to the security of the West.

The Truman administration believed that atomic weapons could play a critical role in the evolving confrontation with the Soviet Union. The US monopoly on these awesome weapons of mass destruction seemed an immediate and direct way to compensate for Soviet conventional military superiority in Europe. To deter Soviet aggression and even compel the Soviet Union to act in a manner acceptable to the West, the United States began deploying nuclear-armed bombers in Europe.

First Attempts at Nuclear Arms Control

US officials realized that the American nuclear monopoly would not last forever. In June 1946 at the United Nations, presidential representative Bernard Baruch presented a bold proposal by the Truman administration to place the development and use of atomic energy under the control of an independent international authority responsible to the UN Security Council. The new agency would ensure that nuclear

Early Strike for Peace

Bernard Baruch at the United Nations in 1946 offered a bold proposal to stop the nuclear arms race before it started.

The Intercontinental Bomber

The US B-36, the first truly intercontinental bomber, was introduced in 1948. Shown here is a B-36H.

materials and technology would not be used to make nuclear weapons. In Baruch's words, "If we fail, then we have damned every man to be the slave of fear. Let us not deceive ourselves: we must elect world peace or world destruction."

The plan called for the United States to destroy its atomic weapons *after* all other nations had turned over their atomic resources to the newly created agency. The United States would have maintained *de facto* control of the agency through the voting majority of its allies in the United Nations, and the Soviet Union would have been unable to veto agency decisions. The Soviet Union rejected the Baruch Plan and returned with an alternative proposal that required the United States to destroy its weapons *before* any international agency was established. The sides failed to reach a compromise, and humankind's first—and perhaps only—opportunity for a future free of nuclear weapons was lost.

The Soviet Atomic Weapon and the Race for the H-Bomb

The Soviet Union detonated its first atomic weapon in August 1949, several years earlier than most US observers had expected. Spurred by the Soviet accomplishment, the United States undertook a crash program to develop the hydrogen, or thermonuclear, bomb. The "H-bomb" was successfully tested in 1952 with a yield a thousand times greater than the bomb that destroyed Hiroshima. The US monopoly on these weapons lasted only until the first Soviet thermonuclear test in 1953.

The nuclear arms competition had now begun in earnest. The United States remained far ahead for more than a decade in its capability to deliver nuclear weapons against the Soviet Union. The first truly intercontinental US bomber, the B-36, was introduced in 1948, and by the end of the Truman administration the United States had nearly 600 aircraft (290 B-29s, 60 B-36s, and 219 B-50s) capable of delivering atomic bombs against the Soviet Union from US or European bases. The Soviet atomic arsenal was much smaller. Though it threatened Europe, it initially posed no serious danger to US territory. The Soviet Union, which did not have any "forward-based" forces near American territory comparable to US bases in Western Europe, did not produce its first long-range bomber, the Bison, until 1956, one year after the United States began deploying its second-generation intercontinental bomber, the B-52.

US Nuclear Dominance: The Eisenhower Administration 1953-1960

Dwight D. Eisenhower

"Our nuclear capabilities have increased to staggering proportions; disarmament has become, literally, a problem of survival for all mankind."

"Massive Retaliation"

The Cold War was at its height when Dwight Eisenhower took office in 1953. The United States was embroiled in a costly land war in Korea against North Korean and Chinese forces and sensed a growing threat from the Soviet Union in Europe and around the world. In 1954, Secretary of State John Foster Dulles announced that any attack on the United States or its allies would be met "in a manner and at a place of our own choosing." The implication was that any Communist aggression, whether direct or through proxies, could well result in "massive retaliation"—large-scale nuclear attacks against the Soviet Union. At the same time, the United States began to integrate nuclear weapons into its forces deployed in the United States, at sea, and on the territory of allied nations.

The Advent of Intercontinental Ballistic Missiles

In 1957, the Soviet Union shocked the United States by orbiting Sputnik, the world's first artificial satellite. Rapid Soviet success in developing nuclear weapons had been widely dismissed as something of a fluke which was highly dependent on espionage. The launch of Sputnik suggested that Soviet technical capabilities had been underestimated and that the Soviet Union would soon be able to develop land-based intercontinental ballistic missiles (ICBMs) capable of delivering nuclear weapons against the United States. Fears grew that the United States would be threatened by a "missile gap." In response, the United States undertook a crash program to develop and deploy its own ICBMs as well as submarine-launched ballistic missiles (SLBMs). As a stop-gap measure, intermediate-range nuclear missiles were deployed in England, Italy, and Turkey between 1957 and 1963. By 1959, the United States began to deploy ICBMs at Vandenberg Air Force Base in California. In 1960, the United States launched the first Polaris ballistic missile submarine.

The development of ballistic missiles gave a new character to nuclear warfare. Previously, nuclear weapons had been carried by bomber aircraft which took many hours to reach their targets. Deployed on ICBMs, nuclear weapons could travel continent-to-continent in 30 minutes. Deployed on submarines in mid-ocean, sea-launched ballistic missiles might strike in even less time. Fears of a surprise Soviet missile attack, designed to destroy US strategic bombers and effectively disarm the country, led the Eisenhower administration to develop and test a plan to maintain some bombers on continuous airborne alert.

Arms Control Efforts

Despite the emphasis of his administration's defense policy on nuclear weapons, President Eisenhower became increasingly concerned with the threat of nuclear war and supportive of arms control efforts. Eisenhower first expressed his interest in controlling the growth of nuclear weapon stockpiles in his December 1953 "Atoms for Peace" proposal. This proposal called on both superpowers to reduce their arsenals and focus their science and engineering work on exploring the peaceful uses of nuclear energy. In 1955 Eisenhower proposed his plan for "Open Skies," which would have permitted each superpower to conduct aerial inspection of the other to build confidence and to prevent suspicion or miscalculation. But the Soviet Union rejected the Open Skies proposal as simply an effort to legitimate US espionage. In 1957, the United States took part in a five-power meeting in London of the UN

Disarmament Subcommittee on General and Complete Disarmament (GCD). Although the meeting failed to make any progress, disarmament remains a declaratory goal of the superpowers.

Concern about the advent of intercontinental ballistic missiles and the evolving strategic situation led to the 1958 Surprise Attack Conference, which studied the technical aspects of reducing the possibility of surprise attack. Although the conference produced no agreement, it did address specific dangers arising from the arms race.

The most serious arms control activity of the period was the proposal for a comprehensive nuclear test ban, which had Eisenhower's strong personal support. The "Conference of Experts," from the United States, the Soviet Union, and their principal allies, convened in the summer of 1958 to discuss the possibility of verifying a comprehensive ban on nuclear tests. On the basis of the conference's positive report, the United States, the Soviet Union, and Great Britain began negotiations in the fall of 1958 for a Comprehensive Test Ban (CTB) and joined in a moratorium on nuclear testing.

Although considerable progress was made in the negotiations, Eisenhower's hopes for a CTB and a new era of cooperation with the Soviet Union did not materialize. US-Soviet relations worsened, following the Soviet downing of a US U-2 spy plane deep inside Soviet territory in the spring of 1960 and the subsequent collapse of the Paris summit between Eisenhower and Soviet leader Nikita Khrushchev. By 1960 the CTB negotiations had foundered, and by 1961 both sides had resumed nuclear testing.

Nuclear Weapons of the '50s

In the 1950s, the United States relied on a variety of delivery vehicles for its nuclear deterrent. Long-range aircraft carried nuclear gravity bombs, such as the multi-megaton Mark 17 (above), the first droppable H-bomb. Ballistic missiles, such as Atlas (right), Thor (below, left) and Jupiter (below, right), were also tipped with nuclear warheads. The Snark (below, center) was an unmanned intercontinental nuclear cruise missile which proved to be an unreliable delivery system.

Mutual Vulnerability: The Kennedy and Johnson Administrations, 1961-1968

The Cuban Missile Crisis

When President John F. Kennedy came to office in January 1961, US-Soviet relations were in a poor state. The Bay of Pigs disaster and the Soviet erection of the Berlin Wall dividing East and West Berlin increased US-Soviet tensions during Kennedy's first year. Nonetheless, the United States and Soviet Union continued discussions on General and Complete Disarmament (GCD) and negotiated a Joint Statement of Agreed Principles for Disarmament Negotiations (the McCloy-Zorin Agreement) in 1961. The two nations also agreed to establish the Eighteen-Nation Disarmament Committee and the following year entered into multilateral GCD negotiations in Geneva that continued until 1964.

US-Soviet relations suffered their severest strain in the postwar period when, in October 1962, US aerial reconnaissance photographs revealed that the Soviet Union was secretly building bases to deploy medium-range nuclear missiles in Cuba. To demonstrate American resolve in face of a threat "90 miles from Florida," Kennedy placed US nuclear forces on increased alert. For seven tense days the world watched the stand-off between Kennedy and Khrushchev. US naval forces blockaded Cuba while the leaders of the two superpowers negotiated. In exchange for a Soviet commitment to withdraw their missiles, the United States pledged not to invade Cuba and indicated informally that intermediate-range US nuclear missiles in Turkey and Italy would be withdrawn. This sobering brush with nuclear war focused the world's attention on the risks of the arms race.

The Missile Gap

President Kennedy had campaigned in 1960 against Eisenhower's strategy of massive retaliation but also had argued for a substantial buildup in ICBMs, largely on the grounds of an alleged "missile gap" between US and Soviet forces. By 1961, however, newly orbited reconnaissance satellites revealed that the Soviet ICBM force was in fact much smaller than US forces. But the United States went ahead with plans to deploy a large force of Minuteman ICBMs.

The United States and the Soviet Union were also starting to deploy submarines capable of launching long-range nuclear-armed missiles.

John F. Kennedy

"Whatever obstacles and disappointments may lie ahead, the world must some day travel the road to disarmament. For in the nuclear age, armaments no longer offer fundamental security to any nation."

Traveling silently underwater throughout vast ocean areas, submarines are extremely difficult to locate and destroy. The United States, with easy access to the sea and extensive experience in naval warfare, was particularly attracted to this weapon system. Submarines would ensure that both sides would have an invulnerable retaliatory deterrent, a condition that continues to this day.

Flexible Response and Assured Destruction

While in the early 1960s the United States remained far ahead of the Soviet Union in the number and quality of nuclear forces, the extraordinary destructive power of nuclear weapons ensured that even with fewer weapons the Soviet Union had the capacity to inflict unacceptable levels of damage on the West. As the Soviet capability to attack or retaliate against US territory grew, the Eisenhower administration's policy of "massive retaliation," which in all probability would have led to general nuclear war and the wholesale destruction of both the United States and the Soviet Union, became less credible. The threat to launch an all-out attack in response to non-nuclear conflicts did not seem to many strategic analysts to provide a credible deterrent to such actions. The Soviet Union might be tempted to call the US bluff. Moreover, events of the 1950s had shown that nuclear superiority could not prevent Communist-supported uprisings in the Third World. Kennedy believed the United States relied too heavily on nuclear weapons and that the challenges of the 1960s would require more sophisticated responses with greater emphasis on conventional forces, counterinsurgency teams, and economic and developmental assistance.

Kennedy thus proposed the replacement of massive retaliation with a strategy of deterrence through "flexible response," which would involve "a range of appropriate responses, conventional and nuclear, to all levels of aggression or threats of aggression." To allow for more non-nuclear options, the Kennedy administration strengthened conventional forces. Kennedy also carried out the deployment, planned by Eisenhower, of some 7,000 "tactical" or "battlefield" nuclear weapons in Europe. The new strategy aimed to

Fire from the Sea

While the superpowers continued to modernize their ICBM and bomber forces in the early 1960s, submarines armed with sea-launched ballistic missiles (SLBMs) were the most significant nuclear weapon development of the period. Shown here is a US Polaris SLBM launched from a submerged submarine.

provide a more credible alternative to a massive retaliation against a Soviet conventional or limited nuclear attack. Some argued that more advanced technology, both in missile guidance systems and in capabilities for monitoring deployments and activities in the Soviet Union, would make precision attacks on enemy military targets possible with a minimal level of civilian casualties or other "collateral damage."

Critics of flexible response, however, did not believe nuclear warfare could be controlled or its damage constrained in any meaningful way. Even the limited use of nuclear weapons on the battlefield in response to a conventional attack by the Soviet Union would almost certainly escalate rapidly to an exchange of weapons between the superpowers and then to uncontrolled general nuclear war and mutual destruction. Many officials and analysts in the United States believed that once the United States and Soviet Union had both deployed large numbers of survivable strategic weapons, mutual destruction was inevitable if these weapons were ever used. This became a fact of life in the US-Soviet nuclear relationship.

Antiballistic Missile Systems

Even before ICBMs were deployed, the superpowers began work on defenses against them. By the mid-1960s, the United States had developed antiballistic missiles (ABMs) with a very limited capability to destroy missile warheads as they descended to their targets. The debate then began over whether to deploy them. Critics opposed ABM deployment because the very costly defensive systems could easily and cheaply be countered or overwhelmed by the deployment of additional offensive missiles and penetration aids. It was also argued that a race between US defenses and Soviet offenses would only result in an acceleration of the overall competition in strategic arms.

After the discovery in 1967 of Soviet ABM deployments around Moscow, the Johnson administration, in response to strong congressional pressure, reluctantly decided to deploy a "thin" ABM defense. Though admittedly ineffective against a Soviet attack, the system was justified as a protection against a fledgling Chinese nuclear-armed missile force (the Chinese tested a nuclear device in 1964) or an accidental Soviet launch of a limited number of missiles. At the same time, the Johnson administration announced that it would forgo this system if the Soviet Union would agree to a treaty banning ABMs.

At the 1967 summit in Glassboro, New Jersey, President Lyndon B. Johnson and Secretary of Defense Robert S. McNamara attempted to persuade Soviet leaders that an arms race in defensive weapons was not in the interest of either side. Initially, the Soviet Union rejected the notion of a ban on missile defenses and was interested only in limiting offensive arms. Eventually, however, talks on both offensive and defensive nuclear arms were scheduled for September 1968, but were postponed when the Soviet Union occupied Czechoslovakia in August of that year.

Other Arms Control Efforts

The October 1962 Cuban missile crisis showed both superpowers how dangerous the nuclear world could be. To improve communications between top US and Soviet leaders in the event of another crisis, the two countries set up a teletype "hotline" in 1963. In the same spirit, when agreement could not be reached on verification provisions for a comprehensive test ban, the United States, the Soviet Union, and Great Britain moved instead to sign the 1963 Limited Test Ban Treaty which prohibited nuclear tests in the atmosphere, outer space, and the oceans. Underground tests, which were more difficult to verify, were allowed to continue.

In 1968, the first three nuclear powers—the United States, the Soviet Union, and the United Kingdom—and 59 non-nuclear nations around the world signed the Nuclear Nonproliferation Treaty (NPT). The non-nuclear parties promised not to develop nuclear weapons if the nuclear powers would assist their peaceful nuclear energy programs. The nuclear powers also agreed to seek negotiated reductions in their nuclear arsenals. The NPT, which has been a principal deterrent to the spread of nuclear weapons to additional countries, has now been signed by over 130 nations. The treaty has not been signed by the other two nuclear weapon states, France and China, but over the years their nuclear power and export policies have come increasingly in line with the provisions and intent of the treaty.

Despite these arms control accomplishments, the United States and the Soviet Union continued to expand and improve their nuclear forces. New technological advances along with the pressure of worst-case analyses and the fear that the adversary might deploy effective ABM defenses fueled

Lyndon B. Johnson

"Arms control is the most urgent business of our time."

the drive for new weapon developments. The superpowers' nuclear arsenals grew in a rapid but asymmetric manner, reflecting different geographical, historical, and technological factors in each country. The US ICBM force leapt from 12 to 1,054 in the Kennedy-Johnson years. The strategic bomber force was modernized and increased from 450 to 650, and SLBMs rose from 48 missiles on three subs to 656 missiles on 41 subs. As these weapons entered the forces, intermediate-range ballistic missiles (IRBMs) and medium-range bombers were reduced.

Soviet forces also increased dramatically during the 1960s, especially in the second half of the decade. The Soviet Union's retreat in the Cuban missile crisis heightened its determination to catch up to the United States, and when Khrushchev, who had favored domestic over military spending, fell from power in 1964, the way was clear for a major buildup. From a handful of ICBMs in 1960, the Soviet force grew to 900 in 1968. Soviet SLBMs increased from 30 in 1960 to 135 in 1968. The number of long-range bombers, 155, remained about the same.

Thus, the first round of competition in numbers of nuclear-tipped *missiles* came to an end, only to make way for technological advances that would dramatically proliferate the number of missile *warheads* in the 1970s.

Photos identified on page 173.

9

10

3

The US-Soviet Nuclear Competition: Nixon to Bush 1969 - 1989

The SALT Era: Nixon, Ford, and Carter 1969-1981

Nuclear Parity, Detente, and SALT I

The Soviet buildup at the end of the 1960s eroded the clear margin of US nuclear superiority, and the superpowers entered the 1970s with large and roughly equal nuclear forces. In 1964 President Johnson faced about 200 Soviet ICBMs; by 1969 President Richard Nixon faced 1,028 Soviet ICBMs. Nixon and his National Security Adviser Henry Kissinger recognized that, for all practical purposes, strategic "parity" existed between the superpowers. Large, surviv-

The MIRV Revolution

The most significant technological advance in strategic nuclear weaponry since the ballistic missile has been the development of multiple independently targetable reentry vehicles (MIRVs). A missile equipped with MIRVs can separately aim and release each reentry vehicle to hit a different target. At left, technicians mount MIRV warheads on a special platform (or "bus") to be placed atop an MX "Peacekeeper" missile. Below and on the facing page are illustrations showing MIRVs in space flight. The missile shroud releases to reveal the warheads; the bus maneuvers in space to dispense separately each reentry vehicle; and they descend to different targets on earth. At the top of the facing page is a time-lapse photo of several MIRV warheads streaking through the atmosphere during a flight test.

able strategic forces on both sides made numerical or technological disparities militarily meaningless.

In recognition of this evolving strategic relationship, Nixon advanced the concept of "strategic sufficiency." The Nixon administration defined the term as "enough force to inflict a level of damage on a potential aggressor to deter him from attacking" and "to prevent us and our allies from being coerced."

Preoccupied with Vietnam and aware that accelerating the arms race could only endanger the security interests of the United States, the Nixon administration decided early to pursue strategic arms control with the Soviet Union. Arms talks were seen as part of a broader policy of "detente," which was designed to involve the Soviet Union in the maintenance of a stable world order. Nixon and Kissinger reasoned that if the Soviet Union had a stake in a network of international economic and strategic agreements, it would be less likely to jeopardize its world position by engaging in military adventure.

During Nixon's first term, the superpowers negotiated the 1972 Antiballistic Missile (ABM) Treaty, which banned nationwide deployment of antimissile weapons, and the SALT I Interim Agreement on Strategic Offensive Weapons, which froze US and Soviet strategic missile launchers at the number deployed at the time of the agreement. The Interim Agreement was intended to last for five years while a more detailed treaty limiting strategic offensive nuclear weapons was being negotiated.

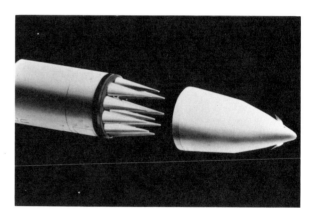

MIRVs

Even as the Strategic Arms Limitation Talks (SALT) proceeded, the arms competition continued apace. As the number of US missiles leveled off in the late 1960s, defense officials increasingly stressed qualitative improvements in weapon performance to maintain an edge in the nuclear competition. Multiple independently targetable reentry vehicles, or "MIRVs," were the most revolutionary of the technological advances. In the mid-1960s, the United States began researching technologies to overcome potential Soviet ABM systems. Putting several warheads, or "reentry vehicles" (so-called because they reenter the atmosphere at the end of the missile flight), on each US missile multiplied the number of offensive warheads the ABM system had to destroy, greatly complicating the task of the defense. MIRVs also allowed the United States to attack a larger number of targets because the missile's upper stage, a maneuvering "bus," could separately aim and release each reentry vehicle to hit a different target.

At the time, many observers recognized that MIRVs would erode the stability of the nuclear balance by giving a single missile the capability to attack several missiles on the other side. Coupled with improved guidance systems with much higher accuracy, MIRVs increased the vulnerability of ICBMs based in silos, even if the silos were "hardened" to withstand the extreme physical effects of large explosions. Theoretically,

a "preemptive" or first strike by a fraction of one side's MIRVed missiles could destroy most of the other side's ICBMs. Although submarines at sea were still invulnerable to MIRVs, and aircraft on strip alert could be launched on warning, the prospect of ICBM vulnerability heightened the perceived risk of a first strike in times of extreme tension.

Despite recognition of the problem, neither side seriously attempted to ban the testing and deployment of MIRVs during the SALT I negotia-

tions. The US testing program was already far advanced and the Soviet Union was anxious to achieve the same technological capability. Without constraints, the United States proceeded to "MIRV" many of its ICBMs and all of its SLBMs until the total number of US missile warheads grew from less than 2,000 in 1970 to over 7,000 by 1978.

The Soviet Union responded with an intensive development effort and tested three different types of MIRVed missiles by 1973. Its arsenal grew from 1,100 warheads in 1968 to 3,300 in 1976 and to approximately 8,000 in 1982. Thus, while SALT I capped the number of missile launchers, the arms race continued in warhead numbers and weapon technology. Although SALT II subsequently limited the overall number of MIRVed missiles as well as the number of MIRVs on particular missiles, the fundamental problem presented by MIRV technology—the ability of a few attacking missiles to destroy a great number of targets—remained.

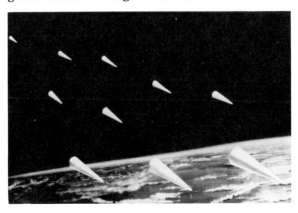

Richard M. Nixon

"I have set as my goal the attainment of a generation of peace. I believe that arms control presents both a necessary and a promising road towards a stable, secure world in which true peace can exist."

Limited Nuclear Options

Technological advances like MIRVs, improved missile accuracy, and the ability to reassign missiles to new targets allowed both sides a greater range of military options. With the advent of the Soviet MIRV program, concerns began to develop in the United States that the Soviet Union would exploit the greater throw-weight (lifting power) of its larger missiles and surpass the United States in numbers of ICBM warheads. These assessments of potential Soviet advantages tended to ignore US superiority in missile technology, strategic bombers, and forward-based systems in Europe.

In 1974 Secretary of Defense James Schlesinger announced a new strategic doctrine which essentially involved creating a wide range of nuclear strike options to provide a strategic "flexible response." The emphasis was on limited "counterforce" strikes against such targets as missile silos, submarine ports, bomber bases, and command and control centers. Schlesinger believed these "limited nuclear options" were necessary in order to maintain the credibility of the US threat to use nuclear weapons in the face of growing Soviet capabilities for such counterforce attacks. He also argued that flexible response would control escalation and reduce collateral damage in the event deterrence failed and nuclear weapons were used.

Schlesinger's critics argued that this view was an anachronistic remnant of the earlier era of US nuclear superiority. They warned that limited nuclear options called for forces indistinguishable from those needed for a first-strike capability. This capability would undermine strategic stability by raising the incentives for both the Soviet Union and the United States to launch a preemptive attack in a crisis. Yet the continued existence of massive survivable retaliatory forces guaranteed that, no matter who struck first, both sides would be destroyed as functioning societies.

During Jimmy Carter's administration, critics of limited nuclear options argued for a position of "rational sufficiency." Proponents of rational sufficiency claimed that the US nuclear arsenal was sufficiently large and diverse to inflict unacceptable damage on the Soviet Union even after a Soviet first strike, and that this capability served as an effective deterrent. However, after extensive internal debate, the Carter administration in 1980 adopted a "countervailing" nuclear strategy that was a refinement of limited nuclear options. Countervailing strategy stressed counterforce targeting, greater flexibility in a protracted nuclear war, and the necessity of survivable command and control centers to conduct such a war.

The Carter administration also approved modernization programs in all legs of the strategic triad. For the land leg, Carter planned the deployment of 200 MX missiles, a highly accurate, 10-warhead ICBM originally proposed for basing in a deceptive, mobile mode. The sea leg was improved through the Trident SLBM modernization program, and deployment of air-launched cruise missiles (ALCMs), to be carried on B-52 strategic bombers, was approved for the air-based leg. Although plans were cancelled for one new bomber program, the B-1, development was begun on a more advanced "Stealth" bomber that would be very difficult for Soviet radar to detect.

SALT II

Despite the continuation of the technological arms race, the superpowers persisted in their attempts to restrain it through arms control. New negotiations for a longer term treaty on strategic offensive weapons began in November 1972, just six months after the SALT I agreements were signed. The basic framework for the new treaty was agreed to at Vladivostok in the Soviet Union in late 1974 by President Gerald Ford and Soviet General Secretary Leonid Brezhnev. After

Gerald R. Ford

"We have embarked on the path of halting and reversing the strategic arms spiral. We must continue both with vigilance and perserverance until we have banned the horrors of nuclear war."

Jimmy Carter

"The fundamental purposes of our arms limitation efforts are to promote our own national security and to strengthen international stability, thereby enhancing the prospects for peace everywhere."

prolonged negotiations, the SALT II Treaty was finally signed by President Carter and Brezhnev in June 1979.

The treaty, which was a complex, detailed undertaking, was far broader in scope than the SALT I Interim Agreement. It mandated equal numerical limits of 2,250 on the aggregate of land- and submarine-based ballistic missile launchers and long-range, nuclear-armed bombers. SALT II also set ceilings on the number of MIRVed missile launchers on each side. While permitting weapon modernization and the freedom to trade in land-based systems for sea- or air-based systems, the treaty placed limits on numbers of warheads on these systems. The treaty also provided the framework for follow-on negotiations to reduce further the number of strategic nuclear delivery vehicles. (See Chapter 5.)

SALT II ratification was delayed by prolonged and bitter congressional committee hearings. Finally, in the wake of the December 1979 Soviet occupation of Afghanistan, President Carter in January 1980 postponed the Senate ratification proceedings. Although SALT II was never ratified, both sides agreed to adhere to its limitations and it became the primary set of constraints on the strategic offensive nuclear forces of the United States and the Soviet Union in the 1980s.

Other Arms Control Efforts

During the SALT era, the superpowers conducted many other negotiations and completed a few modest agreements. These accomplishments included an agreement on crisis management, procedures to prevent provocative incidents at sea, and the Threshold Test Ban Treaty (TTBT), an agreement limiting underground nuclear tests to yields below 150 kilotons. The TTBT was never ratified, but both sides have agreed to observe its 150-kiloton testing limit.

In 1977, the Carter administration resumed the long dormant negotiations for a comprehensive test ban (CTB), and most of the treaty was agreed upon before the negotiations were slowed to a crawl by the SALT II ratification debate and the Soviet occupation of Afghanistan. Carter also initiated negotiations in 1978 for an antisatellite weapons ban, but the talks lasted only until 1979 and did not produce an agreement. Efforts were made unsuccessfully to limit international arms traffic in the Conventional Arms Transfer (CAT) talks. As part of the December 1979 "dual-track" decision, NATO agreed to US deployment of intermediate-range missiles in Europe while at the same time calling for negotiations with the Soviet Union for limits on intermediate-range nuclear forces (INF). Despite the freeze in US-Soviet relations following Afghanistan, the INF talks began in October 1980.

US Nuclear Weapons of the 1980s

After an extensive development program in the 1970s to modernize its strategic arsenal, the United States deployed a number of new nuclear systems in the 1980s, including the B-1 bomber (above), the MX "Peacekeeper" ICBM (shown in a test launch, left), and a fleet of Trident "Ohio-class" ballistic missile submarines (shown below in assembly-line production at the Groton, Connecticut, shipyard). Additional new deployments of the 1980s included modernized SLBMs and air- and sea-launched cruise missiles (ALCMs and SLCMs).

The Reagan Administration 1981-1989

The Reagan Buildup

Ronald Reagan came to the presidency as a long-time critic of detente and arms control. He had argued throughout the SALT era that the United States was falling behind the Soviet Union in the nuclear competition, that US ICBMs were becoming increasingly vulnerable to Soviet attack, and that the unratified SALT II Treaty was "fatally flawed."

In October 1981, President Reagan unveiled his plan for a major strategic modernization program to add thousands of additional warheads and a variety of new delivery systems to the US arsenal, while improving US capabilities for command and control of its forces. The strategic package, which in large part built on programs begun under Carter or before, contained a large increase in bomber forces, including 100 B-1Bs and continued development of the advanced technology bomber (ATB, or Stealth), scheduled for deployment in the 1990s. In addition, more than 3,000 air-launched cruise missiles were planned for deployment on the bomber force. Reagan called for accelerated development and deployment of the Trident II D-5 SLBM and sea-launched cruise missiles (SLCMs).

In response to political criticisms, the basing of the MX missile was changed from the mobile mode of the Carter administration to a fixed silo. The issue of the MX basing mode proved to be a particularly complex technical and political problem. After considering several basing schemes, by the end of 1988, the Reagan administration had deployed only 50 MX missiles in silos and had decided to base 50 additional missiles on railroad trains. Meanwhile, the administration, under congressional pressure, initiated research for a small intercontinental ballistic missile (SICBM or "Midgetman") with one, or possibly two or three, warheads. Midgetman was conceived as a road-mobile system but could also be deployed in silos.

The aims of the US strategic buildup were twofold: to reduce US vulnerability by expanding the number and diversity of nuclear weapons; and to increase Soviet vulnerability so that the United States could acquire the capability to fight and win an extended nuclear war. The prospect of an arms race seemed less frightening to President Reagan—who said in 1978 that "the Soviet Union cannot possibly match us in an arms race" —than to his predecessors. But continued Soviet

Ronald Reagan

"Twice in my lifetime I've seen the world plunged blindly into global wars that inflicted untold suffering upon millions of innocent people. I share the determination of today's young people that such a tragedy, which would be rendered even more terrible by the monstrous inhumane weapons in the world's nuclear arsenals, must never happen again. My goal is to reduce nuclear weapons dramatically, assuring lasting peace and security."

missile programs and a skyrocketing US budget deficit called into question the validity of this judgment.

The US view appeared to be that while vulnerability of US weapons was dangerous, Soviet vulnerability might be desirable for furthering US foreign policy aims. The Pentagon's 1984-88 Defense Guidance document, which was leaked to reporters in 1982, stated that in the event of nuclear war, "The United States must prevail and be able to force the Soviet Union to seek earliest termination of hostilities on terms favorable to the United States." To many observers, this statement appeared to reflect a belief that nuclear war could be won, a view that Reagan and his top aides had attributed to Soviet leaders. In public statements, Reagan denied he held this view and said, "Everybody would be a loser if there's a nuclear war."

Many advocates of arms control argued that Reagan was using dubious claims of Soviet superiority to mask what was in fact a US effort to gain superiority for itself; an effort that would spur the arms race to new heights. Critics of the

Soviet Nuclear Weapons

Although the Soviet Union has begun to modernize its strategic bomber force with cruise-missile-carrying Bear H bombers (top) and the new Blackjack, intercontinental bomber forces continue to lag behind Soviet land- and sea-based missile programs. The Soviets traditionally have emphasized the land-based leg of their strategic triad, as evidenced in the 1980s by the deployment of two mobile ICBM systems, the road-mobile SS-25 and a rail-mobile, ten-warhead SS-24 (middle). The world's largest submarine, the Typhoon-class (bottom), first deployed in the early 1980s, carries 20 nuclear-armed ballistic missiles.

Reagan buildup feared that an effort to make Soviet forces vulnerable could increase Soviet incentives to launch a first strike in a crisis. Fears of war continued to rise in the early 1980s as the superpower relationship degenerated into Cold War-style exchanges of hostile rhetoric between the White House and Kremlin leaders. However, after Mikhail Gorbachev took power in 1985, relations began to improve. With the signing of the INF Treaty at the Washington summit in December 1987, the Moscow summit in June 1988, and Gorbachev's UN speech in New York in December 1988, the two superpowers appeared to be entering into a new period of detente with potentially far-reaching significance for the nuclear arms race.

George Bush

"We want an arms agreement that reduces nuclear weapons. We want an agreement that ensures peace. We want a fair agreement. But, most of all, we want a good agreement. We want an agreement that allows us to coexist with the Soviet Union in an atmosphere of mutual trust, security, and understanding. If we fail in our efforts to reach an arms reduction agreement today, we will be back at the negotiating table tomorrow and the day after that, for as long as it takes."

Arms Control

Despite his opposition to SALT II, President Reagan decided to abide by the limits of the SALT II Treaty after he took office. But throughout 1981 the President resisted calls to begin arms control negotiations on strategic weaponry. However, under strong domestic political pressure and the urging of the NATO allies, late in 1981 the administration resumed the INF talks, which had begun under President Carter, to limit US and Soviet intermediate-range missiles in Europe. At the outset of these negotiations the United States proposed the elimination of all US and Soviet intermediate-range (1,000-5,500 kilometers) nuclear weapons on a global basis, the so-called "zero-option."

In mid-1982 President Reagan agreed to resume talks on strategic weapons. In keeping with Reagan's call for deep cuts in strategic forces, the new negotiations were titled the Strategic Arms *Reduction* Talks (START), to distinguish them from the Strategic Arms *Limitation* Talks (SALT). The initial US START proposal (See Chapter 6.) required much greater cuts in Soviet than in US forces, especially land-based missiles, which comprise the bulk of the Soviet strategic nuclear arsenal. The proposal also omitted constraints in areas where the United States held a lead, such as strategic bombers and air-launched cruise missiles. The Soviet Union rejected the US approach and proposed instead the sides take further reductions within the SALT II framework. After almost two years of fruitless negotiations, the Soviet Union left the bargaining table in late 1983, when the United States began deployment of Pershing II and ground-launched cruise missiles in Europe.

Star Wars and the Post-SALT Era

While the arms talks remained deadlocked, President Reagan initiated a new chapter in the strategic debate when on March 23, 1983, he unveiled his plan to launch a comprehensive research effort aimed at developing space-based antiballistic missile systems to render nuclear weapons "impotent and obsolete." President Reagan called this program the Strategic Defense Initiative, but it was quickly dubbed "Star Wars" because of its reliance on high technology laser and beam weapons deployed in space.

President Reagan and Secretary of Defense Caspar Weinberger repeatedly held out the promise of an antiballistic missile defense system that could provide a "security shield" to protect the population and eliminate the prevailing strategic situation of mutually assured destruction. However, non-governmental critics and many officials involved with the Star Wars program pointed out that a perfect defense could not be achieved and that, far from rendering ballistic missiles obsolete, such a defense system would encourage both sides to expand its offensive strategic nuclear missile arsenal in order to maintain an assured retaliatory capability.

Facing the Future

President Bush, former President Reagan, and Soviet leader Gorbachev met in New York on December 7, 1988. Building on Reagan's progress, Bush has an opportunity to conclude an historic strategic arms treaty with the USSR.

The Star Wars debate involved many of the same arguments that had been advanced in the late 1960s during the ABM debate. Critics of Star Wars asserted that these futuristic defenses would not work effectively, would stimulate a defensive and offensive arms race, and would make war more likely in a crisis by provoking a preemptive strike. The Strategic Defense Initiative also threatened the 1972 ABM Treaty which was designed to constrain such a program and which would have to be abrogated or violated long before a considered deployment decision could be made.

To circumvent these constraints the Reagan administration, in October 1985, advanced a reinterpretation of the ABM Treaty which would allow for the development and testing of space-based and other mobile ABM systems and components. This so-called "broad" interpretation ran directly contrary to the clear language and intent of the treaty, which was to prohibit the testing and development of space-based defenses and to prevent either side from developing the base for a nationwide defense of its territory.

Faced with ongoing US INF deployments in Europe and a potential new dimension of the arms race, the Soviet Union agreed in January 1985 to resume arms control negotiations on strategic, intermediate, and defensive weapons—under the rubric of "Nuclear and Space Arms Talks." In November 1985, President Reagan held a summit meeting in Geneva with new Soviet leader Gorbachev. The meeting brought a new note of civility to superpower relations, but achieved no immediate results. Both sides continued publicly to advocate radical, presumably non-negotiable, solutions to the nuclear dilemma. In January 1986 Gorbachev countered Reagan's "Star Wars" defense with a plan for nuclear disarmament by the year 2000. At the same time, each side continued to develop and deploy new and more advanced weaponry. But prospects for arms control received a major setback when, in May 1986, after several reports alleging Soviet violations of the treaty (see Chapter 15), President Reagan renounced his previous "political commitment" to the SALT I and II agreements on strategic offensive arms. The United States, in November 1986, exceeded one of the key numerical sublimits of SALT II.

The Reykjavik, Iceland, summit between President Reagan and General Secretary Gorbachev in October 1986 defined areas of agreement and remaining problems for a new arms control regime. Although the two sides agreed in principle to the "zero-option" for no intermediate nuclear forces in Europe and to a 50-percent cut in strategic offensive arms, the meeting deadlocked over the issue of strategic defenses and the proper interpretation of the ABM Treaty.

In early 1987 the Reagan administration intensified its efforts to make strategic defenses a key component of US nuclear strategy. A formal move to adopt the new "broad" interpretation of the ABM Treaty and prepare for early deployment of SDI were apparently seriously contemplated by the administration. At this critical juncture, Gorbachev "de-linked" the INF negotiations from the larger strategic discussions and essentially agreed to accept the "zero-option" position of the US. This move set the stage for agreement on an INF Treaty that was signed at a Washington summit in December 1987. (See Chapter 10.)

Some progress was also registered on START issues at the Washington summit and work on the draft strategic arms agreement continued during 1988. The Moscow summit took place in late May and early June, at which time the INF Treaty entered into force as President Reagan and General Secretary Gorbachev exchanged instruments of ratification. Additional issues in START were discussed in Moscow, but the sides failed to resolve crucial differences over the interpretation of the ABM Treaty and the terms of the offense/defense relationship under a START treaty.

President George Bush took office at a crucial moment in the START negotiations. The task of completing the START treaty will be his overriding arms control challenge. The basic outline of the treaty as well as a substantial portion of the text are in place. Although a number of significant treaty issues require resolution, the main obstacle to concluding a treaty remains the future of the US SDI program. If he can overcome these obstacles, President Bush has the opportunity to register a truly historic success in managing US national security policy and superpower arms control. But difficult decisions will have to be made and potentially serious opposition overcome. (See Chapter 6.)

Comparing US and Soviet Strategic Nuclear Forces

The Strategic "Triad"

The United States and the Soviet Union have large strategic arsenals, made up of three types of systems for delivering nuclear weapons, or "warheads," to their targets: intercontinental ballistic missiles (ICBMs); submarine-launched ballistic missiles (SLBMs); and strategic bombers.

These three delivery systems constitute a strategic nuclear "triad," a redundant, survivable force. Each "leg" of this triad has distinct characteristics and implications for both military planning and arms control.

A common method of comparing US and Soviet strategic nuclear forces is to look at numbers of launchers and warheads. (See chart next page.) However, such numerical comparisons overlook the qualitative differences between the arsenals. Moreover, an accurate assessment of the strategic balance requires an understanding of the advantages and disadvantages of the three types of delivery systems, and a comparison of the way each superpower has distributed its weapons within its own strategic triad.

The main characteristics of nuclear weapon systems that affect their performance are:
- survivability,
- controllability,
- promptness,
- penetrability,
- accuracy, and
- yield.

"Survivability," the critical requirement for a reliable deterrent, is a weapon system's capability of withstanding an opponent's attack. "Controllability" refers to the ability of the national leadership to control the targeting, retargeting, launching, and—in the case of bombers—the recalling of a weapon system. "Promptness," the amount of time between the launch of a weapon and its impact, is critical for striking "time urgent" counterforce (military) targets but largely irrelevant to hitting countervalue (industrial) targets.

Once the weapon is approaching enemy territory, three factors determine the ability of a weapon system to destroy its target. The weapon must first be able to "penetrate" enemy defenses, and then must have sufficient accuracy and yield to destroy the target. "Accuracy" is simply a measure of how close a missile can deliver its warhead to its target and is an important factor in calculating the probability of the destruction of a hardened installation. It is usually measured in terms of Circular Error Probable (CEP), the radius of a circle within which half the warheads aimed at a target will land. "Yield" is the energy of the weapon's blast, expressed in thousands (kiloton) or millions (megaton) of tons of TNT equivalent (ordinary chemical explosive). "Hard" targets, such as ICBM silos or underground command and control centers, can only be destroyed by powerful, highly accurate weapons. "Soft" targets, such as cities and troop formations, are extremely vulnerable to nuclear weapons regardless of their accuracy although the extent of damage depends on yield.

Total Launchers	US	USSR
ICBMs	1,000	1,376
SLBMs	608	942
BOMBERS	291	170
	1,899	2,488

Total Warheads	US	USSR
On ICBMs	2,450	6,572
On SLBMs	5,312	3,426
On BOMBERS	4,808	1,000
	12,570	10,998

Figures current as of June 1989

Intercontinental Ballistic Missiles

Intercontinental ballistic missiles (ICBMs) are land-based, multi-stage rockets capable of propelling nuclear warheads over intercontinental distances (i.e., more than 5,500 kilometers). Soviet ICBM forces account for approximately 60 percent of its total strategic nuclear arsenal as compared to approximately 20 percent for the United States.

An ICBM can deliver several powerful warheads with exceptional accuracy to intercontinental targets in under 30 minutes. The development of MIRV (multiple independently targetable reentry vehicle) technology in the late 1960s allows each missile to carry a number of warheads that can be targeted against separate aim points. These characteristics enable ICBMs to carry out "time urgent" missions and make ICBMs potential first-strike weapons. High accuracy also makes ICBMs potentially useful as war-fighting weapons in specialized or "limited options" attacks. Currently deployed in massive concrete and steel silos just below the earth's surface, US ICBMs are very "hard" targets that can only be destroyed by accurate, high yield weapons. ICBMs, unlike bombers, cannot be recalled. Thus, launching ICBMs on warning of an attack, which might be a false alarm, would precipitate a general nuclear exchange. It is reportedly US policy, therefore, to allow ICBMs to ride out an attack, although the capability to "launch on warning" of an enemy missile attack always exists.

Their potential vulnerability as fixed targets increases the likelihood that ICBMs may be used prematurely for fear of losing them to an attacker's weapons. To reduce their vulnerability, ICBMs can be deployed in a mobile mode, as the Soviet Union has done with their new SS-25 missile, which is road mobile, and the SS-24, which is rail mobile. Similarly, the United States is developing both rail and road mobile ICBMs.

Strategic Bombers

Strategic bombers are long-range aircraft capable of carrying nuclear weapons over intercontinental distances and then returning to an overseas recovery base. Bombers were the first means of delivering nuclear weapons, and the United States still relies upon strategic bombers as delivery vehicles for almost 40 percent of its total strategic nuclear arsenal. The Soviet Union has put considerably less emphasis on strategic bombers, with about nine percent of its strategic nuclear arsenal in this category.

Bomber survivability is determined by the readiness of the force. Bombers on the ground are extremely vulnerable to attack. Therefore, a significant portion of the US bomber force (approximately 30 percent) is on constant "strip alert," with crews waiting in "ready rooms," to take off within minutes after receiving warning that an enemy attack is impending. In times of crises, additional bombers can be temporarily added to the alert force in a "generated" alert. Bombers have more flexibility than missiles because they can be recalled and operate under "fail-safe" procedures whereby they automatically return to base unless they receive additional instructions within a fixed time period. While in an intense crisis "scrambling" (launching) bombers could be perceived by the other side as a critical escalation in the confrontation, it also would deprive the other side of the extremely vulnerable and lucrative target of grounded aircraft.

Strategic bombers take many hours to perform intercontinental missions. They are thus not well suited for a preemptive strike against "time urgent" targets such as enemy ICBMs. Large subsonic bombers are also vulnerable to air defenses. To ensure penetration, US bombers fly very low to avoid detection, use electronic countermeasures to jam Soviet radars, employ various tactics to destroy or avoid Soviet air defense radars and missiles, carry low flying air-launched cruise missiles (ALCMs) to overwhelm the tracking and defense capabilities of an adversary, and will employ "stealth" technology to reduce the "visibility" of aircraft and cruise missiles in the future to radars and other sensors. In addition, many US bombers are equipped with nuclear short-range attack missiles (SRAMs) to destroy Soviet air defenses in their path or permit an attack on heavily defended targets from a position many miles away.

The air-launched cruise missile has been the most significant technical development to insure penetration of Soviet air defenses. Cruise missiles, which can be launched outside enemy defenses, fly at very low altitudes (hundreds of feet) to avoid detection and attack by enemy air defenses. About 60 percent of the US strategic bomber force has already been fitted with an average of 12 ALCMs.

Bombers can carry a large number of accurate weapons with high yields. Once they penetrate enemy air defenses, bombers are in principle capable of seeking out and destroying undamaged "hard" and "mobile" targets, but, at least in the case of hardened silos, most of the missiles in them will presumably have been fired by the time the bombers or their ALCMs arrive.

Submarine-launched Ballistic Missiles

Submarine-launched ballistic missiles are similar to ICBMs but are launched from submarines. The United States has concentrated a large percentage of its nuclear forces in SLBMs. Although the United States actually has fewer submarines and SLBMs than the Soviet Union, US SLBMs are extensively MIRVed and carry 5,312 warheads, or 1,886 more warheads than Soviet SLBMs. The US SLBM force with some 5,300 warheads carries about 40 percent of the US strategic nuclear arsenal, while Soviet SLBMs carry slightly more than 30 percent of their strategic nuclear warheads.

SLBMs are inherently the most survivable, and thus the most stabilizing leg of the strategic triad. Deployed on submarines which patrol vast ocean areas, SLBMs are difficult to locate and destroy. As a consequence, they are considered excellent second-strike weapons which add to both deterrence and stability.

For the same reason that submarines and SLBMs are relatively invulnerable, national command authorities may have difficulty communicating with them. They are therefore less suited for coordinated missions against time urgent targets. Current SLBMs are also less accurate than ICBMs and less capable of destroying hardened ICBM silos. However, a new generation of highly accurate SLBMs—the US Trident II (D-5) missile scheduled for deployment in 1989—will give submarine-launched ballistic missiles the capability to destroy hard targets.

Cruise Missiles

Both superpowers are in the midst of deploying a new class of strategic weapons: long-range cruise missiles on aircraft and at sea. Cruise missiles are small, pilotless aircraft, powered by miniature jet engines and capable of flying long-distance, terrain-hugging missions. With modern guidance systems keyed to the terrrain they are overflying, cruise missiles can strike targets with great accuracy. Future cruise missiles will have reduced detectability ("stealth" technology) and increased speeds which will make them even less vulnerable to air defense systems. Moreover, the small size, large projected numbers, and relative ease of production of cruise missiles make their verification more difficult than other delivery systems.

PART II:

The Arms Control Agenda

US Minuteman ICBM in its silo.

4

Strategic Offensive Arms Control: SALT I, 1969 - 1972

Background

By the mid-1960s the United States had assembled a powerful, balanced, and survivable triad of long-range or "strategic" nuclear forces: land-based ICBMs, submarine-based SLBMs, and heavy bombers. Although technologically and economically far behind the United States, the Soviet Union was also well on its way to matching these forces with its own strategic buildup, primarily of ICBMs. The deliberate, seemingly relentless pace of the development and buildup of these forces made it increasingly clear that both sides had sufficient resources and determination to keep up with the other, that neither side could hope to achieve or maintain a position of meaningful strategic superiority, and that any attempt by either side to gain such an advantage in either offensive or defensive systems would only prompt a response by the other side.

A Freeze on Launchers

The SALT I Interim Agreement froze the number of US and Soviet ICBM and SLBM launchers at their existing levels in 1972. At that time, launchers included missile silos, such as the Soviet silo above being loaded with an SS-9 ICBM, and missile-launching tubes on submarines, such as those shown at right on a US Poseidon with hatches open.

During the 1960s, advances in satellite technology provided radically improved surveillance capabilities. A wide range of military activities could now be effectively and confidently monitored without intrusive forms of inspection. In particular, the large and distinctive ICBM launchers and their deployment areas, heavy bombers and their bases, submarines and their construction yards, and antiballistic missile (ABM) radar and interceptor systems could be easily detected and their numbers verified.

These two developments—the emergence and likely persistence of rough parity in strategic forces and the evolution of verification capabilities—laid the groundwork for strategic nuclear arms control. The discovery that the Soviet Union was deploying an ABM system around Moscow further stimulated US interest in arms control. Although, as deployed, the Soviet defensive system was judged to be ineffective, worst case assessments of the potential capabilities of a nationwide deployment of an upgraded version called for a massive increase in US strategic offensive forces to ensure a retaliatory capability.

To avoid this escalation in strategic competition, the Johnson administration sought to put limits on both ABM defensive systems and the strategic offensive arsenals of both the United States and the Soviet Union. President Johnson offered in January 1967 and again at the Glassboro, New Jersey, summit in June 1967 to halt US ABM defense programs if the Soviet Union would agree to mutual limitations on strategic defensive and offensive weapons. The United States argued that without limits on ABMs, capping offensive arms would become impossible and an arms race in both offensive and defensive weapons would be inevitable. The Soviet Union initially did not accept the US arguments, so the United States proceeded with its own ABM program.

By July 1968 agreement was reached with the Soviet Union to begin superpower negotiations to limit strategic arms. However, the United States postponed the scheduled September opening of the talks in the wake of the Soviet occupation of Czechoslovakia in August 1968. After extensive policy reviews, the Nixon administration finally commenced the Strategic Arms Limitation Talks (SALT) on November 17, 1969, in Helsinki, Finland. From the outset, the US delegation, headed by Ambassador Gerard C. Smith, pressed the Soviet delegation, led by Deputy Foreign Minister Vladimir Semenov, for limits on both ABMs and strategic offensive arms.

A number of issues separated the two sides in the negotiations. Because of historical, geographical, doctrinal, and technological dif-

ferences, the strategic arsenals of the two sides were quite dissimilar. The Soviet Union had a large and powerful ICBM force and placed less reliance on sea- and air-based strategic weapons. The United States, on the other hand, as a two-ocean sea-power with extensive World War II experience in strategic bombing, had large and effective sea- and air-based strategic forces. The United States also had significant technological advantages, particularly in the development of multiple independently targetable warheads on its land- and sea-based missiles. This made a comprehensive agreement on strategic offensive forces more difficult to obtain than on antiballistic missile systems. As a result, the United States and Soviet Union decided to work initially towards a permanent treaty on ABMs and to place interim restrictions on strategic offensive forces. These interim restrictions were subsequently to be incorporated into a follow-on treaty on strategic offensive weapons.

The difficulty of negotiating a comprehensive treaty on strategic offensive weapons stemmed partly from disagreement over which systems to include. Because of the proximity of US allies in Europe and Asia to the Soviet Union, US intermediate-range forces stationed there and on aircraft carriers (called "forward-based systems" or FBS) could strike Soviet territory. From the Soviet perspective, US forward-based systems—which consisted mainly of intermediate-range bombers at the time of SALT—were as threatening as intercontinental systems. The nuclear forces of the British, French, and Chinese compounded this imbalance, for no nations friendly to the Soviet Union had comparable forces which could strike the United States. The Soviet effort to deploy nuclear forces abroad in Cuba had in fact led to the Cuban missile crisis in 1962. Thus, the Soviet Union sought to define as "strategic" *all* weapons that could hit the territory of the other side.

The United States, on the other hand, insisted on limiting only long-range systems (i.e., ICBMs, SLBMs, and heavy bombers). From the US perspective, forward-based systems were needed to counter Soviet intermediate-range missiles and aircraft aimed at US allies in Europe. The Soviet Union eventually agreed to restrict ICBMs and SLBMs to the numbers of launchers for these systems existing or under construction at the time. This major Soviet concession allowed the United States to maintain its existing advantage in FBS and intercontinental "heavy" bombers as well as in multiple warhead missiles. The concession also left British, French, and Chinese nuclear forces completely unconstrained. The Soviet Union was allowed to keep its numerical advantage in ICBM and SLBM launchers.

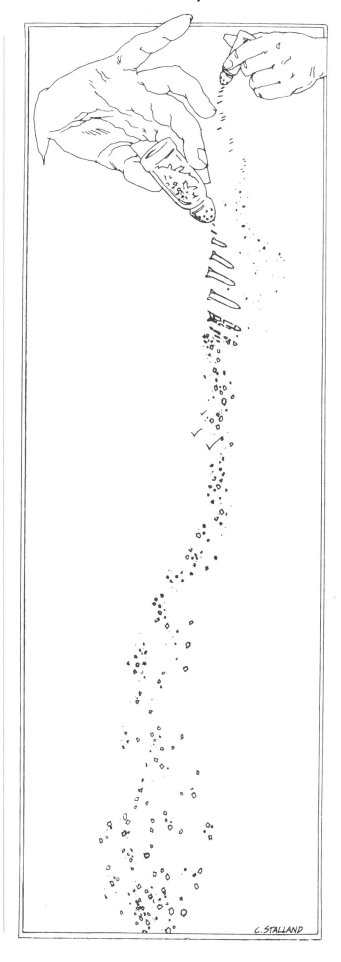

C. STALLAND

Provisions

To halt the buildup in numbers of strategic offensive systems, the superpowers agreed in SALT I to freeze the number of ICBM and SLBM launchers—missile silos and the missile-launching tubes on submarines—at their July and May 1972 levels, respectively. The launchers were much easier to monitor than the missiles themselves. The permitted launcher totals were 2,347 for the Soviet Union and 1,710 for the United States. This disparity in launcher numbers was balanced on the US side by its lead in missile warheads, its superior force of heavy bombers (over 450 highly capable bombers compared to under 150 considerably less capable Soviet ones), some 600 forward-based aircraft, and British and French nuclear forces.

SALT I also addressed US concerns about Soviet reliance on ICBMs. Because of their high accuracy and potential vulnerability to attack, fixed land-based ICBMs were considered to be more destabilizing than sea-based missiles. Of particular concern to the United States were 288 large Soviet SS-9 ICBMs and indications of construction on at least 20 new silos for additional large ICBMs. The SS-9 was deployed with a single 20-megaton warhead or three multi-megaton warheads, and had the potential to deliver a much larger number of smaller weapons. The SALT I freeze on launchers ensured that the number of these "heavy" missiles could not be increased, although the SS-9 was subsequently replaced by an even more capable missile—the SS-18.

The SALT I Interim Agreement also attempted to encourage reduced reliance on land-based missiles by allowing each side to increase the number of its SLBM launchers if corresponding reductions were made in the number of its ICBM launchers. For example, by dismantling 54 older Titan ICBMs, the United States would be permitted to increase its SLBM force from 656 to 710. The Soviet Union could increase its SLBM launchers from 740 to 950 by replacing 210 of its older SS-7 and SS-8 ICBM launchers on a one-for-one basis. Within these limitations on launcher numbers, both sides were permitted to modernize their missiles.

The SALT I agreement formalized the principle of verification by national technical means (NTM). NTM refers to the complex of satellites, radars, seismographs, and other intelligence-gathering systems used to monitor military activity by other nations. SALT I banned both deliberate interference with NTM and attempts to conceal from NTM those forces limited by the agreement. To deal with any questions of treaty implementation and compliance that might arise, SALT I established a joint US-Soviet body called the Standing Consultative Commission.

Status

In view of its limited duration (five years) and the expectation that it would be replaced by a permanent treaty, the SALT I Interim Agreement on Strategic Offensive Arms was treated as an executive agreement rather than a formal treaty. It entered into force on October 3, 1972, following its approval in a Joint Resolution of Congress. The vote was 88 to 2 in the Senate, and 307 to 4 in the House.

The Interim Agreement formally expired five years later on October 2, 1977. Originally, it had been thought that five years would allow sufficient time to negotiate a more comprehensive agreement. As the SALT II talks continued beyond this date, the United States and the Soviet Union both pledged to continue to observe the Interim Agreement. After the signing of SALT II in 1979, the forces of both sides remained within the SALT I limits as an integral part of the 1981 unilateral US and Soviet commitment not to "undercut" existing strategic arms agreements pending further negotiations. However, in May 1986, President Reagan formally repudiated this political commitment to SALT I and II. Although the United States formally exceeded the SALT II numerical limits on MIRVed missiles and bombers equipped with cruise missiles in November 1986, existing programs will not place the United States in excess of the SALT I limits on ballistic missile launchers for several years. Following the US decision to repudiate the SALT limits, the Soviet Union announced its intention to remain within them and has done so up to the beginning of the Bush administration.

Signing of SALT II, 1979.

5

Strategic Offensive Arms Control: SALT II, 1972 - 1979

Background

The United States and the Soviet Union pledged in the SALT I agreement to "continue active negotiations for limitations on strategic offensive arms." These negotiations resumed in November 1972 and continued throughout the remainder of the Nixon and Ford administrations and for two and one-half years of the Carter administration before SALT II was finally signed in June 1979.

The chief objectives of the United States in the SALT II negotiations were to establish equal quantitative limits on the aggregate number of ICBMs, SLBMs, and long-range bombers, and qualitative limits on destabilizing force developments, in particular the addition of large numbers of MIRVs. Despite considerable progress on many issues, basic disagreements over US forward-based systems and Soviet "heavy" ICBMs

Vladivostok

President Gerald Ford and Soviet leader Leonid Brezhnev agreed on the framework for SALT II at a 1974 summit meeting in Vladivostok, USSR. The SALT II negotiations spanned three administrations: Nixon, Ford, and Carter.

(the SS-9 and its replacement, the SS-18) reemerged early in the negotiations.

A major breakthrough occurred in November 1974 at the summit between President Gerald Ford and General Secretary Leonid Brezhnev at Vladivostok, in the Soviet Union. As in the SALT I negotiations, the United States dropped its insistence on reductions in Soviet "heavy" missiles, and the Soviet Union dropped demands that US forward-based systems and British and French nuclear forces be limited in SALT II. Ford and Brezhnev decided to continue the SALT I freeze on ICBM and SLBM launchers and agreed that a new treaty should include heavy bombers in the numerical limits and establish an aggregate ceiling of 2,400 on "strategic nuclear delivery vehicles." Within this overall ceiling there would be a subceiling of 1,320 on MIRVed ICBM and SLBM launchers.

But key disagreements remained. The Soviet Union, wanting to restrain the emerging US cruise missile program, insisted that aircraft carrying air-launched cruise missiles (ALCMs) should be directly accountable under the 1,320 MIRVed missile subceiling. For its part, the United States argued that the Soviet Backfire medium bomber was capable of reaching the United States and thus should be counted as a "heavy bomber" within the 2,400 aggregate ceiling. Faced with a difficult reelection campaign,

President Ford did not attempt to resolve these issues in the last year of his term.

Further complications arose when the newly elected Carter administration in March 1977 proposed consideration of a more radical approach to SALT II than the agreement outlined at Vladivostok. The proposal called for much lower limits on strategic nuclear delivery vehicles, MIRVed ICBMs, and heavy missiles. The Soviet Union took the position that this new approach essentially repudiated past agreements. The Carter administration then agreed to return to the Vladivostok agreement as the framework for the negotiations, although the Soviet negotiators eventually agreed to somewhat lower sublimits.

Provisions

In 1979, the two sides finally agreed on an extremely detailed and technical document which, with its 19 Articles and nearly 100 explanatory "Agreed Statements" and "Common Understandings," attempted to leave as few loopholes and ambiguities as possible. The SALT II Treaty set the initial aggregate number of ICBM and SLBM launchers and heavy bombers at 2,400. The treaty provided for this aggregate number to be lowered to 2,250 by the end of 1981. Both these aggregate figures were under the level of the then existing Soviet arsenal and represented the first agreed reduction in nuclear weapons.

SALT II also established equal subceilings of 820 on launchers for MIRVed ICBMs, 1,200 on launchers for MIRVed ICBMs and SLBMs, and 1,320 on launchers for MIRVed ICBMs, SLBMs, and heavy bombers equipped with long-range ALCMs.

Among its qualitative provisions, SALT II allowed only one "new type" of ICBM for each side. The new ICBM was permitted no more than 10 warheads, and new SLBMs were permitted no more than 14 warheads. Another provision required that the number of warheads on current missile types could not exceed the maximum number already tested. For example, since the Soviet SS-18 ICBM had been tested at a maximum of 10 warheads, the Soviet Union could not test or deploy more than 10 warheads on an SS-18 or its replacement missile in the future. This constraint was especially important since the SS-18 has enough throw-weight (lifting power) to carry 20-30 warheads. Another provision banned the construction of additional heavy missile (SS-18 type) launchers.

SALT II included several limits on heavy bombers. The maximum number of long-range ALCMs allowed on existing heavy bombers was set at 20, and the average load of ALCMs for existing and future bombers was limited to 28. In a separate statement, appended to the treaty, the Soviet Union agreed not to increase the capabilities of its Backfire bomber and not to produce more than 30 such bombers a year.

SALT II, like SALT I, provided for the verification of compliance by national technical means (NTM). In addition to extending the SALT I provisions prohibiting interference with and concealment from NTM, SALT II included a specific ban on encryption of missile telemetry when it impeded verification of treaty compliance. Another cooperative measure required aircraft with different missions (i.e., ALCM-carrying bombers vs. ordinary bombers) to be distinguishable through national technical means by "functionally related observable differences (FRODs)."

National technical means can verify the type of missile launcher deployed, but it cannot directly distinguish the particular missile in a specific launcher or the number of warheads on that missile. To solve this problem a number of "counting rules" were established to simplify verifica-

SALT II Limits

SUBLIMIT — ICBMs: MIRVed INTERCONTINENTAL BALLISTIC MISSILES — **820** MAXIMUM

SUBLIMIT PLUS — SLBMs: THE ABOVE PLUS MIRVed SUBMARINE LAUNCHED BALLISTIC MISSILES — **1,200** MAXIMUM

SUBLIMIT PLUS — BOMBERS: BOTH OF THE ABOVE PLUS LONG-RANGE BOMBERS CARRYING CRUISE MISSILES — **1,320** MAXIMUM

OVERALL CEILING PLUS — TOTAL DELIVERY SYSTEMS: ALL OF THE ABOVE PLUS UNMIRVed MISSILES AND BOMBERS NOT CARRYING CRUISE MISSILES — **2,250** MAXIMUM

tion of the numerical limits. For example, any launcher of a type that had ever been associated with a particular missile during testing would be counted as a launcher of that missile. Moreover, any missile of a type that had ever been tested with MIRVed warheads would always count as a MIRVed missile, whether it was actually deployed with MIRVs or not. As noted above, another rule counted the number of MIRVs on each missile as the maximum ever tested with that type of missile.

Limits and Deactivations

To comply with the SALT I and II accords, the Soviet Union between 1979-89 dismantled or converted 17 Yankee-class ballistic missile submarines (above) as new Delta- and Typhoon-class subs were added to the Soviet fleet. SALT limits also required the Soviet Union to remove hundreds of ICBMs and SLBMs from existing silos as newer missiles were deployed. Although the United States announced in 1986 that it would not ratify SALT II, it remained in technical compliance until November 1986, when the ongoing conversion of B-52 aircraft to carry cruise missiles (below) put the US over the sublimit of 1,320 MIRVed missiles and ALCM-carrying bombers.

In addition to the basic provisions and explanatory detail of the treaty, SALT II also contained a protocol and a "Joint Statement of Principles." The protocol, which was to remain in force until the end of 1981, temporarily banned the deployment of mobile ICBMs and sea- and ground-launched cruise missiles with ranges over 600 kilometers. The ultimate disposition of these systems was in dispute during the SALT II negotiations and the protocol delayed their deployment in order to allow some time for discussion of these systems in follow-on talks. The Joint Statement committed the United States and the Soviet Union to seek "significant and substantial reductions" in follow-on negotiations on nuclear arms for a SALT III agreement.

Status

The SALT II Treaty encountered much more resistance in the Senate than did the SALT I Interim Agreement and the ABM Treaty. Critics challenged not only the treaty's basic provisions but also the broader relationship of the Carter administration's arms control policy to US foreign and defense policies. After the Soviet Union's December 1979 occupation of Afghanistan, Senate ratification appeared very unlikely and President Carter asked the Senate in January 1980 to postpone consideration. However, as long as ratification remained the objective, customary international law obligated both nations not to take actions defeating the object of the treaty. In March 1980, President Carter pledged that the United States would abide by the terms of SALT II if the Soviet Union did likewise.

After Reagan's election to the presidency in November 1980, the future of US adherence to SALT II again became uncertain. During his election campaign, Reagan opposed the treaty and called it "fatally flawed." In 1981, Reagan formally announced that the United States did not intend to ratify SALT II, but pledged not to undercut it if the Soviet Union showed equal restraint. Thereafter, US adherence to the treaty ceased to be a requirement of international law and became a question of political commitment.

The Soviet Union adopted the same "no undercut" policy but made clear that it would not cut its forces to the aggregate limit of 2,400 (to have been reduced to 2,250 by the end of 1981) strategic nuclear delivery vehicles. The Soviets claimed that this provision, which would have required significant Soviet force reductions, was specifically tied in the treaty to the "entry into force of this Treaty." Although not specifically required to do so, the Soviet Union also claims it has maintained its forces at or below its June 1979 level of 2,504. The United States has charged that the Soviet Union has slightly exceeded this limit.

In response to alleged Soviet violations of SALT II (see Chapter 15), the Reagan administration announced in May 1986 that the United States was terminating its commitment to adhere to "the SALT structure," unless the Soviet Union corrected its noncompliance policy, reversed its strategic buildup, and contributed to progress in Geneva. The United States remained in technical compliance with SALT II until November 1986, when the ongoing conversion of B-52 aircraft to carry cruise missiles put the United States over the 1,320 limit on the number of MIRVed missiles and ALCM-carrying bombers. The Soviet Union, for its part, has indicated that it intends to continue to abide by its commitment to the SALT II limits and the evidence indicates that as of 1989 the Soviet Union had remained within the sublimits of the treaty.

Display of ceramic nosecones representing all the warheads in the US nuclear arsenal, Boston Science Museum, 1985.

6

Strategic Offensive Arms Control: START, 1982 - 1989

Background

When President Reagan took office in 1981, the fate of strategic arms control was uncertain. During the 1980 campaign, candidate Ronald Reagan had called the 1979 SALT II Treaty "fatally flawed." Reagan argued that SALT II had helped put the United States in a position of strategic inferiority relative to the Soviet Union. Most alarming, he claimed, was a "window of vulnerability" about to open for US land-based forces. According to this view, SALT II, coupled with an alleged decade of neglecting investment in US strategic forces, had allowed the Soviet Union to exploit its reliance on heavy, land-based missiles and its advantage in missile throw-weight (lifting power) to threaten the survivability of US missiles in fixed silos. Although Reagan's own Special Commission on Strategic Forces (the Scowcroft Commission) ultimately rejected the notion that US strategic forces were vulnerable to a Soviet first strike, the "window of vulnerability" argument had a powerful impact on the administration's basic approach to arms control.

Negotiations on strategic offensive forces under President Reagan did not resume until mid-1982. The administration's marked reluctance to enter into such talks with the Soviet Union stemmed from its belief that until the United States had redressed the perceived strategic imbalance, arms control efforts would be futile, even dangerous. But after seeming to justify its strategic modernization program with the rhetoric of "nuclear warfighting," the Reagan administration came under strong allied and domestic political pressure to resume negotiations. In the spring of 1982, the United States finally agreed to open talks.

President Reagan was careful to distinguish his approach to strategic offensive arms control from that of his predecessors. Citing the growth of US and Soviet strategic arsenals under SALT, he portrayed arms *limitation* as a failed notion of the past and presented arms *reduction* as the chosen alternative for the future. Accordingly, he dubbed the new negotiations the Strategic Arms Reduction Talks, or START.

START

The first set of START talks, held from June 1982 to December 1983, sought to achieve significant reductions in the strategic ballistic missile forces of the United States and the Soviet Union. The five rounds of negotiations were, however, plagued by fundamental differences between the two sides on what forces would be reduced, how the remaining forces would be configured, and how the reductions would be verified.

The primary US objective in the START negotiations was to reduce those Soviet capabilities and force asymmetries most threatening to the United States, particularly the Soviet advantage in "heavy" missiles and missile throw-weight. To this end, the United States used warheads, throw-weight, and missiles, rather than launchers, as the primary units of account in the negotiations. This approach strongly discriminated against land-based ballistic missile forces (the main leg of the Soviet strategic triad), while leaving sea-based forces (the major portion of the US triad) significantly less constrained and air-based forces completely unconstrained. The unspoken but underlying aim of this discrimination was to restructure the Soviet triad, decreasing their reliance on ICBMs and increasing the role of SLBMs, bombers, and cruise missiles, which are considered to be more stabilizing in a crisis situation.

The Soviet Union based its initial approach to the negotiations on the SALT II framework, calling for percentage reductions in the SALT II limits on strategic nuclear delivery vehicles (ICBM and SLBM launchers and heavy bombers) and in the sublimits on MIRVed weapons. It also proposed a new limit on "nuclear charges," or warheads. The Soviet Union dismissed the US approach as one-sided because it required much deeper cuts in Soviet than in US land-based forces and placed no restrictions on strategic bombers and cruise missiles, areas of significant US advantage.

During the first five sessions of START, little progress was made. In November 1983, the United States began the deployment of INF missiles in Europe. When Round V of START came to a close at the end of 1983, the Soviet Union declined to set a resumption date, charging that US INF deployments in Europe had changed "the overall strategic situation." (See Chapter 10.)

Nuclear and Space Arms Talks

After a year away from the negotiating table, the United States and the Soviet Union agreed in January 1985 to resume negotiations on strategic offensive weapons under the umbrella of the Nuclear and Space Arms Talks (NST), which would also include negotiations on intermediate-range nuclear forces and defense and space weapons. When the NST began in March 1985, neither the US nor the Soviet position on strategic offensive weapons had changed significantly. However, the Soviet Union now linked an agreement on strategic offensive arms to an agreement on space-based weapons that would constrain the US program on strategic defensive weapons, which had become a prominent feature of US policy following President Reagan's Star Wars speech in March 1983. (See Chapter 7.) The Soviet Union argued, as did the United States when the ABM Treaty was negotiated, that the development and deployment of strategic defenses would destabilize the US-Soviet strategic balance and force a major buildup of offensive forces.

How START Would Affect US Warhead Deployments

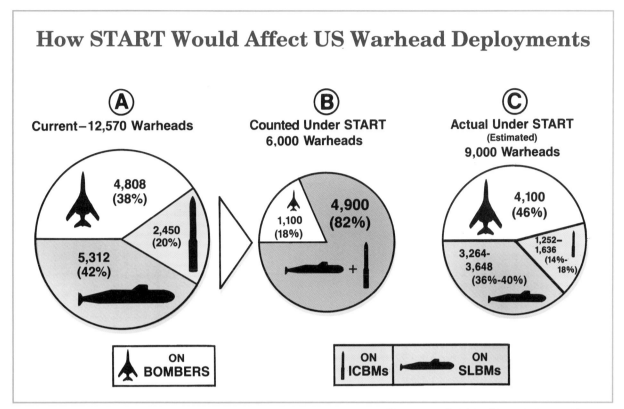

Three pie-charts show the number of US warheads carried by bombers, ICBMs, and SLBMs. Chart A shows US forces as of April 1989. Chart B shows warheads on missiles (both ICBMs and SLBMs) and on bombers as they would be counted under currently agreed terms of a START treaty. Chart C shows an estimated distribution of warheads under START. Because of the START counting rules, the actual number of deployed warheads will exceed 6,000. The Soviet Union currently deploys about 10,766 strategic nuclear warheads, which after START would be reduced to between 6,000-8,000.

Nevertheless, by late 1985, a seed of consensus began to take root in Geneva. In the third round of the NST, the Soviet Union tabled a new proposal that called for a 50-percent cut in ballistic missiles and heavy bombers and limited the number of strategic nuclear warheads to 6,000 on each side. Although the Soviet proposal contained some provisions that were unacceptable to the United States (such as the inclusion of US forward-based systems, a ban on long-range cruise missiles, and linkage to a ban on all "purposeful" SDI research), the United States welcomed the Soviet shift towards the concept of deep reductions.

At the Geneva summit in November 1985, both President Reagan and the new Soviet General Secretary, Mikhail Gorbachev, reaffirmed the goal of a 50 percent reduction in strategic arsenals. By early 1986, both Reagan, by implication in his Star Wars plan, and Gorbachev, in a sweeping proposal for a phased transition to a nuclear-free world by the year 2000, had also endorsed the aim of eliminating all nuclear weapons. However, the Soviet Union continued to link progress in strategic offensive arms reductions with limitations on space weapons.

On May 27, 1986, President Reagan announced that, as a result of alleged Soviet violations and lack of progress in the START talks, the United States would no longer be bound by its political commitment to the limits of the SALT treaties. Two days later in Geneva, the Soviet Union tabled a new strategic offensive weapons proposal, calling for no more than 8,000 nuclear warheads on 1,600 delivery vehicles. Although the Soviet Union had dropped several demands which the United States had found unacceptable, it made its entire proposal contingent upon a commitment by both sides not to exercise the right to withdraw from the ABM Treaty for at least 15-20 years and to adhere to the ABM Treaty's ban on the development and testing of space-based ABM systems.

In September 1986, the United States presented a revised proposal calling for 1,600 strategic nuclear delivery vehicles (which was also the limit proposed by the Soviet Union) and 7,500 ballistic missile and ALCM warheads. This

START Hangups

The START negotiations have been slowed by disagreements over whether and how to limit mobile ICBMs, such as the Soviet SS-25 shown in an artist's concept above, and sea-launched cruise missiles (SLCMs). In the photo at right, a US Tomahawk SLCM rises from the sea after being launched from a submarine (artist's concept, below).

proposal narrowed somewhat the differences between the US and Soviet positions and set the stage for the second Reagan-Gorbachev summit.

In October 1986 Reagan and Gorbachev met on very short notice in Reykjavik, Iceland. The two leaders engaged in a remarkable exchange of wide-ranging and radical proposals on the elimination of ballistic nuclear weapons, and even all nuclear weapons, but the meeting ultimately broke down over the question of limitations on SDI and the interpretation of the ABM Treaty. Nevertheless, the sides did make some progress by agreeing to reduce strategic nuclear delivery vehicles (land-based and submarine-based missile launchers and heavy bombers) to 1,600 in the first five years of a potential 10-year START agreement. They also agreed to cut strategic warheads to an accountable limit of 6,000, which would include all strategic ballistic missile warheads and ALCMs, as well as other bomber armament on a sharply discounted basis (i.e., all the gravity bombs and short-range attack missiles on any individual bomber would only count as a single warhead in the 6,000 aggregate). Sea-launched cruise missiles (SLCMs) would be limited separately from the 6,000 accountable warheads.

Over the next two years, the sides made steady but slow progress towards a START agreement. In May and July of 1987 the United States and the Soviet Union tabled draft treaties based on their respective understandings of the Reykjavik framework. These individual drafts were combined into a Joint Draft Text to serve as the working document of the negotiations.

At the Washington summit in December 1987, at which the INF Treaty was signed, the United States and Soviet Union issued a comprehensive statement outlining the agreed framework for a START treaty based on an aggregate ceiling of 6,000 accountable warheads on 1,600 deployed launchers with a subceiling of 4,900 warheads on ballistic missiles.

At the conclusion of the Washington summit, US and Soviet spokesmen indicated that a START agreement could be ready for signature at a Moscow summit in several months. However, the impasse over how to deal with strategic defenses remained; the United States demanded the ability to terminate a reinterpreted ABM Treaty after a fixed period, and the Soviet Union insisted that the ABM Treaty "as originally" signed be kept in force for at least 10 years. At the June 1988 Moscow summit, despite a further improvement in US-Soviet relations, the START agreement was not ready for signature and very little progress was made on the resolution of remaining differences. At that time, it was reported that there were still over 1,200 "brackets" in the Joint Draft Text indicating disagreements on specific language to be resolved before a START treaty could be completed.

Although negotiation continued after the Moscow summit, little progress was reported for the balance of the Reagan administration. With the existing impasse on strategic defense, it appeared that neither side was prepared to compromise on remaining issues, which themselves tended to be magnified in significance even as they were reduced in number.

Status and Issues

The Bush administration inherited from Reagan an almost completely agreed framework for deep reductions in strategic offensive arms agreed to by both the United States and the Soviet Union. If the United States and the Soviet Union are able to resolve the long-standing impasse over strategic defenses and the future of the ABM Treaty, it should be possible to reach agreement on the remaining elements of this framework and convert it relatively expeditiously into agreed treaty language.

The established START framework would require a reduction of accountable strategic weapons to a common aggregate ceiling of 6,000 on a total of 1,600 deployed launchers. Of the permitted 6,000 weapons, no more than 4,900 could be deployed on ICBMs and SLBMs. A separate sublimit of 1,540 would be imposed on the number of warheads carried by "heavy" ICBMs. Overall missile throw-weight would be reduced to 50 percent of the current Soviet level. Within this aggregate ceiling of 6,000 warheads, bomber weapons would be counted at a greatly discounted rate since all the bombs and SRAMs carried by a single strategic bomber would be counted as one weapon regardless of the number carried. (Current loadings can be 16 or more.)

This negotiated framework would achieve many long-standing US objectives for START by requiring disproportionately large reductions in ballistic missiles, particularly ICBMs, which the United States has long argued are more dangerous and destabilizing than bombers and cruise missiles. In addition, the framework would specifically result in a 50-percent reduction in SS-18 heavy ICBMs, which are particularly destabilizing. Since bomber weapons will be

Reykjavik

At the October 1986 summit in Reykjavik, Iceland, Reagan and Gorbachev agreed on a set of START limits before the talks broke down over disputes about SDI and the ABM Treaty. Fundamental disagreement over the future of strategic defenses has been the main obstacle to the completion of a START agreement.

counted at a greatly discounted rate, the reduction to 6,000 "accountable" weapons by the United States and the Soviet Union will involve an actual reduction of some 30 percent or less rather than the advertised 50 percent. Given the large US quantitative and qualitative advantage in strategic bombers and their associated weapons, the effect of the bomber counting rule would currently favor the United States, although it would also allow the Soviet Union to build up its bomber forces in the future.

The net result of this agreement would be to reduce over a period of years the actual US arsenal of some 13,000 strategic warheads at the end of the Reagan administration to around 8,000-9,000. Similarly, the Soviet arsenal of strategic warheads would be reduced from the approximately 10,600 which existed at the end of the Reagan administration to roughly 6,000-7,000, not counting the currently small numbers of nuclear bombs and short-range nuclear missiles on Soviet strategic bombers. In both cases, the final numbers would have to be adjusted to include the number of nuclear SLCMs eventually permitted under the treaty.

Several important issues remain unresolved as of early 1989. Although the sides earlier agreed to negotiate separate limitations on SLCMs, little progress has been made toward reaching an agreed limit. The Soviet Union has called this dispute a critical issue. The United States wants to leave SLCMs, particularly those with non-nuclear warheads, essentially unrestricted while the Soviet Union wants to have strict limits on both nuclear and conventionally armed SLCMs. The important issue of whether or not to permit mobile ICBMs also remains unresolved. Although the US position is that such missiles should be banned unless acceptable verification provisions are established, the sides have reportedly made some progress towards developing such a verification regime. The question of precisely how to count air-launched cruise missiles is unresolved as well.

Final agreement has yet to be reached on verification procedures, not only for provisions still in contention (SLCMs, mobile ICBMs, and ALCMs), but also for provisions, such as the numbers of warheads on each ballistic missile, where agreement has already been reached.

Agreed verification guidelines—based on the precedents set by the INF Treaty—include data exchanges, several types of on-site inspection, short-notice inspections, a ban on telemetry encryption and other concealment measures, and cooperative measures to enhance observation by national technical means of verification. Ultimately, the details of the verification provisions will depend on how extensive and how intrusive the agreed on-site inspection will be. For its part, the United States has apparently already decided that it does not want to seek unlimited inspection rights, because it is reluctant to allow Soviet inspectors access to sensitive US facilities.

Even before the START treaty has been completed, its basic framework has been strongly criticized by some US security analysts. These analysts question both the specific effect of START on the survivability of US strategic forces and the overall desirability of reducing strategic forces in the absence of improvements in the conventional balance, on the grounds that this would undermine the effectiveness of the US nuclear deterrent in the face of Soviet superiority in conventional weapons facing NATO.

The criticism of START's effect on US strategic forces holds that START would actually make US land-based and sea-based forces more vulnerable to attack and would result in reduced crisis stability. Specifically, it is argued that in the absence of a US decision to deploy mobile ICBMs the reductions required by START will leave ICBMs more vulnerable to a Soviet attack than without START. In the case of sea-based systems, it is argued that START would force the United States to deploy its sea-based weapons in a smaller number of submarines, which would make this leg of the strategic triad more vulnerable to potential advances in Soviet antisubmarine warfare (ASW) capabilities.

Senior officials of the Reagan administration and other security experts have rejected these criticisms. They have argued that the provisions of START will actually reduce the overall threat to US strategic forces, including ICBMs, while permitting the United States the flexibility to deploy whatever mix of fixed and mobile land-based missiles it deems appropriate. With regard to the effect of START on submarines, these observers point out that the reduction in the number of submarines deployed by the United States is not due to START but to a conscious decision that the increased range, quietness, and efficiency of Trident submarines as compared to older Poseidon submarines justify concentrating SLBM warheads in 20 rather than 35 boats. Senior administration officials have argued that this reduction in numbers does not reduce the survivability of sea-based systems because US intelligence foresees no significant threat to our nuclear missile submarines through at least the end of the century. Moreover, START would not prevent the United States from distributing SLBM warheads on a larger number of platforms if Soviet ASW were to improve significantly.

Some critics have also argued that START should not be completed until perceived Soviet and Warsaw Pact advantages in conventional arms in Europe have been reduced or eliminated. This view has been rejected by the Joint Chiefs of Staff, the Reagan administration, and officials within the NATO alliance. Moreover, following Mikhail Gorbachev's pledge at the United Nations in December 1988 to withdraw unilaterally a significant portion of Soviet tanks and troops from Eastern Europe, this argument is unlikely to be persuasive. If the Bush administration moves towards the completion of START, beyond the fundamental issue of strategic defenses, the domestic debate will probably center on the question of survivability of US strategic forces and the closely related issue of what missiles and bombers the United States should deploy in the coming decades under the treaty.

The Missile Site Radar of the Safeguard Ballistic Missile Defense System deployed in North Dakota in the 1970s.

7

Strategic Defensive Arms Control: The ABM Treaty and Star Wars

Background

Over the ages, military technology has seen a continuous competition between offense and defense. The machine-gun was the answer to the infantry or cavalry charge; the tank was the answer to the machine-gun. But the development of nuclear weapons suddenly increased the destructive power of offensive weapons a million-fold, creating a fundamentally new situation in warfare.

After trying and failing to find effective defenses against the devastating power of nuclear weapons, the United States and the Soviet Union agreed to the Antiballistic Missile (ABM) Treaty of 1972. The treaty banned nationwide defenses against ballistic missiles and was intended to prevent the development of the sort of

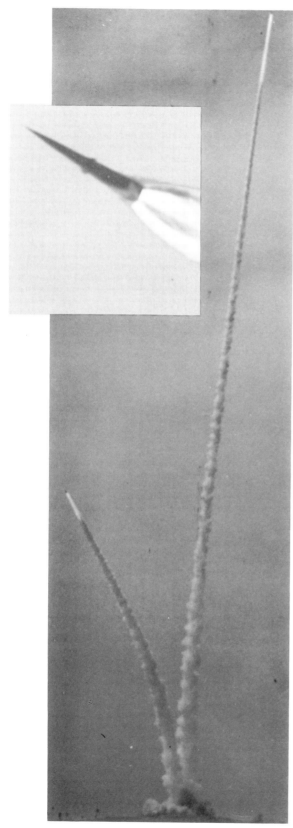

Pre-SDI Defense

ABM systems of the 1960s and '70s relied on nuclear-armed missile interceptors. Above are two Sprint ABM missiles fired in salvo. Inset shows a Sprint during launch.

offense/defense arms race that had long plagued military technology in other fields. In signing the treaty, the two sides recognized that strategic offenses and defenses were closely linked and that deployment of defenses would only encourage increases and improvements in offensive forces in order to overcome them.

Then in 1983, President Reagan rejected the conclusions that had led to the ABM Treaty—that a truly effective defense could not be found, and that attempts to build defenses would only stimulate an offense/defense arms race—and called for a massive research program to develop a defense that would render nuclear weapons "impotent and obsolete." Since then, there has been increasing tension between the ABM Treaty and Reagan's Strategic Defense Initiative (SDI), impeding progress in strategic arms control.

Defense Before Star Wars

Efforts to develop a defense against nuclear weapons stretch back to the beginning of the nuclear age. In the early 1950s, the United States began a major air defense program to protect US territory from attack by anticipated Soviet long-range bombers. The defense system involved a network of radars for detecting and tracking bombers and surface-to-air-missiles (SAMs) to intercept them.

The advent of Soviet intercontinental ballistic missiles (ICBMs) in the late 1950s forced a reevaluation of the air defense program. The system was judged ineffective against a future threat from Soviet aircraft, could not intercept ICBMs, and was extremely vulnerable to direct ICBM attack. Consequently, the program was gradually phased out.

Even before the first Soviet ICBM was tested, the United States had initiated research on antiballistic missile (ABM) defenses. The Nike-Zeus ABM system, which emerged from this program, was based on mechanically steered radars and nuclear-armed interceptor missiles. Nike-Zeus would have been able to destroy some incoming warheads, but officials recognized that it could not have protected the nation from any sizable attack, especially if an adversary employed countermeasures (such as decoys or bits of radar-reflecting foil, called chaff) to overwhelm the system. Nike-Zeus evolved into the more sophisticated Nike-X, which used more powerful phased-array radars and the high-acceleration Sprint missile along with the longer

Deployments Under the ABM Treaty

The ABM Treaty and its 1974 protocol allow the United States and the Soviet Union one ABM site armed with no more than 100 interceptors. Above is an artist's concept of a Soviet Galosh interceptor, one of two types of ABM missiles deployed at the Soviet Union's single permitted site at Moscow. Below is a 1975 photograph of the US ABM site at Grand Forks, North Dakota. The United States shut down the facility because it did not believe the protection provided by the system was worth the cost of continued operations and maintenance.

range Zeus missile. But the growing size of Soviet offensive arsenals also rendered Nike-X ineffective and neither system was ever deployed.

In the mid-1960s a public debate grew in the United States over the costs and dangers of antiballistic missile systems. Soviet ABM activities, including initial ABM deployments around Moscow, as well as China's initiation of a ballistic missile program, increased pressures in the United States for deployment of an ABM defense. Advocates argued that the United States had to match Soviet ABM developments. They held that new technologies showed promise of providing the nation with a defense against nuclear attack, and that any such promise should be vigorously pursued.

Critics responded that ABMs simply would not work. An attacker could easily disable the entire ABM system by destroying its few highly vulnerable radars. Even if the radars somehow survived, the system could not possibly track and destroy a large number of incoming warheads in a nuclear-war environment. The destructive power of nuclear weapons ensured that the large number of weapons that would leak through any foreseeable defense would completely devastate the country. ABM critics also argued that, as envisioned, an ABM system would cost far more than enemy countermeasures, such as an increase in relatively inexpensive nuclear weapons or even cheaper decoys, which could be easily developed.

Other critics held that limits on ABMs were essential for slowing the arms race. Even if these systems were unable to defend the country over

the long term, many feared that the superpowers would be forced in the short term to expand the size of their offensive forces to maintain confidence in their retaliatory capabilities. With each side compensating for its adversary's new offenses by building more defenses, a costly, spiralling arms race in both offensive and defensive weapons would be unavoidable.

The final and perhaps most decisive criticism of ABM defensive systems was that they would increase the risk of nuclear war. In a world of less-than-perfect ABMs, each side might believe that by attacking first it could penetrate an opponent's ABM defenses and destroy a substantial portion of the other side's nuclear forces. The attacker could then use its own ABM weapons to intercept the adversary's reduced and ragged retaliation. Even though it is highly unlikely that effective defenses could be developed, each side might believe its defenses were just enough to gain a significant advantage by initiating an attack—precisely the situation that could precipitate a war in a crisis.

The arguments against deploying antiballistic missile defenses persuaded President Johnson and Secretary of Defense Robert McNamara to try to prevent an ABM arms race. At a June 1967 summit in Glassboro, New Jersey, Johnson and McNamara attempted to convince Soviet Premier Alexei Kosygin of the advantages of an agreement to limit ABM systems. But Kosygin was reluctant to abandon the Soviet ABM program and argued that no Soviet leader could reasonably forgo any effort to defend his country.

Under pressure from Congress and unable to bring the Soviet Union to the negotiating table, President Johnson decided in September 1967 to deploy the Sentinel ABM system, the successor to Nike-X. Paradoxically, McNamara announced the decision to deploy in a speech that emphasized that a nationwide ABM defense was probably not feasible, would be very expensive, and would only accelerate the arms race. The stated purpose of Sentinel was not to protect against a determined Soviet attack but to offer protection from a limited Chinese attack or an accidental Soviet missile launch.

In 1968, after the US decision to deploy its own ABM system, the Soviet Union reconsidered the US arguments against missile defenses and agreed to initiate negotiations. But the talks, which were scheduled to begin in September 1968, were postponed by President Johnson after the Soviet occupation of Czechoslovakia in August 1968.

ABM Negotiations

The Nixon administration, which took office in 1969, questioned the Sentinel ABM system on strategic grounds and decided to deploy a somewhat different system called Safeguard. Safeguard, while technologically similar to Sentinel, had an entirely different rationale. It was intended to protect Minuteman ICBM fields, Strategic Air Command bases, and the National Command Authority in Washington rather than to provide a thin defense of the entire nation.

Plans to develop and deploy the Safeguard system fueled the debate within the United States regarding the utility, wisdom, and feasibility of strategic defenses. But as this debate intensified, the United States and the Soviet Union agreed to begin the Strategic Arms Limitation Talks (SALT). From November 1969 to May 1972, US and Soviet delegations discussed complex questions related to what kind of limitations were desirable for defenses as well as what, if any, limits should be placed on offensive systems.

After the first year and a half of negotiations, the parties were able to reach an agreement on ABM limitations. The Soviet Union then sought to restrict the SALT negotiations to ABM systems and to defer the limits on offensive systems. As a result of the continuing deadlock over offensive limits, the sides finally agreed to conclude an

Head to Head

Ambassador Gerard C. Smith (right) led the US team in negotiations with Vladimir Semenov (left) and his Soviet delegation during the two and a half years of talks that produced the ABM Treaty.

ABM Eyes

The ABM Treaty places strict limits on the deployment of large phased-array radars (LPARs). The critical guiding eyes of ground-based ABM systems, LPARs also provide for early warning, space tracking and verification.

ABM Treaty of unlimited duration and an interim five-year agreement to limit certain offensive arms, to be followed by negotiations to achieve a more comprehensive offensive treaty.

The signing of the ABM Treaty signified formal recognition by the United States and the Soviet Union that deterrence, based on the inherent mutual capability for assured destruction, was the basis of security in the nuclear age. Without ABM defenses, neither power could delude itself into thinking it could survive and win a nuclear war. Because of the inherent link between defenses and the offenses needed to overcome them, the treaty also laid the basis for curbing the ongoing strategic offensive arms race. The ABM Treaty is thus the keystone of strategic arms control.

ABM Treaty Provisions

The ABM Treaty was designed to prevent either side from building a nationwide or "territorial" defense against strategic ballistic missiles. It accomplishes this through a series of quantitative and qualitative limits on development, testing, and deployment of ABM systems and components. The United States and the Soviet Union were each allowed only two 100-interceptor ABM sites, one to defend the national capital and one to defend an ICBM field. A 1974 protocol reduced the number of permitted sites to one, which could be either the national capital or an ICBM field. The Soviet Union has maintained its single permitted ABM site around Moscow and is currently modernizing it, but in 1975 the United States abandoned its Grand Forks, North Dakota, site because the protection provided by its 100 interceptors to the adjacent missile field was judged not to be worth the cost of maintaining the system.

The ABM Treaty contains detailed provisions designed to prevent either side from gaining the capability to "break out" from its limitations and rapidly deploy a nationwide defense. Since large phased-array radars (LPARs) were then the critical guiding eyes of ABM systems and the long lead-time items in constructing a nationwide defense, the ABM Treaty places strict limits on their deployment. ABM radars may only be deployed at the single permitted site or at agreed ABM test ranges, and new early-warning radars can only be constructed along the periphery of the country and oriented outward.

Similarly, since mobile ABMs have an inherent potential for rapid deployment to protect broad areas, the development, testing, and deployment of all sea-based, air-based, space-based, and mobile land-based ABM systems and

Presidential Orders

In his instructions to the US delegation at the ABM talks, President Nixon ordered chief US negotiator Gerard Smith to seek limits on future ABM systems to prevent circumvention of the treaty by unforeseen technological developments. During the reinterpretation debate, Nixon said the ABM Treaty he presented to the Senate in 1972 conforms to the strict interpretation of the agreement.

components is banned. Only research on mobile systems and components may be conducted. Under the traditional view of the ABM Treaty, this ban on mobile systems applies equally to both traditional-technology ABMs, such as interceptor missiles and radars, and those based on "other physical principles," such as lasers and particle beams. Such new-technology ABM systems and components may be developed and tested if they are fixed and land-based, but they cannot be deployed unless the treaty is amended.

In addition, the development, testing, and deployment of multiple-warhead or rapidly reloadable ABMs is banned, to protect the limit on ABM firepower implicit in the 100-interceptor limit at the single permitted ABM site. The treaty also prohibits giving non-ABM systems and components—such as air defense missiles or antisatellite weapons—an ABM capability, or testing them in an ABM mode. While the treaty only applies to the United States and the Soviet Union, neither side is permitted to give ABM systems and components (or the technical descriptions to build them) to other countries or to deploy them outside its national territory.

To facilitate verification of these provisions, the treaty prohibits interference with national technical means of verification, which include such intelligence systems as radars and photoreconnaissance satellites, and bars deliberate concealment to impede verification. The treaty also created a bilateral forum, the Standing Consultative Commission (SCC), to resolve details of implementing the accord, clarify compliance questions, and discuss possible means of strengthening the treaty.

ABM Treaty Status

On May 26, 1972, President Nixon and General Secretary Brezhnev signed the SALT I Agreements: the ABM Treaty and the five-year Interim Agreement on Strategic Offensive Arms. The US Senate gave its advice and consent to the ABM Treaty and approved the Interim Agreement by votes of 88 to 2, reflecting the broad consensus in the United States regarding these difficult issues.

The ABM Treaty is of unlimited duration, continuing forever unless one or both sides decide to withdraw. Either side can withdraw from the agreement on six months' notice if "extraordinary events" jeopardize its "supreme national interest." Under international law, a party can also withdraw from a treaty if the other party commits a "material breach," defined as the violation of "a provision essential to the accomplishment of the object or purpose of the treaty."

Every five years, the two countries are obligated to hold a review conference on the treaty. In 1977 and 1982, the review conferences reaffirmed the importance and effectiveness of the ABM Treaty. In early 1983, however, the debate over strategic defensive systems was renewed when President Reagan announced a major new ABM research program called the Strategic Defense Initiative (SDI), a program designed to develop exactly the kind of nationwide defense the ABM Treaty was intended to ban. Although the third review conference ended in discord in 1988, with each side accusing the other of violations, the treaty remains in force.

The Treaty Reinterpretation

At the outset of SDI, President Reagan assured Congress, US allies, and the Soviet Union that the program would be conducted entirely in accordance with the ABM Treaty. But early on, the Department of Defense announced plans for space tests that some experts believed would undermine the treaty's ban on testing of space-based ABM components. The Department of Defense argued that the planned tests were not of "components" but of "adjuncts," or "subcomponents," or of technologies not yet powerful enough to serve as ABM components. Eventually, even if the announced tests could be considered legal, violations of the treaty would be inevitable as the program progressed, since the program was explicitly directed toward deployment of a system that the treaty was designed to prevent.

In an effort to widen the area of permitted activity under the ABM Treaty, the Reagan administration announced in October 1985 a major reinterpretation of the ABM Treaty that had the effect of exempting much of the SDI program from the treaty's restrictions. Administration lawyers claimed that although the treaty banned the development and testing of space-based and other mobile ABM "systems or components," a close reading of the treaty's text and its negotiating record indicated that the Soviet Union never agreed to include restrictions on the development and testing of exotic-technology systems such as lasers and particle beams.

Many experts, however, including all but one of the US ABM Treaty negotiators, immediately condemned this "broad" interpretation as directly contrary to the language and intent of the treaty itself, to the negotiating record, to the ratification record as explained by the Nixon administration to the Congress, and to 13 years (1972-85) of subsequent practice by the parties to the treaty. Every administration since 1972, including the Reagan administration through 1985, agreed with the original interpretation, which was also supported by the Soviet Union. In April 1988, former President Nixon said he never anticipated that a subsequent administration might try to reinterpret the treaty, and confirmed that, "As far as what was presented to the Senate was concerned, it was what we call the narrow interpretation. There is no question about that."

Supporters of the traditional view argue that, while the ABM Treaty allows extensive research (to the point of field-testing), it specifically bans the development and testing of mobile systems, whether "conventional" or "exotic." This provision was built into the treaty because mobile systems are inherently suitable for a nationwide defense, which the treaty sought to ban. Reinterpreting the treaty to remove the ban on mobile systems would render the treaty "a dead letter," in the words of the chief US negotiator of the ABM Treaty, Ambassador Gerard C. Smith.

In addition to these legal criticisms of the broad interpretation, supporters of the traditional view maintain that an effective SDI research program can be carried out for many years under the narrow interpretation, particularly since exotic weapons such as lasers and particle beams are still in their infancy, far from the point at which space-based testing against strategic missiles is necessary. Moreover, supporters of the traditional view argue that the broad interpretation would undermine not only the ABM Treaty but the prospects for arms control generally.

After heated criticism of the reinterpretation from Congress and the allies, the Reagan administration announced that although it considered the new interpretation to be "fully justified" and "legally correct," it would continue to abide by the original, "restrictive" interpretation of the treaty. This position muted criticism, but left the door open for the United States—and the Soviet Union, if it chose to do so—to develop and test exotic ABM weapons in the future.

At the beginning of 1987, the issue came to the fore again as the Defense Department sought authorization to proceed with testing and development of SDI systems under the broad interpretation, and a heated battle ensued in the Senate. Then State Department Legal Adviser Abraham Sofaer released a series of studies defending the broad interpretation, while Senator Sam Nunn (D-GA), chairman of the Senate Armed Services Committee, released a series of studies supporting the traditional view. Nunn and other senators argued that if the administration could ignore the meaning of the treaty as described to the Senate in 1972, the Senate's constitutional role in the treaty-making process would be seriously undermined.

By the end of 1987, a provision limiting SDI tests to those certified by the Defense Department as compliant with the traditional interpretation had been passed into law, as part of the fiscal year 1988 Defense Authorization Bill. This was repeated the following year. In addition, in May 1988 the Senate attached a provision to the INF Treaty resolution of ratification barring the President from changing the meaning of treaties from that presented to the Senate.

The Strategic Defense Initiative

On March 23, 1983, President Reagan reopened the debate over missile defense, calling on the scientific community to develop an ABM system that would render "nuclear weapons impotent and obsolete." Such a defense, he argued, could completely replace deterrence based on the threat of nuclear retaliation. "Wouldn't it be better," he asked, "to save lives rather than to avenge them?" The President's speech launched the Strategic Defense Initiative, more popularly known as "Star Wars." Since then, SDI has become the most expensive and far-reaching military research program in US history, consuming some $17 billion in its first six years. Because a Star Wars defense would need a variety of weapons, sensors, communications, and new rockets to lift the satellites into orbit, SDI is an extremely broad research program, covering high technology from lasers to rocket nozzles, from radars to computer software.

Unlike previous US missile defense programs, which concentrated on attacking missiles at the very end of their flight, the SDI program has focused on the concept of a "multi-layered" defense, attacking missiles throughout their flight, but centering particularly on boost-phase defense, intercepting Soviet missiles in the minutes just after launch. (See box on page 75.)

Because a boost-phase defense would have to intercept Soviet missiles while they are still over the Soviet Union, most of the defense would have to be based on satellites in space. SDI planners envision networks of hundreds of satellites, carrying both weapons and sensors, the eyes of the system, to detect and track Soviet missiles. In the near term, such a boost-phase defense would rely on space-based interceptors (SBIs), rockets designed to home in on Soviet missiles and destroy them by direct impact. In the longer term, SDI scientists are developing space-based laser battle stations, or ground-based lasers whose beams would flash up into space and be reflected by a series of orbiting mirrors, finally flashing onto Soviet missiles on the other side of the earth. Another, even more exotic possibility is the X-ray laser, which theoretically would focus the power of a nuclear bomb into multiple high-power laser beams to blast Soviet missiles from enormous distances.

These plans involve extremely complex technology, still in its infancy. In 1987, an authoritative report by the American Physical Society, the national professional organization of physicists,

SDI Research

Although several proposals have been offered for near-term deployment of strategic defenses, the exotic technologies being pursued under the Strategic Defense Initiative are in an early stage of research. Above is a laboratory facility for an electromagnetic launcher, or railgun, which fires high-velocity bullets.

concluded that at least 10 years of research would be required to determine whether "directed-energy weapons" such as lasers or particle beams could be effective. The report warned that each of these technologies seems likely to be even more effective in an offensive role—shooting down enemy satellites (including ABM satellites)—than in a defensive role.

In addition to these space-based weapons and sensors, SDI planners envision eventually building thousands of ground-based rocket interceptors and linking the whole system with an extremely complex network of radars, computers, and communications equipment. Because thousands of Soviet missiles would have to be intercepted within a few minutes, much of the operation of the defensive system would have to be controlled by computers. By SDI planners' own estimates, this will require computer software far more complex than any yet created. And the entire high-technology global system would have to work the first time it was ever tried, in the midst of an all-out nuclear attack, an environment in which it could never be tested beforehand. Former Secretaries of Defense James Schlesinger and Harold Brown have roughly estimated the total cost of a "thick" defense at $1 trillion, though SDI supporters argue that probable costs (particularly of "thin" defenses that would intercept only a small fraction of Soviet missiles) would be much less.

Phases of a Missile's Flight

The Strategic Defense Initiative is intended to develop a multi-layered defense to attack missiles throughout their flight. The flight of a ballistic missile can be divided into four phases, each of which presents different problems and opportunities to possible defenses.

Flight begins with the "boost phase," the few minutes between ignition and burnout of the missile's rocket. Missiles in the boost phase are high-value targets because they have not yet released their complement of warheads. A successful attack on a missile in boost phase may destroy as many as a dozen or more nuclear warheads at once as well as possible warhead-mimicking decoys. But attacks on missiles in the boost phase generally require space-based weapons which are likely to be costly and vulnerable. Although the missile's rocket flare is easily detectable during the boost phase, the time for boost-phase attack is short: the rockets of current long-range missiles burn for three to five minutes, and future "fast-burn boosters" may complete their boost phase in a minute or less, making boost-phase attack extremely difficult.

The "post-boost phase" is the period during which the missile's "bus" maneuvers to place its warheads and decoys on the proper trajectories to their targets: the advantages and disadvantages of attacking a missile in the post-boost phase are similar to those of the boost phase, though the engines of the missile bus are smaller and more difficult to detect than the missile's main rockets.

The "midcourse phase" is the relatively long central portion of the flight in which the warheads coast through space, possibly accompanied by hundreds of thousands of decoys and other "penetration aids." For an ICBM, the midcourse phase lasts some 20 to 25 minutes, giving the defense more time to attack. However, discriminating the warheads from the thousands of cheap decoys would be very difficult.

The "terminal" or "reentry phase" is the few tens of seconds of a missile's flight when the warheads reenter the atmosphere (hence the term "reentry vehicle") and eventually detonate over or on their targets. Defense in this phase is technologically less demanding than in the other phases, but timelines are extremely short, and very large numbers of interceptors would be required for a nationwide defense, since each target area would have to be defended separately.

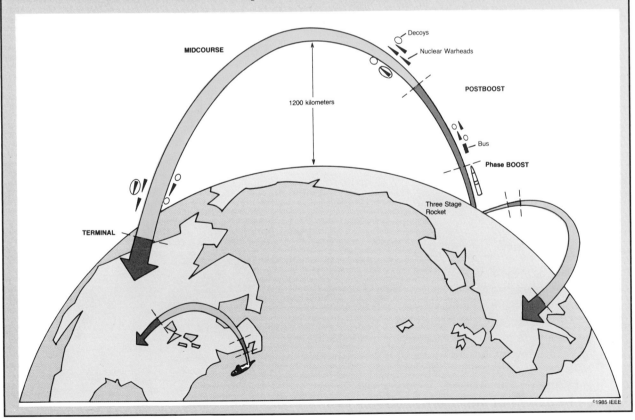

Infrared Sensor

The Airborne Optical Adjunct (AOA), carried in the hump of this modified jetliner, is designed to test the effectiveness of infrared sensors for tracking and discriminating ballistic missile warheads. Critics have questioned the experiment's compliance with the ABM Treaty's ban on development and testing of mobile ABM components.

The SDI Debate

SDI has been the subject of intense controversy, replaying many of the 1960s arguments for and against missile defenses. Advocates argue that new defenses will dramatically reduce the nuclear threat, while critics hold that they will provide no real protection and will intensify the nuclear arms race. SDI advocates argue that dramatic advances in such areas as infrared sensors, lasers, particle beams, and high-speed computers have created a new situation, calling into question the conclusion that real defense is unachievable, which led to the ABM Treaty. Advocates also cite ongoing Soviet ABM and ABM-related programs as reasons for pursuing a vigorous SDI program. Critics disagree, arguing that the awesome destructive power of nuclear weapons has not changed and continues to make highly effective defenses an unachievable goal.

A Defense of Cities?

Many supporters of SDI, most notably former President Reagan, hold out the possibility of a perfect or near-perfect defense. In June 1986, Reagan described SDI as leading to "a shield that missiles could not penetrate—a shield that could protect us from nuclear missiles just as a roof protects a family from rain." On June 1, 1988, after the Moscow summit, Reagan predicted that SDI "can just make it impossible for missiles to get through the screen." However, as former Strategic Defense Initiative Organization (SDIO)

Director Lt. General James Abrahamson has often acknowledged, "Nothing is perfect and there is no such thing as a perfect defense."

Critics of SDI point out that because of the incredible destructive power of nuclear weapons, only a near-perfect defense could actually protect US cities from Soviet attack. As was demonstrated at Hiroshima and Nagasaki, a single atomic bomb can devastate a city. If a city's defense missed even one attacking warhead, it would leave the city in ruins. Today, the Soviet Union has some 10,000 warheads capable of reaching the United States, each many times

Pointing and Tracking

The Sealight Beam Director was developed for use with the MIRACL high-energy laser. This experimental pointing and tracking system is designed to track targets in flight and direct a high power laser beam to selected aimpoints.

more powerful than the bombs dropped on Japan. Hence, critics of SDI argue, the ability of the United States and the Soviet Union to destroy each other is simply a fact of the nuclear age, resulting from the power of nuclear weapons and the vulnerability of cities—factors that no plausible defense system will be able to change.

These critics argue that, while technology has changed since 1972, the fundamental problems facing a missile defense remain the same. They contend that Soviet countermeasures would be much cheaper and less complex than the defense system itself. For example, the Soviet Union could attack the defense satellites, perhaps with weapons similar to those developed in the SDI program. Or the Soviet Union could deploy hundreds of thousands of warhead decoys during an attack, confusing and overwhelming the defense. Nuclear explosions or offensive jamming might blind the defense's sensors. Fast-burning missiles could drastically increase the cost of the critical boost-phase defense by requiring the deployment of many more satellites to insure coverage. Bombers and cruise missiles would avoid a ballistic missile defense entirely.

The most obvious countermeasure, and the most troubling for the future of arms control, is to increase radically the size of offensive forces. The Soviet Union might step up production of offensive missiles or increase the number of warheads on each missile to overwhelm the defense.

Supporters of SDI acknowledge these possibilities but maintain that new technologies may someday lead to defenses able to overcome even a determined and sophisticated offense. Paul Nitze, President Reagan's senior arms control adviser, outlined three basic requirements for such a defense, which have been incorporated into law. Before a defense can be deployed, it must be: *1)* militarily effective, *2)* survivable against Soviet attack, and *3)* "cost-effective at the margin," meaning that the United States could maintain a defense capability more cheaply than the Soviets could increase their forces or deploy countermeasures to overcome it.

Former Secretary of State George Shultz added two criteria: that each phase of defensive deployments must be carefully managed to avoid creating instabilities, and that the first phase of a defensive system must not be deployed before the final concept is understood. SDI critics believe that these criteria cannot be met. Cities, they say, are precious, rare, and vulnerable, while nuclear weapons are cheap, numerous, and incredibly destructive, creating a fundamental advantage for the offense.

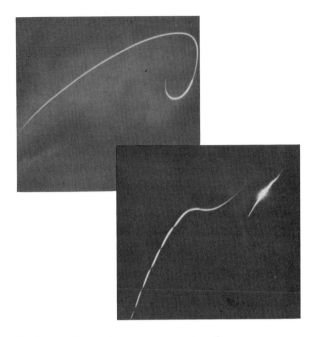

Defense Countermeasures for the Midcourse and Reentry Phases

Maneuvering reentry vehicles (MaRVs), such as the Mk500 Evader shown above in flight tests, could avoid defensive systems by changing course during reentry. The United States and the Soviet Union could also equip their missiles with thousands of penetration aids to confuse SDI systems. The photo below shows the deck of a proposed penetration aid system for the MX missile. Such a system might release chaff, aerosols, and warhead decoys in the form of lightweight balloons or small radar-jamming reentry vehicles.

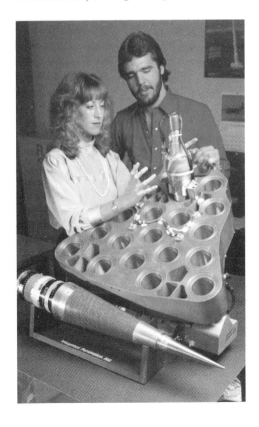

Imperfect Defenses and the Arms Race

Some SDI advocates argue that even a partial defense would be valuable and might be one step toward the long-term goal of a nearly perfect defense. Even an imperfect defense, they argue, could create "uncertainty" in Soviet war plans, particularly if the Soviet Union contemplated a first-strike attack to destroy the US nuclear deterrent. A limited defense might also provide protection against an accidental Soviet missile launch, and if it achieved a high level of effectiveness might limit the damage if a nuclear war occurred.

Critics reply that the United States already has an assured deterrent, with thousands of warheads constantly at sea in invulnerable submarines and more on board alert bombers. Hence a missile defense is not necessary to create uncertainty in the mind of the opponent or improve the survivability of US forces. Moreover, deployment of even an imperfect nationwide defense would raise a number of profound strategic risks. It would irrevocably destroy the ABM Treaty, possibly dooming prospects for agreements reducing strategic offensive arms. SDI critics believe that the fundamental rationale for the ABM Treaty is still valid: deployment of nationwide defenses would only encourage each side to build up offenses to overcome them, leading to a costly and dangerous arms race.

Some types of partial defenses would not conflict with the ABM Treaty as directly as the nationwide defenses proposed by SDI advocates. The ABM Treaty allows deployment of 100 ABM interceptors at a single ABM site. The Soviet Union has such a site at Moscow. In early 1988, Senator Sam Nunn (D-GA), chairman of the Senate Armed Services Committee, urged consideration of possible measures to deal with the risk of an accidental or unauthorized launch of nuclear missiles, possibly including a limited missile defense he dubbed the "Accidental Launch Protection System" (ALPS). Some defense contractors have proposed reopening the US ABM site at Grand Forks, North Dakota, and deploying 100 new-generation ABM interceptors there to create a rudimentary ALPS defense. However, a single site in the center of the country could not protect the coasts against submarine-launched missiles. Moreover, since some Soviet submarines carry up to 200 warheads, considerably more than 100 interceptor missiles would be needed to defend against some possible un-

authorized launch scenarios. As a result, providing a complete ALPS system would require several ABM sites and major amendments to the ABM Treaty. To permit several sites, each armed with more than 100 interceptors, would seriously undermine the treaty, allowing each side to build a base for a nationwide defense. Critics question the cost and effectiveness of an ALPS system and argue that the risk of accidental or unauthorized launches is small. The threat, if worrisome, might be more cheaply and effectively handled by emplacing better PALs (permissive action links) on all systems, including ballistic missile submarines, and "command destruct" systems on operational missiles to allow them to be destroyed in flight in the event of an accident, as is already done with test missiles.

In another approach, short-range interceptors could be used to defend some US missile silos near the Grand Forks site, in what is often referred to as "hard-site defense." Defenses of hardened missile silos, which rely on somewhat different technology than widespread defenses of cities and population, might bolster deterrence by making retaliatory forces less vulnerable to surprise attack. However, many analysts dispute whether this is a problem, and, if so, whether an expensive missile defense is the best way to solve it. Some analysts believe that the ABM Treaty could be loosened somewhat to allow more widespread defenses of hardened missile silos without compromising the fundamental objective of banning nationwide defenses that might undermine deterrence. Others argue, however, that allowing deployment of thousands of ABM interceptors would gravely weaken the ABM Treaty, providing a base for rapidly upgrading the system to a broad-area or even nationwide defense. In any case, technology for hard-site defenses is not being vigorously pursued in the SDI program.

Kinetic-Energy Interceptors

Kinetic-energy interceptors destroy enemy missiles or warheads by high-speed collision. In 1984 the US Army conducted the Homing Overlay Experiment (HOE), shown in an artist's concept on the facing page (bottom), in which an ABM homing vehicle launched from a Pacific island intercepted an inert ICBM warhead. Currently under development are two ground-launched systems similar in principle to the HOE, the Exoatmospheric Reentry Vehicle Interception System (ERIS) and the High Endoatmospheric Defense Interceptor (HEDI, middle). A space-based kinetic-energy system is also under development, known as the Space-Based Interceptor (SBI, top).

Early Deployment

In early 1987, a push for "early deployment" of SDI came to the fore. Advocates argued that a limited system of more "mature" technologies—interceptor rockets rather than more exotic lasers and particle beams—could be in place by the mid-1990s. Such a system, they argued, would enhance US security in the near term, and provide a foundation for a more capable system in the future. Some advocates acknowledged, however, that part of the motivation was political, stemming from a desire to lock in future administrations to construction of a strategic defense and a fear that support for SDI might wane if the benefits seemed far in the future. Early deployment could serve these goals by undermining the ABM Treaty or forcing a US withdrawal.

By 1988, however, the schedule for even this rudimentary "Phase I" defense had slipped, with program managers acknowledging it could not be fully deployed until after the turn of the century. As of early 1989, this near-term defense was planned to include thousands of space-based and ground-based interceptors guided by several types of sensors, and netted together by a complex of communications and battle management computers. The Phase I defense would be designed to intercept only a small fraction of Soviet missiles—30 percent of a limited first-wave attack, according to press reports. But the administration argued that it would eventually be replaced by more capable defenses, including lasers and other more exotic technologies. The administration estimated the cost of such a Phase I system at $69 billion, not counting operations costs or the cost of developing the more expensive follow-on systems. Critics argued that this estimate is likely to be far too low. While the Defense Department approved continued work on a somewhat modified version of the Phase I plan in October 1988, many analysts expected that budget and arms control pressures would eventually lead the Bush administration to deemphasize the Phase I concept, focusing again on research for longer-term defenses.

Opponents of such a Phase I deployment argued that the system is too expensive for its limited planned effectiveness, and could be easily overcome by Soviet countermeasures. SDIO officials have acknowledged that the space-based interceptors intended for boost-phase defense could be overcome by Soviet "fast-burn boosters." The proposed smaller version of the space-based

Zenith Star

Zenith Star, shown in this artist's concept, is a proposed space-based laser experiment that will explore the feasibility of using laser devices in future SDI systems. Critics believe it could violate the ABM Treaty's ban on testing of space-based ABM components.

interceptor system known as "brilliant pebbles" would not solve this fundamental problem. Critics believe the defense satellites would also be extremely vulnerable to attack. Moreover, critics argued that the ground-based interceptors intended for the second layer of the defense would be overwhelmed by swarms of cheap warhead-mimicking decoys.

SDIO officials argued that by the time such countermeasures become available, more exotic (and presumably more expensive) technologies such as lasers and particle beams would be available to improve the effectiveness of the US defense. Others, however, argue that the feasibility of such technologies is still uncertain. The 1987 American Physical Society report and a June 1988 report by the Congressional Office of Technology Assessment (OTA) both concluded that the effectiveness of directed-energy weapons would not be proven for at least a decade. As the OTA report put it, "Commitment in the mid-1990s to phase-one deployment would require an act of faith" that later phases would prove effective and in the end, "The long-run ability of the Strategic Defense Initiative (SDI) to stay ahead of an ever-changing threat . . . is questionable."

Such large-scale deployments of missile defenses would clearly be inconsistent with the ABM Treaty. How long the treaty could survive if a formal decision were made to deploy is difficult to judge. The necessary test program would require withdrawing from or violating the ABM Treaty several years before deployment could begin. Some in the Reagan administration argued that the testing of space-based interceptor rockets would be allowed under the broad interpretation, but even under that interpretation the treaty clearly bans space-based testing of all "ABM interceptor missiles." Critics of early deployment are concerned about the threat it poses to the ABM Treaty and argue that a decision to deploy would probably mean the end of arms control and touch off a dangerous offense-defense race.

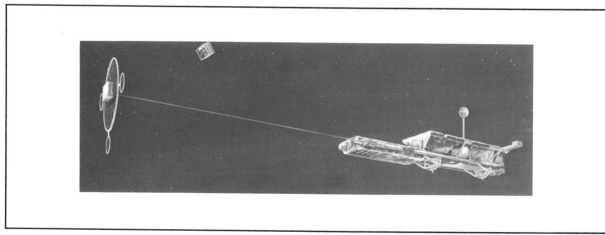

Neutral Particle Beam

This artist's concept of a proposed Neutral Particle Beam Space Experiment shows the beam firing at the target satellite (left). A small detector satellite (above) is monitoring beam-induced radiation from the target satellite. Neutral particle beams could be used to destroy ballistic missiles or warheads or for warhead and decoy discrimination.

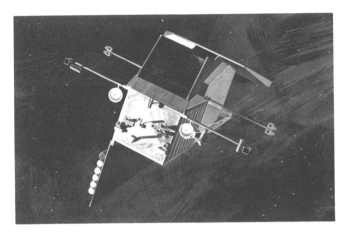

Surveillance and Tracking

The Boost Surveillance and Tracking System, shown in this artist's concept, and the Space Surveillance and Tracking System are proposed satellites that would carry infrared sensors to track Soviet missiles.

SDI and Arms Control

The impact of SDI on arms control has become the subject of intense debate. The Soviet Union has bitterly opposed the program from the beginning and has focused many of its arms control proposals on limiting it. Soviet leaders Andropov, Chernenko, and Gorbachev have each stated their belief that the true aim of SDI is to gain the capacity to strike first and intercept a Soviet retaliatory strike with Star Wars weaponry. They see SDI as an aggressive drive by the United States to regain nuclear superiority.

SDI advocates argue that Soviet fears of SDI have brought the Soviet Union back to the negotiating table and forced the Soviets to offer reductions in offensive strategic forces. Moreover, SDI supporters argue that development and eventual deployment of defenses will make the Soviets more willing to bargain, since defenses would reduce the value of offensive ballistic missiles.

SDI critics disagree, pointing out that the Soviet Union was already at the negotiating table and offering major reductions in offensive forces when Reagan first proposed SDI. In fact, the Soviet Union actually walked out of the negotiations in late 1983 in response to the US deployment of intermediate-range missiles in Europe. These critics argue that the Soviet return to the table in 1985 was not caused by the continuation of SDI, but was more the result of the Soviets' effort to recapture popular opinion in the West after the public relations failure of their 1983 walkout tactic. As for the future, SDI critics repeat the arguments that led to the ABM Treaty, that defenses on one side will only provoke more offenses on the other designed to overcome them. They point out that the US response to Soviet defensive programs has always been improved countermeasures and increased offensive forces, rather than agreement to reduce the systems threatened by the Soviet defenses.

The SDI program and the ABM Treaty have been the subjects of intense disagreement in the Nuclear and Space Talks (NST), which began in 1985. At the outset of those talks, the two sides agreed that the purpose of the negotiations included "preventing an arms race in space," but there is continuing dispute as to what that phrase means.

More Launch Capability

A future SDI system would require an extensive space launch capacity. This artist's concept of an Advanced Launch Vehicle is a possible candidate.

In the Defense and Space Talks portion of the NST negotiations, US negotiators have attempted to convince the Soviets that a mutual transition to reliance on defenses would be beneficial. The US side has insisted that it should have the right to nearly unfettered development and testing of SDI under the "broad" interpretation of the ABM Treaty and has proposed converting the unlimited-duration ABM Treaty into a new agreement that would allow either side to deploy defenses after a period of years. Though President Reagan repeatedly offered to share SDI technology with the Soviet Union, few other officials took the proposal seriously; indeed, former SDIO Director James Abrahamson told Congress that any sharing plan "would be necessarily conditioned on safeguarding our own national defense technology." US negotiators have, however, proposed a "predictability package" on missile defense work. Although no technology would be shared, the package would include exchanges of data on planned missile defense efforts, observation of tests, and visits to selected areas of missile defense laboratories.

The Soviet Union has adamantly rejected the notion that deployment of defenses is desirable and has strongly opposed the Reagan administration's "broad" interpretation of the ABM Treaty. At the outset of the negotiations, the Soviets sought to ban all SDI work, claiming that even research on space-based systems and components was prohibited by the ABM Treaty, ignoring their own research program on SDI-like technologies. (See page 84.) The Soviet Union subsequently moderated its position to endorse the traditional interpretation, which permits research but not development and testing on space-based systems and components, and proposed

Star Wars Laser Battle-Stations

A variety of laser platforms designed to destroy Soviet missiles in their boost and mid-course phases have been proposed for SDI systems, including space-based lasers (left, top) and ground-based stations (left, bottom) that would reflect a beam off space-based mirrors (left) to hit their targets. Although such futuristic technologies sparkle with imagination, their effectiveness, according to analyses by such institutions as the American Physical Society and the Office of Technology Assessment, cannot be proven for many years. Even if such systems can be developed and deployed, they may be vulnerable to enemy countermeasures or direct attack, and may be deemed too costly both in actual dollars spent and in the opportunity costs of scientific and engineering ingenuity that could be applied to other pursuits. The most serious effects of such systems, however, would be to destabilize the superpower nuclear confrontation, block progress in arms control, and create a greater risk of nuclear war.

that the two sides agree not to withdraw from the ABM Treaty for 10 years. After the non-withdrawal period, the treaty would remain in force, as it is of unlimited duration; but either side could withdraw on six months' notice if its "supreme national interests" were jeopardized.

At the Washington summit in December 1987, President Reagan and Soviet General Secretary Mikhail Gorbachev agreed to an ambiguous statement on the ABM Treaty, but failed to bridge the gap between the two sides' positions. The statement committed both sides to observe the ABM Treaty "as signed," which the Soviet Union interpreted as meaning the traditional interpretation, while conducting missile defense testing "as required," which the United States interpreted as allowing SDI testing under the broad interpretation. The continuing disagreement was apparent as the negotiations reconvened in 1988, with both sides accusing the other of backing away from the Washington language.

The Moscow summit in mid-1988 failed to make any progress on these issues, leaving them for the Bush administration to resolve.

As of early 1989, the impasse over SDI remained the single most important barrier in the path toward a strategic arms reduction agreement. The Reagan administration argued that reductions in offensive forces should not be dependent on strict limits on defenses, and the Soviet Union took the position that reductions in offense cannot be undertaken without certainty as to the defenses those reduced offensive forces would have to overcome. Hence, the Soviet Union maintains that any SDI development or deployment in violation of the traditional interpretation of the ABM Treaty would nullify a strategic arms reduction agreement. The approach of the Bush administration to the SDI program will be the critical factor in determining the prospects for a START agreement and future progress on arms control.

Soviet ABM Programs

The Soviet Union has a long history of interest in strategic defense. It began antiballistic missile research nearly 30 years ago and currently has the world's only operational ABM system (at Moscow), a robust ABM research and development program, and the world's largest air defense (antiaircraft) system. Nevertheless, though the Soviet Union initially opposed limits on ABM systems, it changed its position in 1968 and agreed to strict limitations on its missile defense program in the 1972 ABM Treaty.

After 1972, the Soviet Union continued a large ABM research and development program and completed construction of the Moscow ABM system, which is permitted by the ABM Treaty. A major upgrade of the Moscow system also permitted by the ABM Treaty began in 1978 and is nearing completion. In addition, the Soviet air defense system includes some 10,000 small radars and antiaircraft missiles, as well as hundreds of interceptor aircraft. The US Defense Department has estimated that the Soviet Union spends approximately $20 billion a year on strategic defense, including air defense, ABM work, and civil defense, roughly as much as is spent on Soviet strategic offensive forces. Nearly $15 billion of that amount, however, is for air defense, not ballistic missile defense.

Soviet ABM-related programs are often divided into two broad areas: so-called "conventional" ABMs—rocket interceptors guided by large radars—and "exotic" systems such as lasers and particle beams. The conventional Moscow ABM system includes nuclear-armed rockets for midcourse interception and new rockets for terminal interception, guided by a large phased-array radar near Moscow. Defense Department officials have acknowledged that this system, which is not yet fully deployed, is technologically no more advanced than the US Safeguard system that was abandoned as not cost-effective in the 1970s. In 1987, the Reagan administration's deputy undersecretary of defense for strategic and theater nuclear forces told Congress that the Moscow system could be overcome "with a small number of Minuteman missiles equipped with highly effective chaff and decoys."

The Soviet Union has worked on other conventional ABM systems, including a so-called "rapidly-deployable" system that was tested in the 1970s. The Reagan administration expressed concern that this system might represent preparations to break out of the ABM Treaty and rapidly deploy a nationwide defense. However, these systems, with their smaller and less powerful radars, would clearly be far less effective than the Moscow ABM system. The radars associated with this system were never deployed and do not appear to have been in active development for some years. Most of the half-dozen radars set up at test sites have been dismantled. While the Reagan administration charged that the movement of parts of the dismantled radars to other locations is itself a violation of the ABM Treaty, other US experts have rejected the charge, including Sidney Graybeal, the US Standing Consultative Commissioner who negotiated the regulations governing dismantling of ABM systems and components. Upgraded air-defense missiles, or even anti-tactical ballistic missiles, would provide little defense against a large-scale attack by modern strategic ballistic missiles.

The Soviet Union is building a large radar near Krasnoyarsk, which violates the ABM Treaty's provision limiting the emplacement of early warning radars to the periphery of the country. The Reagan administration has argued that Krasnoyarsk and other similar early-warning radars at legal locations could form an ABM radar network for a nationwide defense. The CIA has reportedly concluded, however, that Krasnoyarsk is "not well designed" for an ABM battle management role, because of its location, orientation, and frequency (which is less than one-tenth the frequency used by modern ABM radars and therefore is potentially vulnerable to nuclear blackout effects). In mid-1987, a US congressional team that was permitted to inspect the radar confirmed that it was not likely to be able to serve effectively as an ABM radar, finding it shoddily constructed and far from completion. Later that year, the Soviets announced a unilateral cessation of construction at Krasnoyarsk, while arguing that the US radar soon to be constructed at

The Gazelle silo-based missile, shown in this artist's concept, is a new component of the Moscow ABM system.

Fylingdales Moor, U.K., also violates the ABM Treaty. (See Chapter 15.) Since then, the Soviet Union has proposed turning Krasnoyarsk over to an international space agency and dismantling some parts of the facility.

The Soviet Union also has an active program investigating exotic technologies, such as lasers and particle beams. As Gorbachev acknowledged in 1987, "Practically, the Soviet Union is doing all that the United States is doing, and I guess we are engaged in research, basic research, which relates to those aspects which are covered by SDI."

In 1985, the CIA judged that US and Soviet directed-energy weapons technology was "comparable." In particular, the Soviet Union has a strong military laser program, including lasers at the Sary Shagan test range judged capable of damaging the sensors of low-orbit US satellites, and a mysterious new laser facility, which may be designed to track or attack satellites, under construction close to the Afghanistan border near the city of Dushanbe. But the CIA and the Defense Department have both concluded that the Soviet Union lags in chemical lasers, the type considered most applicable for near-term ABM applications, and the Defense Department has recently added that the Soviets are also slightly behind in free-electron lasers, the type considered most promising for ballistic missile defenses in the long-term.

The Soviet Union also has a particle-beam program, though the CIA estimates that it has received considerably less emphasis than lasers, and "the technical requirements are so severe that we estimate that there is a low probability they will test a prototype [of a space-based particle beam weapon] before the year 2000."

Soviet technology is farther behind US technology in other areas critical to any high-technology defense. The 1988 SDI *Report to Congress* estimates that the Soviet Union is 10 years behind in SDI sensor technologies and nearly 10 years behind in military computers. "These limitations," the report concluded, "undoubtedly prevent the Soviets from deploying defenses with the level of sophistication and capability envisioned for SDI." A late 1987 Defense Department assessment of the 20 technologies most likely to affect the military balance over the next two decades found the United States ahead in 15, and the two superpowers tied in the other five. Nowhere did the Soviets lead. Overall then, as the Department of Defense's *Soviet Military Power* puts it, the US SDI program enjoys "significant benefits from the West's broad and deep technical superiority."

Satellites essential to US security would be threatened by an ASAT arms competition

Antisatellite Weapons

Background

Satellites play a key national security role, providing a range of capabilities from reliable global communications to early warning of attack, strategic intelligence, and verification of arms control agreements. Threats to satellites, such as those posed by antisatellite (ASAT) weapons, therefore represent a significant national security issue. In addition, because satellites in orbit are similar in many respects to ballistic missiles in mid-flight, there is an important overlap between the capabilities of ASAT and antiballistic missile (ABM) systems. Future efforts to develop strategic defenses are likely to create powerful ASAT weapons long before they lead to effective defenses, and some types of ASAT development could serve as a surrogate for ABM testing, possibly undermining the ABM Treaty.

The ASAT Problem

Since the 1957 flight of Sputnik, the first man-made satellite, the United States, the Soviet Union, and several other countries have developed satellites for a wide range of tasks, both military and civilian. For almost as long, both the United States and the Soviet Union have pursued the possibility of weapons to destroy satellites in space. Early ASATs were simply modified ballistic missiles or antiballistic missiles. Armed with high-yield nuclear warheads, they did not require high accuracy because in space they could destroy satellites at great distances. The United States maintained such a system, utilizing Thor missile boosters, on Johnston Island in the Pacific in operational status through 1970 and in semi-operational status through 1975. However, aside from deterring the Soviet Union from attacking US satellites in conventional war or peacetime, it was not clear when such a system could be used without leading at least to the loss of US satellites (on which the United States depended more than the Soviet Union) or even to escalation to nuclear war.

By 1968, the Soviet Union began testing the first crude non-nuclear ASAT. The Soviet ASAT is a multi-ton shrapnel warhead lofted into orbit by a modified SS-9 ICBM. The warhead maneuvers into the path of the target satellite and destroys it with a conventional explosion. Ths Soviet ASAT system has proved to be somewhat unreliable, however, having failed five of 14 tests using a radar guidance system and all six

tests using a more advanced infrared homing system. In addition, the Soviet ASAT can only reach targets orbiting at low altitudes and cannot threaten satellites in high or geosynchronous orbits, where most US satellites are placed.

The Carter administration adopted a two-track response to this Soviet ASAT program, developing a non-nuclear, low-altitude ASAT while simultaneously attempting to negotiate bilateral ASAT restraints. Although some progress was made in the 1978-79 negotiations, a number of differences were left unresolved when the talks were recessed.

Meanwhile, the United States began development of a "miniature homing vehicle" (MHV) ASAT, which was lofted into space on a small rocket carried by an F-15 fighter aircraft. The MHV used infrared guidance to home in on the target satellite and destroy it by direct impact. In principle, the MHV would be more capable and

Early ASAT

Early US ASATs were simply modified ballistic missiles armed with nuclear warheads, such as this Thor missile stationed on Johnston Island. X-ray and other radiation from the explosion could knock out unshielded satellites at great distances.

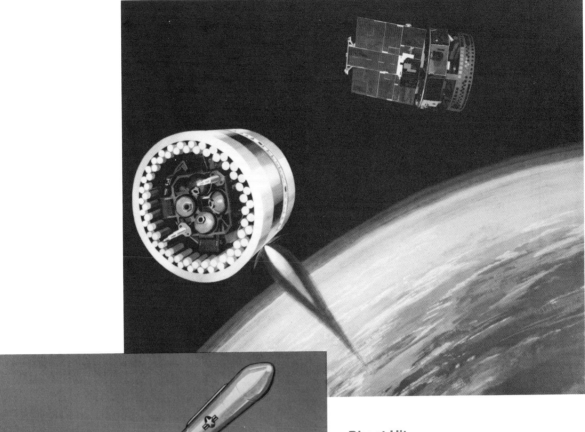

Direct Hit

In the 1980s the United States tested the miniature homing vehicle (MHV) ASAT, which was shot into space on a rocket carried by an F-15 fighter aircraft (artist's concept, left). In 1985 the MHV (above left) successfully destroyed the Solwind research satellite (above right) by direct impact.

flexible than the Soviet ASAT because the F-15 launch platform could be deployed rapidly worldwide to permit more or less simultaneous attacks on all low-altitude Soviet satellites. The system was tested once against an actual satellite, successfully destroying the Solwind research satellite in 1985, and has been tested successfully homing on the light from a star.

Testing of both the US and Soviet ASATs has been halted for several years as a result of separate unilateral testing moratoriums. In 1983, the Soviet Union announced a unilateral halt in ASAT testing and submitted to the United Nations a draft treaty banning space weapons. Since then, the Soviet Union has repeatedly proposed a ban on all space weapons, including ASATs. The US moratorium was mandated by Congress over the objections of the Reagan ad-

ministration, as part of the budget process starting in late 1985.

The Reagan administration rejected the Soviet ASAT proposals, arguing that they are unverifiable and that a US ASAT is needed to match the "operational" Soviet ASAT capability, to deter Soviet attacks on US satellites, and in time of conflict to permit selective attack on Soviet satellites that might track and target US naval forces.

Advocates of ASAT arms control argue, by contrast, that with unrestricted ASAT testing it will be difficult or impossible to ensure the survivability of critical US satellites in the future. Limits on ASAT testing would prevent development of those ASATs which could threaten high-altitude satellites, which are the most important to the United States. Moreover, these advocates

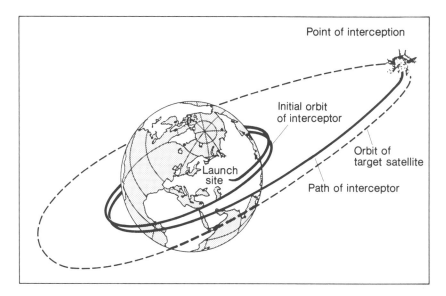

Point of interception

Initial orbit
of interceptor

Orbit of
target satellite

Launch
site

Path of interceptor

Explosion in Orbit

The Soviet ASAT is launched into orbit, maneuvers into the path of the target satellite, and destroys it with a conventional explosion. The Soviet Union has not tested its orbital antisatellite system since it declared a unilateral moratorium on ASAT testing in 1983.

of ASAT arms control argue that the verification problems are surmountable, particularly with regard to potentially more threatening future systems. Finally, advocates assert that the threat to our naval forces posed by Soviet surveillance capabilities during a conventional war are greatly exaggerated and can be countered by means other than attacking the surveillance satellites themselves, such as spoofing the Soviet satellite sensors with radar decoys.

Congress has taken a particularly active role on this issue. In 1984, in response to the Soviet moratorium, Congress specified that tests of the new ASAT against objects in space could not be conducted unless the President certified that the United States was pursuing an ASAT agreement. In August 1985, President Reagan certified that he was "endeavoring in good faith" to develop a security-enhancing ASAT proposal, but criticized the concept of ASAT arms control. The following month, the MHV was tested against the Solwind satellite. The Soviet moratorium continued, and in December 1985, Congress halted further tests against objects in space, conditioned on the Soviet Union exercising parallel restraint. The congressional moratorium continued through fiscal year 1988; in its fiscal year 1989 budget request, the administration canceled the MHV program because of the congressional testing restriction.

The United States is continuing research on future ASAT systems. In early 1989, the US secretary of defense called the lack of an ASAT the "single most vulnerable point" in US defenses and proposed a major new ASAT program, including work on rocket interceptors and other technologies derived from the SDI program. In addition, the defense secretary reportedly

decided in December 1988 to upgrade SDI's Mid-Infrared Advanced Chemical Laser (MIRACL) for tests against US satellites, probing their vulnerability to attack and the effectiveness of such ground-based lasers, which the Soviet Union is also developing. Both programs are likely to face opposition in Congress, as they pose the risk of upsetting the current ASAT moratorium.

The Star Wars-ASAT Connection

As is evident from the new focus of the US ASAT program, the ASAT issue is complicated by the technological overlap between ASATs and ABMs. Ballistic missiles in mid-flight and satellites in orbit follow similar trajectories. But satellite trajectories are generally more predictable, making them easier to intercept than ballistic missiles, and an effective ASAT need only intercept a few satellites, possibly over a period of days, while a nuclear defense might be forced to contend with thousands of missiles arriving over minutes or hours. Hence, development of SDI systems will lead to severe threats to satellite survivability long before the technologies offer any potential for effective nationwide ABM defenses. Indeed, these advanced ASAT capabilities could pose severe problems for space-based missile defenses, which might be shot down by opposing missile defenses or ASATs. As former Secretary of Defense Harold Brown has pointed out, "Everything that works well as a defense also works somewhat better as a defense suppressor."

Moreover, critics of SDI fear that since satellites in orbit and ballistic missiles in mid-flight follow similar trajectories, antiballistic missile technologies, severely restricted by the 1972 ABM Treaty, could be developed and tested surreptitiously as ASAT programs. In September 1986, for example, the Delta 180 SDI-related test destroyed a satellite. The test was designed to develop sensors for Star Wars interceptors, but administration officials argued that since only a satellite was destroyed and not a strategic missile, the test did not violate the ABM Treaty. Extensive tests of this kind could fuel suspicions that one or both sides was preparing to break out of the ABM Treaty, possibly leading to an ABM arms race. Hence, advocates of ASAT arms control argue that an ASAT ban would also be important to close this potential loophole in the ABM Treaty.

As of mid-1989, the US Defense Department hoped to begin testing new ASATs by 1991, despite the continuing Soviet ASAT moratorium. Although no ASAT negotiations were under way, members of Congress continued to press for talks with the Soviet Union. Meanwhile, the Bush administration was considering some ASAT negotiating proposals as part of its review of defense and arms control policies.

SAC underground command post, Nebraska.

9

The Command and Control of Nuclear Forces

Background

The nuclear forces of the superpowers involve more than just warheads and delivery systems. While actual weapons are the muscles of the nuclear giants, the complex systems and procedures designed to acquire information and then command and control the weapons are the eyes, ears, and brains. Some knowledge of how these command, control, communications, and intelligence networks function in peacetime, during a crisis, and in wartime is crucial to an appreciation of the complexities of our nuclear environment.

Command, control, communications, and intelligence—often labelled C^3I—include the equipment and procedures used to detect and evaluate enemy actions, to transmit information to leaders and link them to their forces, and to direct and coordinate the war plans. Broadly speaking, C^3I has two primary objectives: to prevent the

unauthorized or accidental use of nuclear weapons *and* to ensure that nuclear weapons could actually be used, once authorization was received, before they are destroyed or disabled.

In addition to making unilateral C^3I improvements to enhance their control over their respective nuclear arsenals, the United States and the Soviet Union have negotiated several bilateral arms control agreements to reduce the risk that nuclear weapons would be used as a result of miscommunication, misperception, or accident. Such confidence-building measures have increased the superpowers' abilities to interpret each other's actions in the nuclear realm and have improved the lines of communication available to US and Soviet leaders in a crisis, making inadvertent nuclear war less likely.

US Command and Control Systems

The US intelligence system would probably receive advance "strategic" warning of an impending Soviet "surprise" attack because the system is constantly monitoring the movement and communications of Soviet military forces. However, such strategic warning is neither certain nor unambiguous. Warning that a Soviet missile

attack had actually been launched against the United States would come first from infrared sensor satellites positioned over both hemispheres in synchronous orbits at 35,000 kilometers, where satellites can remain fixed over a point on the earth's equator. These satellites would sense the heat from the rocket exhaust of Soviet missiles as they rose through the atmosphere. A second net of ground-based early warning radar systems in Massachusetts, California, Alaska, Georgia, Texas, North Dakota, Canada, Greenland, and Great Britain would detect and track these missiles, confirming the satellite warning. All of this data would be collected by the North American Aerospace Defense Command (NORAD) at Cheyenne Mountain, Colorado, and transmitted to the Pentagon in Washington.

Official control over US nuclear weapons belongs to the National Command Authority, which, according to a Pentagon directive, "consists of the President and secretary of defense or their duly deputized alternates or successors." If the President decided to use nuclear weapons, either in response to a NORAD warning of a Soviet attack or to launch a US retaliatory strike, he would authorize an Emergency Action Message. This message would direct the execution of a preplanned option from the Single Integrated Operational Plan (SIOP, pronounced "sigh op") through the secretary of defense and the Joint Chiefs of Staff to nuclear force commanders, who would in turn pass the orders to operational officers.

Before they can execute the war SIOP, the officers responsible for operating land-based in-

On Alert

The Defense Support Program satellite (facing page, left), which detects and reports on missile launches and nuclear detonations, is an integral part of the US missile warning system. In the event of a crisis or alert, the Airborne Command Post (facing page, right) would take to the air, where key military and political personnel would hope to maintain communication with and control over US nuclear forces. Part of the military communication network is provided by the Defense Satellite Communications System (artist's concept, left).

tercontinental ballistic missiles and strategic bombers would have to receive the codes needed to unlock the permissive action links (PALs), which are sophisticated, tamper-proof electronic locks that prevent nuclear weapons from being used without proper authorization. Submarine-launched missiles do not have permissive action links on their warheads but have elaborate weapons release routines that involve the coordinated actions of the captain and several officers after receipt of an order to fire. Upon warning that an attack might be under way, strategic bomber aircraft on runway "alert" would normally take off and fly to holding positions, pending further orders on receipt of the Emergency Action Message. If the action message is not received, the bombers return to their bases. This "fail-safe" procedure is intended to insure the survival of vulnerable bombers by getting them in the air while preventing an unauthorized attack on the Soviet Union.

Vulnerability

The ability of top officials to transmit orders personally to retaliate against a Soviet attack is obviously limited by the vulnerability of ground-based command posts. These include the White House, the Pentagon, the Alternative National Military Command Center near Fort Richie, Maryland, and the Strategic Air Command headquarters in Omaha, Nebraska. These centers could be destroyed within a few minutes by the initial Soviet attack.

Such vulnerability raises the threat of "decapitation"—a Soviet attack on key US command centers that might cut off the "head" of US strategic forces and prevent top leaders from assessing the situation and ordering the appropriate level of retaliation. To improve the chances that some of the top leadership will survive, the United States maintains a fleet of emergency command airplanes. The President's "doomsday plane," stationed at Grissom Air Force Base, Indiana, stands ready to rendezvous with a White House helicopter if the President can be evacuated in time. The Strategic Air Command, in charge of directing strategic forces, operates a fleet of command aircraft, and at all times keeps at least one plane airborne. These airplanes can transmit orders to missile crews on the ground or even launch the missiles directly if necessary. Other commanders of US nuclear forces in the Atlantic, the Pacific, and Europe also have backup aircraft.

Despite the vulnerabilities of the system, decapitation of the US C^3I system is not a simple or rewarding strategy from a Soviet perspective. The Soviet Union cannot be sure who all of the "duly deputized alternates or successors" might be. While the presidential succession is a matter of law, others may have predelegated authority in certain defined circumstances to launch nuclear weapons. Only a reckless Soviet leader would assume that the release of a US retaliatory strike would be dependent on the survival of a few highly vulnerable individuals. But from the US perspective, a decision on which the fate of civilization depends should be made at as high and responsible a level as possible.

To maintain communication between command and control centers and with missile and bomber crews, the United States deploys multiple redundant systems, ranging from commercial telephone lines to satellites and aircraft that broadcast radio messages. The Navy maintains a fleet of aircraft (TACAMO, for "take charge and move out") on continuous alert over the Atlantic and Pacific Oceans. These aircraft are designed to transmit commands on low-frequency radio to submarines beneath the ocean. In addition, the first site of a new extremely low frequency (ELF) communication system became partially operational in 1986. The ELF system uses miles of buried cable to transmit messages to submerged submarines worldwide. The system is scheduled to become fully operational in 1989.

The human dimension of command and control is as important as the hardware. Thousands of individuals work in the US command and control network. But how they would behave in a severe crisis, with nuclear forces on full-scale alert and the prospect of nuclear destruction imminent, is difficult to predict.

Soviet Command and Control

There is little public information about the Soviet nuclear C^3I structure, but it appears to be highly centralized. Authority to launch nuclear forces rests in the Defense Council, a special subcommittee of the Politburo. Because of the Kremlin's desire to restrict nuclear authority to top leaders, it has developed an elaborate system of alternate command centers, including a number of underground posts in the Moscow area, to protect those leaders. The Soviet Union also has airborne command posts and extensive backup communication systems. However, like the US system, the Soviet system is unlikely to survive intact—with adequate communications between top leaders and nuclear force commanders—much beyond the outset of a nuclear war.

Nuclear Alerts and Accidents

In peacetime, the United States concentrates nuclear authority in the hands of the President to prevent unauthorized use and emphasizes safety procedures to minimize the chance of accidental release. But during attack, the emphasis would shift to insuring with high confidence the ability to release and use forces according to prearranged plans. Once these steps are taken, the authority to fire nuclear weapons is placed in many hands and procedures are set in motion that initiate preparations for launching. Under these circumstances, the possibility that a decapitating attack would prevent retaliation is essentially eliminated, but the risk of accidental or unauthorized release of nuclear weapons is greatly increased.

US warning systems have made errors in peacetime. For example, in the 1950s a flock of Canadian geese was identified by a US air defense radar as a Soviet bomber attack, and in 1980 false warning of a Soviet missile attack was triggered by a malfunctioning computer chip. Fortunately, the peacetime environment in which such mistakes have occurred has facilitated quick assessment of the source of the warning and cross checking with alternative sources of information that did not confirm the false alarm. But the potential impact of such an error in a period of superpower confrontation is a matter of grave and continuing concern. These incidents also underscore that complex technical systems are not infallible, an underlying problem that has been brought into sharp focus by the Strategic Defense Initiative, where unprecedentedly critical decisions would have to be made automatically in seconds.

We Deliver

Missileers for the Strategic Air Command, such as the two lieutenants at far left, work 60 feet underground in a capsule near a missile field. In the event of nuclear war, the missileers would take part in a procedure to activate launch codes to fire a flight of missiles. The photo on the near left shows a bomber crew scrambling to their aircraft during a drill. A number of strategic bombers and their accompanying crew remain on runway strip alert at all times.

In a crisis, alerting nuclear forces—putting more bombers on runways or in the air, sending more nuclear-armed submarines to sea, even putting a top official like the Vice President aboard the "doomsday plane"—might be carried out as a defensive action, designed to guard against a Soviet attack. The Soviet Union, however, would probably regard these actions with extreme alarm, viewing them as possible preparations for a preemptive attack. The United States ordered nuclear alerts during the 1962 Cuban Missile Crisis and the 1973 Middle East war, primarily to signal political resolve. The world is fortunate that, in both cases, the Soviet Union did not respond with a significant nuclear alert of its own. In a future crisis, however, the Soviet Union might match the US nuclear alert, which might lead to a higher level of US alert, and the escalation of alert levels could continue. In such a situation, with tensions high and forces ready to fire, a false alarm or other accident could trigger a nuclear war, or one side might decide that nuclear war had become inevitable and that it was better to preempt than be struck first.

Launch on Warning

Concerns about the vulnerabilities of US land-based missiles to Soviet attack, coupled with the vulnerabilities of the US command and control net, have led some to advocate a declaratory "launch on warning" policy. Under such a policy, the United States would not wait until Soviet missiles had landed on US territory before striking back. The United States would instead launch its counterstrike after "positive" detection of the attack, but before any missiles had arrived. This policy would insure that all of the potentially vulnerable ICBMs were launched before they had been destroyed.

Advocates of "launch on warning" argue that such a posture, if made clear to Moscow, might help discourage a Soviet first strike by increasing Soviet certainty that the United States could strike back. But critics of "launch on warning" believe it would significantly increase the possibility of an attack launched by a false alarm. Although extensive redundancy in US warning systems reduces the likelihood that a false alarm generated by one part of the system would not be corrected by information from another part, the risk that "launch on warning" could accidentally lead to a general nuclear war is a terrible chance to take. But regardless of declaratory policy, the knowledge that the other side probably has the technical capability to "launch on warning" is a further deterrent against a first strike.

Improving Command and Control Systems

Over the years, the US C^{3}I system has been continuously upgraded. A wide range of additional programs have been proposed to improve these systems: additional hardening against the electromagnetic pulse effects of nuclear explosions, improved command aircraft, new jam-resistant communications systems, mobile ground-based command posts, deep underground command and control posts, more survivable satellites, and improved procedures for processing and transmitting information. But there are disagreements over which improvements should have priority.

Some analysts are concerned that this effort to upgrade C^3I, unless combined with a change in nuclear doctrine, could actually increase the risk of nuclear war. This concern reflects the fact that current US strategy commits the United States to achieving the capability to fight and "prevail" in a prolonged nuclear war that might last weeks or even months. In that light, attempts to achieve a very robust command and control system could be associated more with the development of a "nuclear war-fighting" strategy than with the avoidance of unintended nuclear war. Critics of a "nuclear war-fighting" strategy are concerned that, although it may serve as a deterrent by increasing the credibility of the limited, controlled use of nuclear weapons, any use of nuclear weapons in a superpower conflict would almost certainly escalate into a general nuclear war.

While this controversy divides command and control analysts, there is general agreement that the superpowers must continue to improve the capabilities of their command, control, and communication systems to avoid accidental or unauthorized use of nuclear weapons. There is probably also a consensus that even the most robust C^3I system would not survive effectively for more than a few hours, possibly days, in a general nuclear war.

Crisis Prevention and Confidence-Building Measures

Unilateral improvements in C^3I have been supplemented by bilateral crisis prevention agreements and confidence-building measures (CBMs) designed to render superpower intentions and behavior more "transparent" and thereby reduce the possibility of a war caused by accident, misperception, or surprise. Several US-Soviet agreements improve communication channels and regulate military activities in an effort to create a higher level of predictability and confidence than might otherwise exist in the superpower relationship. By promoting increased communication and cooperation before and during a crisis, CBMs can help prevent inadvertent war.

Direct communication between the leaders of opposing nations can be an important means of preventing or resolving crises. In the aftermath of the 1962 Cuban missile crisis, US and Soviet leaders recognized that existing communication facilities were inadequate for effective consultation. Their concern led to the 1963 Hotline Agreement, which created a direct teletype link between Washington and Moscow for quick and reliable communication. Teletype was chosen over a voice connection on the grounds that it would insure dispassionate exchanges between the US President and the Soviet General Secretary. Teletype transmissions would also allow the recipients time to provide considered responses. In the midst of conflicts in the Middle East (1967 and 1973) and South Asia (1971), the hotline allowed the superpowers to exchange views and make clear their intentions without excessive delay.

The teletype link was the first of a series of hotline measures intended to enhance crisis stability by facilitating the flow of time-urgent information. Further superpower agreements in 1971 and 1984 led to improvements in the hotline, including the establishment of satellite communications circuits between the United States and the Soviet Union, with a system of multiple terminals in each country. Today, US and Soviet leaders can exchange detailed information, including satellite images of incipient trouble areas. In 1985, further agreement was reached on the transmission of messages on the hotline in the event of nuclear terrorism.

Other bilateral agreements aimed at enhancing crisis stability are the 1971 Nuclear Accidents Agreement and the 1973 Agreement on the Prevention of Nuclear War. In the Nuclear Accidents Agreement, the superpowers pledged to improve command and control safeguards against accidental or unauthorized use of their nuclear weapons and consult with each other immediately should the risk of nuclear war arise from such use, from detection of unidentified objects by early warning systems, or from any incident involving the possible detonation of a nuclear weapon. The agreement also required advance notification of all extra-territorial missile tests launched in the direction of the other party.

These CBMs were supplemented by the Agreement on the Prevention of Nuclear War in which the United States and the Soviet Union declared their shared objective of eliminating the danger of nuclear war and agreed to consult each other immediately should the risk of nuclear con-

Risk Reduction

Soviet Foreign Minister Eduard Shevardnadze (seated, left) and former Secretary of State George Shultz (seated, right) signed an agreement in 1987 establishing Nuclear Risk Reduction Centers (NRRCs) in Washington and Moscow. (President Reagan stands to the far left and Senators Warner and Nunn, original cosponsors of the crisis control center idea, stand directly behind Secretary Shultz.)

flict arise. Most recently, the two countries signed a pact to give each other at least 24 hours advance notice of all launches of strategic ballistic missiles, including the date and location of the launch and where the missile is expected to land.

In 1981, Senators Sam Nunn (D-GA) and John Warner (R-VA) proposed that the United States and Soviet Union create a crisis control center, to be jointly staffed by Soviets and Americans. The center would monitor worldwide conflicts and provide for rapid and direct communication in a crisis. An additional function of the center would be to serve as a meeting place for ministerial-level visits and discussions relating to risk reduction and military doctrines, forces, and activities.

Supporters of the crisis control center argued that it would go far beyond the hotline in facilitating superpower communication and cooperation. But some critics maintained that such a center would simply duplicate existing capabilities within and between governments and would, in any case, be bypassed during a real crisis. In such a situation top-level officials would become personally involved and would want direct contact that was not filtered through a jointly staffed,

middle-level organization. Others suggested that such an organization could be used for espionage or disinformation.

But supporters of the idea were persistent and well organized, and in September 1987 the United States and Soviet Union signed an accord establishing two Nuclear Risk Reduction Centers (NRRCs), one in Washington and one in Moscow. The accord is only distantly related to the original Nunn/Warner proposal. Instead of joint staffing, the centers are manned only by officers of each country at national command centers. Rather than actual crisis management, the centers are specifically limited to the exchange of information already required by existing arms control agreements. For example, the NRRC facilitates the data exchange required under the INF Treaty and the exchange of information related to missile tests, naval maneuvers, and other military activities.

In sum, negotiated agreements have reinforced improvements in the C^3I system. They further reduce the risk that a decision to use nuclear weapons would result from inaccurate information, unexpected or misperceived events, or a lack of communication.

Mobile Pershing II missiles in West Germany.

10

Nuclear Forces in Europe

Background

Shortly after the conclusion of World War II, the United States withdrew its military forces from Europe and began to demobilize them. But a series of Soviet actions in the immediate post-war period, aimed at consolidating its position in Eastern Europe, forced the United States to recommit itself to the protection of Western Europe and to support the formation in 1949 of a Western defensive alliance called the North Atlantic Treaty Organization (NATO).

The NATO nations, weary of war and reluctant or unable to provide the funds and manpower required to match the more numerous Soviet conventional forces, early on decided to rely on US nuclear weapons to deter and repel a Soviet conventional attack against Western Europe. With an initial monopoly and later an overwhelming superiority in these weapons, the United States was in a credible position to threaten massive retaliation against the Soviet homeland in the event of conventional war in Europe.

tems, the warheads remained under US control and could only be armed through a "two-key" system in which the United States held one of the keys. In the late 1950s, the United States stationed intermediate-range, nuclear-armed missiles (Thors and Jupiters) in England, Italy, and Turkey with sufficient range to strike the Soviet Union.

The growth of Soviet nuclear forces, including deployment between 1959 and 1961 of SS-4 and SS-5 intermediate-range missiles, led to a reevaluation of NATO policy in the early 1960s. New Soviet battlefield, intermediate-range, and strategic nuclear forces diminished the credibility of NATO's threat of "first use" of nuclear weapons. Western military planners began to recognize that even a battlefield nuclear war would devastate Europe and almost certainly escalate into a superpower exchange, a prospect made increasingly perilous for the United States by the growth of Soviet long-range nuclear forces. As a consequence, the Kennedy and Johnson administrations urged NATO to place more emphasis on conventional defenses and to adopt a policy of "flexible response." Under the proposed doctrine of "flexible response," NATO would improve its conventional forces while retaining the option to use tactical nuclear weapons if conventional defense failed. The United States, in turn, would maintain its commitment to use strategic nuclear forces, if necessary, to defend the NATO allies from a Soviet attack.

The NATO allies initially resisted adoption of the "flexible response" strategy. They favored continued reliance on nuclear weapons to avoid the heavy burden of conventional defense and to securely tie or "couple" the United States to the defense of Europe. It was argued, especially by France, that deemphasizing the nuclear threat in favor of non-nuclear defenses would remove the US nuclear umbrella and leave Europe more vulnerable to Soviet attack or coercion.

These doubts about the reliability of the U.S. nuclear umbrella had already led Britain (in 1952) and France (in 1960) to acquire their own nuclear weapons. After France withdrew from the joint military command of the alliance in 1966, the other members of NATO finally agreed to increase their contribution to conventional defenses and adopt the "flexible response" doctrine in 1967. Although flexible response has been the official doctrine ever since, NATO has actually made little progress in reducing its reliance on the threat of nuclear escalation to forestall a Soviet attack.

The United States initially stationed in England intermediate-range nuclear-armed bombers capable of reaching the Soviet Union, and during the 1950s deployed in Europe a growing array of "battlefield" or "tactical" nuclear weapons: short-range aircraft armed with nuclear gravity bombs, land-based missiles, artillery shells, and "atomic demolition munitions," or land mines. Although other NATO nations owned and operated many of the delivery sys-

INF

The role of intermediate-range nuclear weapons and the issue of "decoupling" was further underscored in the 1970s by the SALT agreements, which were seen as codifying strategic parity between the Soviet Union and the United States. The Soviet Union, whose intermediate-range forces (INF) had been unconstrained by the arms control agreements of the 1970s, began to modernize these forces by replacing the old fixed-based, single warhead SS-4s and SS-5s with the mobile, triple-warhead SS-20. Former West German Chancellor Helmut Schmidt and other European leaders argued that, faced with superpower parity and growing Soviet INF capabilities, NATO needed new US intermediate-range forces to match the growing Soviet threat and to "couple" more securely the US strategic arsenal to the defense of Europe.

In December 1979, NATO agreed on a "dual-track" approach to the Soviet INF challenge. One track called for the deployment of 464 ground-launched cruise missiles (GLCMs) and 108 Pershing II ballistic missiles on NATO soil in West Germany, England, Italy, the Netherlands and Belgium. These new intermediate-range weapons would have the capability to strike targets in the Soviet Union. It was argued that these weapons provided a more credible deterrent in an age of nuclear parity. They represented a direct threat to the Soviet Union in the event of a Soviet invasion of Western Europe. Because the Soviet Union would probably respond to an INF attack on its own territory by striking the United States—an act that would certainly provoke a response from US strategic forces—these weapons were also seen by Europeans as a mechanism to link US strategic forces in a credible fashion to a European deterrent of Soviet conventional attack.

The second track of the 1979 NATO decision called for a parallel effort to obtain an arms

Intermediate-range Missiles

The US Pershing II (top) and Soviet SS-20 (bottom) mobile intermediate-range nuclear missiles held center stage in the INF debate. The Soviet Union found the single-warhead Pershing II particularly threatening because its range and high accuracy would allow the United States to strike from Europe at hardened targets deep within Soviet territory. NATO was deeply troubled by the large number of triple-warhead SS-20s deployed by the Soviet Union.

No-First-Use and Tactical Nuclear Weapons

Whether NATO policy should call for the "first use" of nuclear weapons in the event of a major conventional attack by the Warsaw Pact has been a persistent political, military, and ethical controversy. In this context, the "first use" of nuclear weapons in response to a conventional threat is distinguished from a "first strike," which is a sudden, large-scale nuclear attack against the homeland and war-making potential of an adversary.

The Soviet Union has declared its intention to adhere to a policy of "no-first-use" of nuclear weapons. On the other hand, the US position, as put forward in the United Nations, is one of "non-use" of nuclear weapons against a non-nuclear state in a conflict unless it is allied with a nuclear power, clearly leaving open the option of using nuclear weapons in a European conflict. NATO military commander Gen. John Galvin claims he "can guarantee only two weeks against an all-out Warsaw Pact attack—then we will have to use nuclear weapons." This option to use nuclear weapons to deter a conventional attack on Western Europe is an integral part of NATO's doctrine of "flexible response" adopted in 1967.

Proponents of first use believe the risk that a conventional war in Europe could become nuclear, and thus threaten the Soviet homeland, introduces an element of uncertainty into the military equation and contributes substantially to deterring a Soviet conventional attack on Western Europe. First-use proponents, especially in Europe, argue that renouncing first use would decouple US nuclear forces from the defense of Europe and increase the likelihood of conventional war.

Critics of the NATO first-use policy argue that any Western use of nuclear weapons would almost certainly be met by a Soviet nuclear response. The resultant nuclear exchange, even if it were intended to be limited or simply "demonstrative" of alliance will, would risk escalating into an all-out nuclear war. In any event, critics argue, even a limited use of nuclear weapons in Europe would totally devastate the territory being defended. Consequently, they conclude that a first-use policy lacks both sense and credibility and that NATO should strengthen its conventional forces and declare a policy of no-first-use.

Critics of first-use point to another, operational problem with NATO's current policy. To maintain the credibility of the first-use threat, NATO has over the years kept thousands of battlefield nuclear weapons in forward battle areas. If Warsaw Pact forces were to break through, NATO field commanders would be faced with "using or losing" their battlefield nuclear weapons. While pressure on NATO to use nuclear weapons early in a conflict raises the risk for the Soviet Union, it also poses grave risks for the West. The forward-basing of nuclear weapons by NATO reduces the time available to negotiate a ceasefire or to de-escalate a crisis before having to make a crucial decision to fire.

To address this operational problem, an intermediate concept of "no-early-first-use" has evolved. Supporters of this concept believe that, even if the first-use policy is not changed, NATO should "raise the nuclear threshold" (i.e., delay the moment when it must turn to nuclear weapons) by strengthening conventional defenses and by reducing and redeploying battlefield nuclear weapons in order not to be forced to "use them or lose them." In fact, since 1979 NATO has withdrawn thousands of battlefield weapons, mainly older nuclear artillery shells, air-defense weapons, and nuclear land-mines.

However, several thousand tactical and battlefield nuclear weapons and bombs on aircraft will remain in Europe even after INF missiles are withdrawn, and NATO forces continue to train for their use in response to a conventional Warsaw Pact attack.

Short-range Missiles

After the INF Treaty was ratified in 1988, short-range nuclear systems became the focal point of the European nuclear arms debate. Missiles with less than 500 kilometers of range, such as this nuclear-capable Lance deployed by NATO, were not covered by the INF Treaty.

control agreement on INF with the Soviet Union. The United States proposed unspecified equal worldwide levels of US and Soviet intermediate-range forces at talks in Geneva in the fall of 1980. A "zero" level for these systems was specifically not advanced because the NATO allies wanted to maintain at least the symbolic coupling provided by US forces capable of striking the Soviet Union from Europe (like the earlier Thors and Jupiters which had been removed from Europe in the years following the Cuban missile crisis). When President Reagan resumed the INF negotiations in November 1981, the new US position called for a worldwide limit of zero on US and Soviet INF missiles. This proposal became known as the "zero-option." These worldwide limits included Soviet intermediate-range SS-20s based in the Soviet Far East, because as mobile systems, they could be redeployed within range of Europe.

The Soviet Union, for its part, initially sought to ban any new US INF missile deployments and to limit to equal levels all Warsaw Pact and NATO intermediate-range missiles and bombers based, or "intended for use," in the European theater. The underlying disagreement between the two sides was related to different assessments of the forces involved in the nuclear balance in Europe. The US view was that the Soviet Union had a six-to-one advantage in intermediate-range weapons while the Soviet Union insisted that rough parity existed between the two sides prior to the US INF deployments. The

great difference between these assessments stemmed from the US exclusion of French and British forces (on the grounds that they are independent nuclear forces not under US control) and inclusion of a large number of Soviet fighter-bombers (on the grounds that they could deliver nuclear weapons or could easily be converted to do so).

When the West German government approved the actual initiation of INF deployments in November 1983, the Soviet Union walked out of the INF talks and threatened (and later actually undertook) to deploy additional forward-based nuclear forces and to augment its ballistic missile submarine patrols off US coasts. When the companion START talks recessed in December 1983, the Soviet Union declined to set a resumption date, asserting that the new US deployments had undermined the basis for negotiation on strategic weapons as well as INF.

The United States and the Soviet Union resumed negotiations on INF in March 1985 as part of a new set of umbrella talks (the Nuclear and Space Arms Talks) in Geneva which also included strategic offensive and defensive weapons. Initially, the two sides remained as far apart as ever. But at the Reykjavik, Iceland, summit in October 1986, the Soviet Union essentially agreed to the US position on INF and both sides agreed to eliminate all European-based US and Soviet INF missiles and to retain only a token level of 100 INF warheads. Other issues related

Missile Deployments Eliminated by the INF Treaty

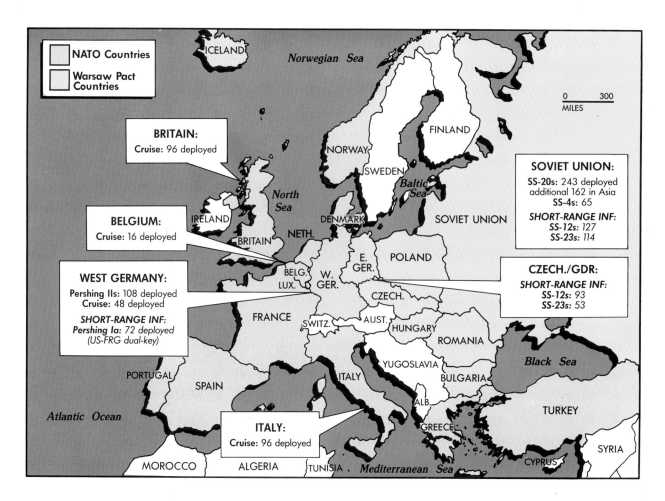

BRITAIN:
Cruise: 96 deployed

BELGIUM:
Cruise: 16 deployed

WEST GERMANY:
Pershing IIs: 108 deployed
Cruise: 48 deployed

SHORT-RANGE INF:
Pershing Ia: 72 deployed
(US-FRG dual-key)

ITALY:
Cruise: 96 deployed

SOVIET UNION:
SS-20s: 243 deployed
additional 162 in Asia
SS-4s: 65

SHORT-RANGE INF:
SS-12s: 127
SS-23s: 114

CZECH./GDR:
SHORT-RANGE INF:
SS-12s: 93
SS-23s: 53

The INF Treaty eliminated all US and Soviet missiles with ranges between 500 and 5,500 kilometers. The official figures above show missiles deployed November 1, 1987, shortly before the INF Treaty was signed. The treaty also required destruction of 430 US missiles and 979 Soviet missiles which were in storage or otherwise not deployed. The treaty prevented the planned deployment of an additional 208 GLCMs in the Netherlands, Britain, Belgium, Germany, and Italy. The Pershing IAs, under joint US-German control, were not formally covered by the INF Treaty but were also to be eliminated by US and West German agreement.

to the INF talks, such as constraints on shorter-range nuclear weapons and the nature and extent of required verification, were not resolved at Reykjavik. But after the failure of the Reykjavik summit to reach a broader agreement on strategic forces, the Soviet Union relinked an INF agreement to a resolution of the strategic arms impasse.

Faced with a beleaguered US administration in the aftermath of the Iran/Contra scandal, General Secretary Gorbachev in February 1987 announced that the Soviet Union was prepared to delink an intermediate-range nuclear forces agreement from other issues and to negotiate an accord along the lines agreed at Reykjavik. In the

following months, the Soviet Union indicated its willingness to constrain shorter-range INF missiles as well, provided that the Federal Republic of Germany disposed of its 72 Pershing IA missiles and delivery systems and that the United States removed and dismantled its nuclear warheads for these systems. The Soviet Union also agreed to eliminate the residual 100 INF warheads, opening the way for a so-called "double zero" agreement (i.e., "zero" INF and "zero" short-range INF missiles). The treaty, calling for the elimination over three years of all ground-based missiles with ranges between 500 and 5,500 kilometers was signed on December 8, 1987, and entered into force on June 1, 1988.

INF Treaty Provisions

General Terms

The INF Treaty was signed by President Reagan and General Secretary Gorbachev on December 8, 1987. The treaty requires the United States and the Soviet Union to eliminate all intermediate-range missiles, shorter-range missiles, associated launchers, equipment, support facilities, and operating bases worldwide. Intermediate-range missiles include all ground-launched missiles with ranges between 1,000 and 5,500 kilometers, and shorter-range missiles include all those with ranges between 500 and 1,000 kilometers. The treaty bans flight testing and production of these missiles as well as production of their launchers.

The 17-article treaty is supplemented by two detailed protocols, one relating to elimination (i.e., dismantlement and destruction) procedures and the other to on-site inspections. An accompanying Memorandum of Understanding (MOU) provides an unprecedentedly detailed accounting of the number and location of all US and Soviet missiles, launchers, equipment, and facilities subject to the terms of the treaty.

The treaty will result in the destruction over a three-year period of a total of 2,695 deployed and nondeployed missiles: 1,836 by the Soviet Union and 859 by the United States. The Soviet Union will scrap 826 intermediate-range missiles (650 SS-20s, 170 SS-4s, and six SS-5s) and 1,010 shorter-range missiles (726 SS-12s, 200 SS-23s, and 84 SSC-X-4s). All are single-warhead missiles except for the powerful SS-20 which carries three warheads. The United States will destroy 689 intermediate-range missiles (247 highly accurate Pershing IIs and 442 ground-launched cruise missiles) and 170 shorter-range missiles (all Pershing IAs). Each US missile carries only one warhead.

Although the treaty does not require the elimination of any warheads *per se*, it will result in the removal of some 2,200 warheads from deployed missiles (including 100 US warheads on West German Pershing IA missiles) to the United States and the Soviet Union where they will be returned to stockpiles or recycled.

The treaty outlines the numerous and precise notification procedures. The US-Soviet Nuclear

Removal and Destruction

The trains in these photos are loaded with Soviet nuclear missiles and launchers being withdrawn from Eastern Europe and returned to the Soviet Union where they will be destroyed under the provisions of the INF Treaty.

Closing the Deal

President Ronald Reagan and Soviet leader Mikhail Gorbachev exchange the INF Treaty instruments of ratification on June 1, 1988.

Risk Reduction Centers (NRRCs), agreed to on September 15, 1987, will provide ongoing communication between the parties for notifications of elimination and inspections as well as requests for the implementation of cooperative measures. NRRCs will also serve as the channel through which treaty-relevant data will be updated. The treaty also establishes the Special Verification Commission (SVC), where US and Soviet representatives are to "resolve questions relating to compliance with the obligations assumed" under the treaty and "agree upon such measures as may be necessary to improve the viability and effectiveness of this Treaty."

Verification Provisions

At the heart of the INF Treaty is the most comprehensive and intrusive verification regime ever established to monitor compliance with a US-Soviet arms control agreement. Integral to the regime is on-site inspection (OSI), both within the United States and the Soviet Union and at US and Soviet bases in Belgium, Italy, the Netherlands, the United Kingdom, West Germany, East Germany, and Czechoslovakia. On-site inspection is permitted only for the first 13 years of the treaty's duration—that is, during the three-year elimination period and 10 years thereafter. During that time, it is meant to serve five different functions:

• *To establish a baseline inventory.* Between 30 and 90 days after the treaty takes effect, each party has the right to conduct inspections at all missile operating bases and support facilities specified in the Memorandum of Understanding (MOU)—including sites where missiles are stored and repaired but excluding missile production facilities—and at all elimination facilities to verify the number and location of all missiles, launchers, and other items to be destroyed.

• *To witness the elimination of missiles and launchers.* Each party is permitted to have inspectors observe the actual destruction of the other party's missiles and launchers at elimination sites. Inspectors may also observe missiles being launched to destruction.

• *To confirm the elimination of a facility.* Within 60 days after a given missile operating base or missile support facility (other than a missile production facility) is eliminated, each party has the right to conduct close-out inspections to verify that the process of destroying missiles, their launchers, and support equipment has been completed.

• *To conduct short-notice "challenge" inspections.* During the first three years after the treaty enters into force, each party will be permitted up to 20 short-notice inspections per calendar year at sites listed in the MOU (except elimination sites, which are subject to OSI during the actual dismantlement and destruction process, and production facilities). During the next five years, each will be allowed 15 inspections annually, and during the final five years 10 annually.

• *To monitor specified production facilities.* Thirty days after the treaty takes effect and for the duration of the 13-year period, each party has the right to station, 24 hours a day, up to 30 resident inspectors at the exits and around the perimeter of a missile production facility. In the Soviet Union, the US will monitor the Votkinsk Machine Building Plant, west of the Urals, where both the SS-20 IRM (covered by the treaty) and the SS-25 ICBM (*not* covered by the treaty but which uses a rocket stage outwardly similar to a stage of the SS-20) are assembled. Although no parallel dual-production facility exists in the United States, the Soviet Union will be permitted to monitor the portals of the Hercules Plant at Magna, Utah, which now manufactures boosters and other components for the MX and Trident missiles and once produced boosters for the Pershing II missile.

The treaty also includes a standard prohibition against interference with National Technical Means (NTM) such as photo-reconnaissance satellites, the backbone of any verification regime. The use of concealment measures which impede verification of compliance is forbidden, as well as the transmission of telemetry from missiles being launched to destruction except for unencrypted data transmitted to ensure that a missile is following a safe flight path.

Although strategic offensive arms are not limited by the INF Treaty, they are subject to some of its verification provisions. Cooperative measures will be used to ensure that intermediate-range missiles banned by the treaty are not hidden at bases where Soviet mobile SS-25 ICBMs are deployed. For three years or until a treaty limiting strategic offensive arms enters into force, the United States may ask the Soviet Union to open the roofs of garages housing SS-25s, remove the missiles and launchers, and display them openly for US satellites to photograph.

Atomic bomb test, Bikini atoll, South Pacific, 1946.

11

Nuclear Weapon Testing

Background

The first nuclear weapon test was in July 1945 at Alamogordo, New Mexico. After two nuclear weapons were used in the war against Japan in August 1945, the US resumed its nuclear weapon testing program in the southwest United States and US Pacific Island Territories. The Soviet Union tested its first weapon in 1949.

With supplies of nuclear materials assured, nuclear tests became the critical element in the burgeoning nuclear arms race. In the early years of the nuclear age, weapons technology, driven by a massive test program, progressed very rapidly. Fission weapons with yields almost 50 times that of the Hiroshima bomb were soon tested, and in 1951 a thermonuclear device with a yield of around 10 megatons (about a thousand times the yield of the original Hiroshima bomb) was detonated in the Pacific. Two years later, the Soviet Union tested its first thermonuclear device. Then the two sides began to tailor these fission and thermonuclear devices to every conceivable type of delivery system. There seemed to be no limit to the power and diversity of nuclear weapons. These rapid developments depended in large part on massive and uninhibited US and Soviet programs of atmospheric tests undertaken with little regard or even appreciation of the potential environmental problems.

By the mid 1950s, there was a widespread and growing belief that the only way to bring the nuclear arms race under control was to stop nuclear testing. This belief was reinforced by popular opposition to and fear of nuclear testing as a pernicious worldwide health hazard. The environmental health concern was fueled by the belated discovery of unexpected high-radiation effects of fallout from the large US tests in the Pacific. Concurrently, President Eisenhower, along with scientists close to the nuclear weapons program impressed by the surprisingly rapid rate of success of the Soviet test program, became increasingly concerned about the long-term security implications of an unconstrained nuclear arms race. A ban on nuclear weapon testing, an area where the United States still possessed a clear advantage, appeared to be the one practical and verifiable path to the control of future nuclear weapon developments. Then existing technical collection systems outside the Soviet Union could easily detect atmospheric tests worldwide by their airborne radioactive debris.

In March 1958, the Soviet Union declared a moratorium on nuclear testing and President Eisenhower proposed technical talks to discuss the possibility of verifying a comprehensive ban on nuclear testing. Scientists from East and West met that summer in Geneva, Switzerland, at the "Conference of Experts" and agreed that a network of monitoring stations could detect and identify nuclear tests in the atmosphere and underwater down to very small yields. It was also concluded that even underground tests—of which there had only been one—could be identified down to a few kilotons.

In October 1958, the three nations that had then tested nuclear weapons (the United States, Great Britain, and the Soviet Union) began negotiations on a comprehensive test ban treaty (CTBT). To emphasize the serious nature of these talks, Eisenhower announced a one-year testing moratorium. Verification arrangements were the focus of the negotiations, with the Soviet Union resisting the US proposals for on-site inspections, international control of the seismic stations on Soviet territory, and revisions of the Conference of Experts' technical data on underground tests.

In 1960, in an effort to resolve a negotiating impasse on verification, the United States proposed a partial ban on underground tests with seismic magnitudes greater than 4.75 (on the Richter scale). Such a limit would have allowed tests of weapons with yields under 10-20 kilotons. But the negotiations failed to make progress after a US U-2 reconnaissance plane was shot down in May 1960 over the Soviet Union, and the subsequent Paris summit between Eisenhower and Khrushchev collapsed.

The Kennedy administration resumed the trilateral test ban talks, pursuing the threshold idea on underground tests. But little progress was made, especially after the Soviet Union—citing France's first nuclear tests in 1960 and 1961—resumed testing in August 1961. Although the moratorium had officially ended by 1960, the suddenness of the Soviet announcement and the large number and high yields of its test series came as a shock to the United States, which responded with a massive test series of its own.

Seismometer readings of underground nuclear tests...

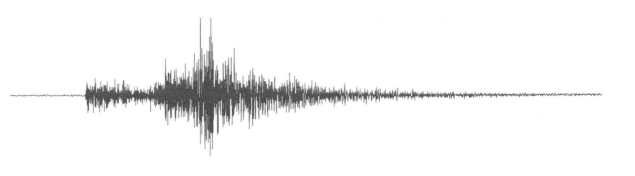

The Limited Test Ban Treaty

The massive nature of the renewed Soviet and US atmospheric testing and the sobering Cuban missile crisis of October 1962 revived international interest in a test ban. Although negotiators agreed on the importance of a CTBT, agreement could not be reached on several important issues, including the number of allowed on-site inspections and the number of unmanned seismic stations to be located in each country. President Kennedy insisted on at least seven inspections and Khrushchev would not accept more than three. In the summer of 1963, the United States, the Soviet Union, and Great Britain reached a less comprehensive prohibition, the Limited Test Ban Treaty (LTBT), which banned all nuclear explosions except for underground tests. Thus, the LTBT ended the immediate environmental problems associated with atmospheric nuclear testing. But underground testing has continued to the present at a very substantial level. Since the LTBT entered into force there have been up to the end of 1988 approximately 1,200 underground tests worldwide, including more than 600 US and about 450 Soviet tests. (See Chart, page 115.)

The US Senate ratified the LTBT in the fall of 1963 and the three original parties continue to adhere to its provisions. Over 100 other nations are now parties to the LTBT. Fifteen more have signed the treaty but have not ratified it. France, the only other nuclear power in 1963, has refused to sign the treaty but did cease atmospheric tests in 1974. China, which conducted its first nuclear explosive test in 1964, has also refused to sign the agreement but has stopped atmospheric testing. India, which is a party to the LTBT, conducted an underground explosion in 1974 which it claimed was for "peaceful" purposes.

TTBT and PNET

Despite a commitment in the preamble "to achieve the discontinuance of all test explosions of nuclear weapons for all time," the LTBT has not led to a ban on nuclear weapon tests. Nuclear testing received little attention between the mid-1960s and the mid-1970s, partly because the LTBT had diminished environmental concerns and had removed testing from public view. Meanwhile, the emphasis of arms control shifted to limitations on strategic offensive and defensive systems, where rapid technological developments were occurring.

Finally, in 1974 progress was made towards limiting underground tests by the Threshold Test Ban Treaty (TTBT), which was followed in 1976 by the Peaceful Nuclear Explosion Treaty (PNET). The TTBT, signed by President Nixon and General Secretary Brezhnev in 1974, placed a 150-kiloton limit on underground nuclear weapon tests. The two sides were to rely on national technical means and external seismic monitoring stations for verification of the TTBT. Verification was to be enhanced through "cooperative measures." These would include the exchange of technical data on the geology of testing areas and on the explosive yields of two nuclear tests at each testing site to help both sides calibrate their seismic instruments and calculations.

The PNET, signed by President Ford and General Secretary Brezhnev in 1976, closed a major loophole in the TTBT by limiting to 150 kilotons individual nuclear explosives used for peaceful purposes, such as large-scale earth moving. The PNET permitted group explosions, or "salvos," of individual explosions with combined yields up to 1.5 megatons for earth moving projects; but, if the total yield of a salvo was to be

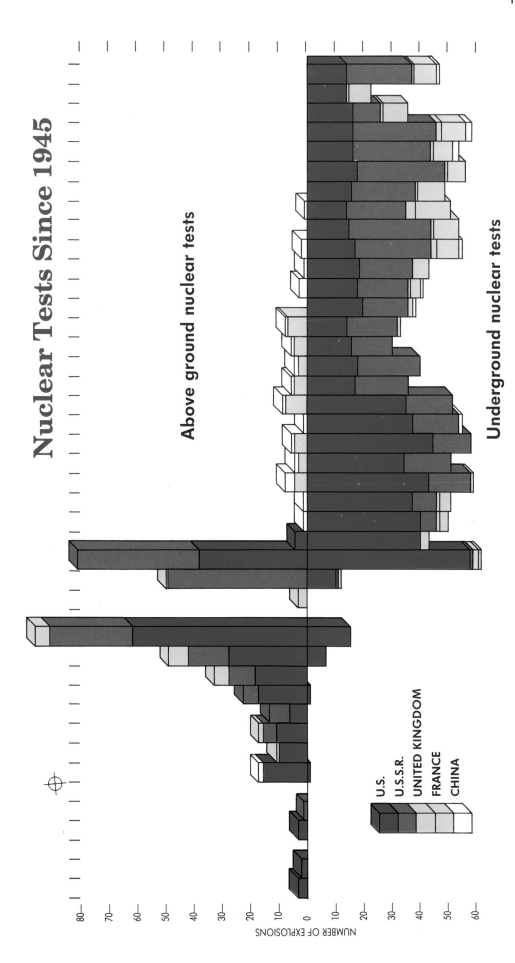

Nuclear Tests Since 1945

Above ground nuclear tests

Underground nuclear tests

NUMBER OF EXPLOSIONS

80—
70—
60—
50—
40—
30—
20—
10—
0—
10—
20—
30—
40—
50—
60—

U.S.
U.S.S.R.
UNITED KINGDOM
FRANCE
CHINA

|1945| '46 | '47 | '48 | '49 | '50 | '51 | '52 | '53 | '54 | '55 | '56 | '57 | '58 | '59 | '60 | '61 | '62 | '63 | '64 | '65 | '66 | '67 | '68 | '69 | '70 | '71 | '72 | '73 | '74 | '75 | '76 | '77 | '78 | '79 | '80 | '81 | '82 | '83 | '84 | '85 | '86 | '87 |

The above graph reflects the number of nuclear tests from the beginning of the nuclear era through 1987. Since the Limited Test Ban Treaty of 1963, all U.S., British, and Soviet tests have been conducted underground. Also note the virtual lack of testing in 1959 and 1960, when the United States and the Soviet Union adopted testing moratoriums. Photographs on the preceding page show three types of nuclear tests. At left, a mushroom cloud rises from an above ground explosion at the US test site in Nevada, 1955. The soldiers are standing about five miles from Ground Zero. At top right, an underwater explosion creates a cloud chamber at Bikini atoll in the South Pacific, 1946. The ships are unmanned. At bottom right, dust rises and a crater begins to form one minute after an underground explosion in Nevada, 1969.

above 150 kilotons, on-site monitoring was required to insure that none of the individual explosions exceeded 150 kilotons.

Although the TTBT and the PNET have never been ratified, the United States and the Soviet Union have abided by the 150-kiloton limit on underground nuclear explosions. The Reagan administration at first opposed the TTBT as an unnecessary constraint on the US test program and then accused the Soviet Union of violating the 150-kiloton limit, a charge that is denied by the Soviet Union and strongly disputed by many knowledgeable US scientists. (See Chapter 15.) The Reagan administration insisted that seismic methods of verification are inadequate to determine Soviet compliance with the 150-kiloton limit and proposed protocols to the TTBT and PNET that would incorporate more advanced—and intrusive—means of verification. The administration's preferred method was a "hydrodynamic" system called "CORRTEX," which requires independent measurements within a few meters of the exploding test device. In the summer of 1988 the two superpowers conducted the Joint Verification Experiment (JVE) to demonstrate the operation of the CORRTEX system, as well as a similar Soviet system, and evaluate its applicability as a routine means of nuclear test verification in the future.

Comprehensive Test Ban

In 1977 President Carter renewed active trilateral negotiations for a CTBT with the Soviet Union and Great Britain. The newer nuclear weapon states, France and China, did not participate in these talks. A great deal of progress was made toward an agreed treaty text, including detailed verification procedures. These provisions included: agreed numbers of in-country, unmanned seismic monitoring stations, detailed procedures for "challenge" on-site inspections, and the exchange of geological and geophysical information. Final agreement on a complete treaty text had not been reached when the talks recessed at the end of the Carter administration.

The Reagan administration did not continue the negotiations and announced in 1982 that a CTBT would not be in the security interests of the United States "at this time." But the CTB has not been dropped from the arms control debate. In August 1985, the Soviet Union began a unilateral moratorium on Soviet nuclear weapon testing, which it extended two times. A year and a half later, the Soviet Union resumed testing after the United States repeatedly refused to join in the testing moratorium.

The Reagan administration argued that a CTBT would be dangerous to US security interests for the following reasons: there is a pressing requirement to test more advanced "third-generation" weapons, such as the nuclear-pumped X-ray laser, a possible kill mechanism for a "Star Wars" antimissile system; nuclear tests are necessary for the development of new warhead designs for strategic systems already planned for deployment; tests are required to maintain the reliability of the existing stockpile of nuclear weapons; and such an agreement could not be verified. In support of its case, the administration reported instances where testing had been used to correct reliability problems discovered in stockpile weapons. It was also argued that the Soviet Union could conduct militarily useful underground testing below the identification threshold of a seismic detection system and could use various concealment schemes to hide much larger yield tests. This might be accomplished by testing in large underground

cavities to muffle seismic signals or by testing during earthquakes that generate a seismic background in which the test signal would be drowned out.

CTBT advocates argue that the development of advanced nuclear weapons should be halted because, in the hands of the Soviet Union or other countries, they might threaten US security. Furthermore, they argue that nuclear testing is not needed for planned modernizations of US strategic forces because warheads for the MX and cruise missiles have been fully tested, and suitable warheads already exist for the Midgetman and Trident II systems.

CTBT advocates also reject the argument that nuclear tests are needed to ensure the continued reliability and safety of existing weapons. They point out that the discovery and remedy of reliability problems have not been, and need not be, dependent on nuclear testing. Reliability can be insured by subjecting weapon components to non-destructive testing and non-nuclear tests, and by replacing defective or aging components when necessary. Some test ban advocates acknowledge that over a period of decades a CTBT might to some extent diminish confidence among military and political leaders in the precise capabilities of their strategic arsenals. However, they argue that the resulting situation would actually contribute to strategic stability. While both sides' confidence in their ability to launch a successful first strike might be reduced, deterrence would be maintained since the weapons would be sufficiently reliable to assure an effective retaliatory capability.

CTBT advocates argue that a complete ban can be "adequately" verified. Most seismologists agree that, using only seismic monitoring stations outside the two countries, testing down to a few kilotons can be verified with high confidence. With manned or unmanned in-country monitoring stations, as were agreed in CTBT negotiations, the United States could detect and identify Soviet testing at very low levels (well below one kiloton), even if elaborate schemes for cheating were utilized. Advocates of a ban argue that testing below this level has little technical or military significance and would certainly not be useful for developing new nuclear weapons, which the ban is designed to prevent.

Advocates also emphasize that a CTBT would strengthen the nuclear nonproliferation regime. Without testing, a nation would have great difficulty achieving a nuclear capability based on anything other than a relatively primitive device. Since a CTBT would ban nuclear explosions on a worldwide basis, it would probably be acceptable to countries, such as India, which have not signed the NPT on the grounds that it is inherently discriminatory. Even those potential nuclear states that refused to sign a CTBT would find it more difficult to test in the face of a worldwide ban on nuclear testing.

Reagan administration representatives, however, have tended to reject or minimize the significance of a CTBT as a deterrent to nuclear proliferation on the grounds that potential nuclear states are concerned with their own security problems and not superpower relations. Thus, in assessing the security implications, technical issues, and desirability of the CTBT, the Reagan administration and advocates of such an agreement have been in almost total disagreement.

Status at the Beginning of the Bush Administration

The United States and the Soviet Union agreed in late 1987 to resume stage-by-stage talks on nuclear testing. The joint communique establishing the goals of the talks states that the two nations "as the first step, will agree upon effective verification measures which will make it possible to ratify the US-USSR Threshold Test Ban Treaty of 1974, and Peaceful Nuclear Explosions Treaty of 1976, and proceed to negotiating further intermediate limitations on nuclear testing, leading to the ultimate objective of the complete cessation of nuclear testing as part of an effective disarmament process."

With the advent of the Bush administration, the first stage of the talks on enhanced verification measures for the TTBT and PNET had not yet been completed. The second stage, generally considered to be directed at establishing an annual quota of underground tests, a decreasing threshold for permitted underground tests, or both, is apparently not intended to begin until the TTBT and PNET are ratified. To the end, the Reagan administration maintained its position that a CTBT would not be possible until the United States no longer depended on nuclear weapons for deterrence.

Research reactor at India's Bhabha Atomic Research Center.

12

Nuclear Proliferation

Background

Arms control has understandably focused on the immense nuclear arsenals of the Soviet Union and the United States and on the smaller but still substantial nuclear forces of Great Britain, France, and China. First priority has been given to controlling and reversing this "vertical" proliferation of nuclear weapons. Looking to the future, however, the spread or "horizontal" proliferation of nuclear weapons to additional countries would be a new, serious threat to world peace and the security of the superpowers themselves. The arms control process has made a major contribution to containing horizontal proliferation by establishing an international nonproliferation regime. But the underlying problem remains, and further horizontal proliferation could occur at any time.

The horizontal proliferation of nuclear weapons increases the possibility that nuclear weapons will actually be used deliberately or accidentally in a local conflict that could then esca-

Israel's Dimona nuclear complex.

US Nonproliferation Policy in the '40s and '50s

late to involve the United States and the Soviet Union. It also increases the risk of a "catalytic" nuclear war between the superpowers, sparked by the provocative use of nuclear weapons by a third nation, or even by terrorists.

In addition to the five declared nuclear-weapon states, two countries, India and Israel, probably already have some nuclear weapons and Pakistan and South Africa may have, or soon can have, a few nuclear weapons or the components for rapid assembly of weapons. India tested a nuclear device in 1974, but insists that the test was for peaceful purposes and denies that it has a nuclear weapons program. Although Israel has not conducted a full scale nuclear test, it does have a major weapons development program and production capability and is generally believed to have a stockpile of nuclear weapons or the necessary components ready to assemble on short notice. Pakistan is also actively developing a weapons capability and South Africa is probably in a similar position.

Many other nations are technically capable of undertaking a nuclear weapons program. But most nations without nuclear weapons, including such technological giants as Japan and Germany, have forsworn the nuclear option.

A few non-nuclear weapon states may believe an independent nuclear capability is desirable to deter or intimidate their adversaries; others may be tempted by the international prestige and influence associated with nuclear weapons. The nuclear arms race between the superpowers has clearly tended to encourage these perceptions in some nations. Nevertheless, most non-nuclear weapon nations have so far decided that it is in their self-interest not to develop nuclear weapons and to support an international effort to limit the number of nuclear-capable states.

At the end of World War II, the United States recognized that its monopoly on nuclear weapons could not last in the absence of an international agreement. In early 1946, the United States proposed the Baruch Plan to prevent nuclear proliferation by placing all nuclear materials and technology under international control. The plan was rejected by the Soviet Union and it soon became evident that the Soviet nuclear weapons program was already well-advanced at that time. (See Chapter 2.)

In the absence of an agreement, US nuclear exports were banned by the 1946 McMahon Act. Despite these early efforts to deny the spread of US technology, four other countries tested nuclear weapons over the next 18 years: the Soviet Union in 1949, Great Britain in 1952, France in 1960, and China in 1964. Meanwhile, many other countries began to investigate peaceful nuclear power, which was widely believed to be the energy source of the future. The resulting proliferation of interest in nuclear power concerned the United States because much of the technology and materials used in civilian nuclear programs could be used in the manufacture of nuclear weapons.

President Dwight Eisenhower addressed this emerging dilemma in his "Atoms for Peace" speech of December 1953. Rather than deny nuclear materials and equipment, Eisenhower proposed to help non-nuclear nations develop peaceful nuclear power if they would disavow nuclear weapons. In 1957, the International Atomic Energy Agency (IAEA), an autonomous specialized agency of the United Nations, was founded to help nations develop peaceful nuclear programs under careful monitoring to ensure that materials were not diverted for nuclear weapons.

The task of the IAEA has been difficult because of the considerable overlap in the nuclear technologies used for military and peaceful purposes. For example, uranium enrichment and plutonium reprocessing plants, which may be part of a legitimate nuclear power program, can also produce weapons-grade nuclear material. As more nations have acquired these advanced facilities, the IAEA has had more difficulty ensuring that material has not been diverted to weapon programs.

The Potential for Nuclear Proliferation

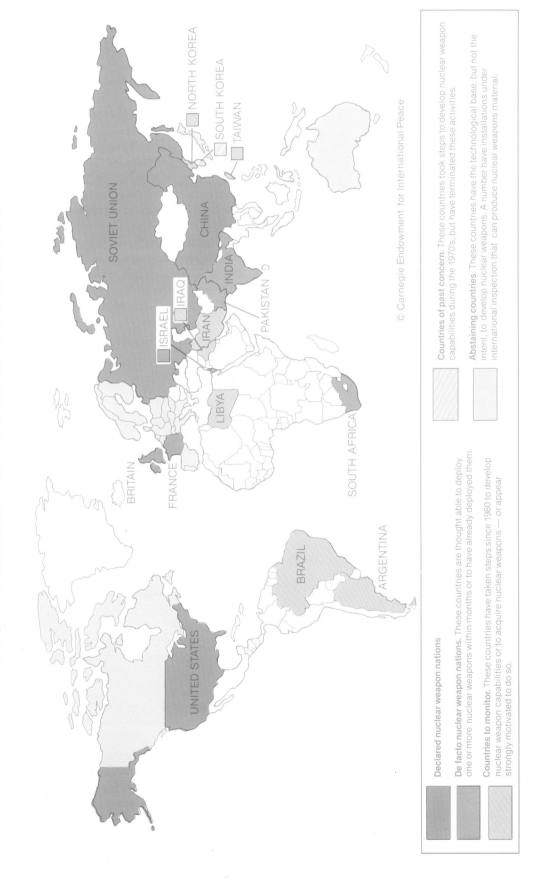

Declared nuclear weapon nations

De facto nuclear weapon nations. These countries are thought able to deploy one or more nuclear weapons within months or to have already deployed them.

Countries to monitor. These countries have taken steps since 1980 to develop nuclear weapon capabilities or to acquire nuclear weapons — or appear strongly motivated to do so.

Countries of past concern. These countries took steps to develop nuclear weapon capabilities during the 1970's, but have terminated these activities.

Abstaining countries. These countries have the technological base, but not the intent, to develop nuclear weapons. A number have installations under international inspection that can produce nuclear weapons material.

© Carnegie Endowment for International Peace

SOVIET UNION

CHINA

NORTH KOREA

SOUTH KOREA

TAIWAN

INDIA

IRAQ

IRAN

ISRAEL

PAKISTAN

LIBYA

BRITAIN

FRANCE

SOUTH AFRICA

BRAZIL

ARGENTINA

UNITED STATES

The Nonproliferation Treaty

Multilateral negotiations began in 1965 on a formal treaty to prevent the spread of nuclear weapons. In June 1968, after protracted negotiations, the United States, the Soviet Union, Great Britain, and 59 non-nuclear-weapon states finally signed the Nuclear Nonproliferation Treaty (NPT). Since then, 74 other non-nuclear-weapon states have signed the treaty.

The NPT essentially adopted Eisenhower's Atoms for Peace bargain: the non-nuclear weapon states agreed to renounce the development and acquisition of nuclear weapons in exchange for a pledge from the three nuclear-weapon states to share peaceful nuclear technology. Thus the NPT, which was founded on the premise that preventing nuclear proliferation is in the interest of all countries, provided an additional incentive to non-nuclear states to join the regime. To relieve the pressure on non-nuclear-weapon states to develop nuclear weapons, the signatory states already possessing nuclear weapons also agreed to seek an end to the nuclear arms race.

By establishing a number of legal, political, and practical obstacles to the acquisition of nuclear explosives, the NPT attempted to strengthen and preserve each party's commitment to nonproliferation. Each non-nuclear-weapon signatory state agreed to open its entire peaceful nuclear program to a "full safeguards" system managed by the International Atomic Energy Agency. IAEA inspectors check the inventory of fissionable materials in the peaceful programs by on-site inspections involving direct measurements and audits to uncover diversions that might go to a clandestine weapons program. IAEA inspectors, however, can only visit "declared" facilities and not sites "suspected" of illegal activities. While not designed to prevent an illegal program or diversions to such a program, the IAEA system is meant to sound an alarm if illegal diversion or activities are underway or have occurred.

The signatories of the NPT agreed to be bound by its provisions for an initial period of 25 years, at the end of which a conference would decide by majority vote whether to extend the treaty indefinitely or for another fixed period.

Several nations have refused to sign the Nonproliferation Treaty. In addition to France and China, which had already developed and deployed nuclear weapons by the time the treaty was signed, these so-called "holdout" states include India, Pakistan, Israel, and South Africa, which are now suspected of having developed initial nuclear weapons capabilities.

The holdout states notwithstanding, the NPT has helped build a barrier against further proliferation. India, the only new country to explode a nuclear device since the treaty was signed, felt compelled at the time to assert that the test was for peaceful purposes and has not tested since then. A number of additional countries have signed the NPT in recent years, indicating growing worldwide awareness of the security benefits of nuclear nonproliferation efforts. NPT signatories now include all NATO countries (except France, which nevertheless now informally supports the treaty's provisions), all the Warsaw Pact countries, and, with the important exception of the holdout states, most other countries with significant nuclear programs.

Export Controls

The NPT requires that safeguards be placed on all materials or equipment exported by the signatories for use by any non-nuclear-weapon state. This provision, when combined with the required "full scope" safeguards on all nuclear facilities of non-nuclear weapon states, provides a powerful deterrent to evasion by signatories to the treaty. In the case of nonsignatories, however, this provision has only limited impact since they are not required to accept "full scope" safeguards on existing facilities as a condition for importing sensitive equipment provided it was safeguarded. Moreover, without specific guidelines for the application of safeguards, nuclear suppliers might be tempted to cut corners to gain advantage in the highly competitive international nuclear market. India's "peaceful" nuclear explosion in 1974, and anticipation of increased worldwide demands for sophisticated nuclear power facilities capable of producing weapon-grade material, led to greater interest in tightening the nonproliferation regime.

From 1974 to 1976, representatives of all the "nuclear suppliers" of the NPT regime and France developed guidelines for nuclear exports. As a result, every major nuclear supplier except China agreed to common "trigger lists" of sensitive materials, equipment, and technology which cannot be exported without IAEA safeguards. In 1984 and 1985, China reversed itself and agreed to follow the nuclear export guidelines of the other nuclear suppliers. The nuclear suppliers have also agreed on certain common procedures, such as requiring purchasers of nuclear equipment not to transfer safeguarded items to third nations unless they too accept safeguards.

These multilateral export controls have been supplemented by unilateral legislation that further restricts sensitive exports. The United States, along with France and West Germany, forswore the sale of plutonium reprocessing technology in the mid-1970s. In 1978, the US Congress passed the Nuclear Nonproliferation Act, which provided for tighter safeguarding procedures than those required under the NPT and attempted to discourage nuclear power based on the plutonium fuel cycle by prohibiting the international transfer of plutonium and plutonium reprocessing technology. The US Congress also enacted legislation prohibiting economic and military assistance for any nation supplying or receiving sensitive nuclear equipment or technology, but under pressure from the Reagan administration has backed off enforcing these provisions in the case of Pakistan.

Some non-nuclear NPT parties have criticized export controls as inherently inconsistent with the treaty's goal of promoting peaceful nuclear power. Supporters of export controls argue that the NPT intended discretion to be used in promoting nuclear power. Advocates of a very restrictive regime argue that controls should be applied even-handedly to avoid additional charges of discrimination. Others hold that nations like Japan and West Germany, which have strong political commitments not to build nuclear weapons and which already have access to weapon-grade material, should not be subject to the same restrictions as nations such as South Africa and Libya. The issue has been considerably diffused for the time being by the decreasing commercial attractiveness of nuclear power in general and the noncompetitive status of nuclear reprocessing and breeder reactors in particular. But the problem is inherent in the present regime and will continue to be an issue in implementing nonproliferation policy.

Unilateral diplomatic efforts have also bolstered the nonproliferation regime. In some cases, nuclear weapon states have used diplomatic leverage to dissuade their allies from pursuing a nuclear weapons capability. The United States, for example, successfully pressured South Korea and Taiwan—two allies which had demonstrated an increasing interest in acquiring nuclear weapons—to forego the nuclear option. Other efforts at dissuasion have, however,

foundered on their potential costs to the interstate relationships involved. The United States has not, for example, brought its diplomatic muscle to bear over Israel's nuclear weapons program for fear of jeopardizing the "special relationship." In some cases, multilateral diplomatic efforts have overcome the difficulties of coordination and have been quite effective. When a Soviet photo-reconnaissance satellite discovered what appeared to be preparations for a nuclear test in the Kalahari Desert of South Africa in 1977, the Soviet Union notified the United States, which then led its European allies in a successful diplomatic campaign to keep South Africa from exploding a nuclear device.

Nuclear-Free Zones

Another constraint on the proliferation of nuclear weapons has been the creation of nuclear-free zones by the 1959 Antarctic Treaty, the 1968 Treaty for the Prohibition of Nuclear Weapons in Latin America (also known as the Treaty of Tlatelolco), and the 1985 South Pacific Nuclear-Free Zone Treaty (also known as the Treaty of Rarotonga).

The Antarctic Treaty, which involves on-site inspections of facilities of all countries in the region, has been in effect for over 25 years. The Treaty of Tlatelolco, though not fully in force (it must first be ratified by all Latin American countries—Argentina has not ratified and Cuba has neither signed nor ratified), has contributed to restricting the presence of nuclear weapons in Latin America for almost two decades. It has been signed by three countries that have not signed the NPT—Argentina, Brazil, and Chile. In Latin America, only Cuba remains entirely outside of both accords. The South Pacific agreement must still be ratified by a number of its signatories.

Nuclear-free zone agreements differ from the NPT by prohibiting both the acquisition and *stationing* of nuclear weapons within a specific, geographic area. Both the Latin American and South Pacific treaties have protocols that require other countries with territories in the area to respect their denuclearized status. Another protocol in both treaties calls upon nuclear-weapon states to respect the zones and not to use or threaten to use nuclear weapons within the zones. This protocol in the Latin American treaty has the unique distinction among arms control agreements of having been signed and ratified by all five nuclear powers. All three nuclear-free

Latin American Nuclear-Free Zone

STATUS OF COUNTRIES, TREATY OF TLATELOLCO

■ TREATY FULLY IN FORCE

□ SIGNED AND RATIFIED BUT TREATY NOT IN FORCE*

▨ TREATY SIGNED BUT NOT RATIFIED

▨ TREATY NOT SIGNED

*COUNTRIES HAVE THE OPTION OF PUTTING TREATY IN FORCE ONLY WHEN *ALL* LATIN AMERICAN COUNTRIES HAVE RATIFIED.
TERRITORIES IN WHITE NOT ELIGIBLE TO SIGN

Living Without the Bomb

The Latin American, South Pacific, and Antarctic treaties form a nuclear-free zone stretching from the western border of Australia to the eastern shores of Latin America, and extending south from the United States through Antarctica.

South Pacific Nuclear-Free Zone

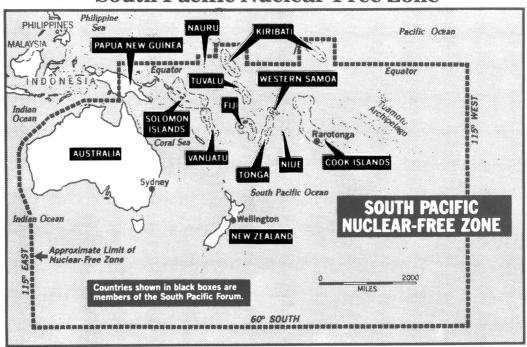

Countries shown in black boxes are members of the South Pacific Forum.

zones permit the transit of nuclear-armed aircraft and ships of other powers.

The three existing nuclear-free zones form a broad nuclear-free expanse from the western border of Australia to the eastern shores of Latin America and extending from the southern border of the United States through Antarctica. Attempts have been made in the past to create similar zones in Africa, the Middle East, and South Asia; but these proposals, which involve difficult political issues, have had little success to date.

A Comprehensive Test Ban

A ban on nuclear testing could also help restrain the spread of nuclear weapons. (See Chapter 11.) Indeed, the Preamble and Article VI of the NPT commit the parties "to achieve the discontinuance of all test explosions of nuclear weapons for all time and to continue negotiations to this end," and "to pursue negotiations in good faith of effective measures relating to cessation of the nuclear arms race."

Besides responding to frequent charges of the non-nuclear-weapon signatories that the nuclear-weapon parties to the treaty are failing to meet this commitment, a comprehensive test ban (CTB) would create an additional barrier to proliferation. Non-nuclear nations that forswore all nuclear testing would find it difficult to build reliable nuclear weapons and impossible to build more sophisticated thermonuclear weapons. In addition, some nations would not be interested in developing nuclear weapons if they could not demonstrate their capability to their adversaries or their domestic constituencies. Above all, it would be politically much more difficult for those nations which are not members of the NPT to test nuclear weapons if most nations, including the superpowers, were observing a ban on nuclear tests.

Some opponents of a comprehensive test ban argue that such a treaty would have little impact on the decision of Third World countries to go nuclear since that decision would be made for domestic and regional reasons largely unrelated to the status of US-Soviet relations. Others have argued that a comprehensive test ban might actually encourage hitherto undecided nations to undertake a nuclear weapons development program because they could lose confidence in the ability of one or the other of the superpowers to maintain a satisfactory deterrent posture.

The Future

Despite nationalistic complaints over "discrimination" and technical concerns about constraints on the peaceful uses of nuclear energy, there is probably more general agreement on the wisdom of restraining the proliferation of nuclear weapons than on any other arms control measure. Both superpowers, the other nuclear-weapon states, as well as most of the world's non-nuclear states, now believe that a non-proliferation regime is clearly in their national security interests. A complex of multinational arms control agreements and informal agreements, national legislation, and unilateral diplomatic initiatives have made this non-proliferation regime possible.

The coming years will tell whether the regime can survive growing regional pressures. In 1990, the Bush administration will be faced with the fourth Five Year NPT Review Conference at which many of the non-nuclear-weapon states will be highly critical of the United States and the Soviet Union if they have failed to reach agreement on a strategic arms treaty in partial fulfillment of their NPT commitment to work toward nuclear disarmament. In 1995, the 25th anniversary of the NPT's entry into force, the members of the treaty will have to decide in accordance with the treaty whether the NPT, which has been the keystone of the nonproliferation regime, will continue in force indefinitely or for a fixed period.

Artillerymen prepared for gas warfare during World War I.

13

Chemical and Biological Warfare

Background

In such forms as poisoned arrows and the catapulting of diseased corpses into besieged cities, chemical and biological warfare (CBW) has existed for thousands of years. But the 20th century has seen the first mass use of poison gases in war as well as the development of other extremely deadly chemical and biological agents and the means to deliver them.

Concern over the potential of chemical warfare was already widespread at the turn of the century, as manifested by the bans on gas warfare negotiated at the Hague conferences of 1899 and 1907. These measures did not prevent the mass use of chemical weapons in World War I. Gas was used by all the major participants, and resulted in more than a million casualties. The international repugnance for this indiscriminate weapon led to the Geneva Protocol of 1925, which banned the use of chemical and biological weapons in warfare.

Although chemical weapons were used in Ethiopia by the Italians in the mid-1930s, in World War II both sides refrained from employing chemical warfare in actual combat despite the existence of large stocks of chemical weapons. It should be noted, however, that countless non-combatant Jewish and other prisoners were killed in Nazi concentration camps by gases suitable for chemical warfare. In recent years, Iraq has used chemical weapons in its war with Iran, and the US government has charged that the Soviet Union or its allies have made limited use of chemical and toxin weapons in Southeast Asia and Afghanistan.

Agents of Death

Chemical weapons are toxic chemicals—referred to as "agents"—used to injure, incapacitate, or kill. At the outset of World War I, chemical weapons were relatively primitive, sometimes consisting of little more than tanks of common industrial gases, such as chlorine or phosgene, which were opened when the wind was blowing toward the enemy. A standard agent in World War I was mustard gas, which causes severe blistering of the skin, damage to the lungs, and blindness. Since then, there has been a revolution in both the deadliness of the agents and the effectiveness of the means of delivery.

In the 1930s, an extremely lethal family of agents, the "nerve gases," was developed. The nerve gases, which are similar to some pesticides in their chemical structure, attack the central nervous system by interfering with enzymes in the brain. The primary nerve agents in modern chemical stockpiles include Soman, Sarin, and VX. All of these agents would be extremely deadly if used against unprotected troops or civilians.

Nonlethal chemical agents, such as tear gas, have been developed for riot control and other purposes where the intention is not to kill or permanently injure the exposed individuals. These riot control agents are rarely useful in combat. Military interest in developing more effective "incapacitant" agents has been limited by their highly unpredictable effectiveness in battle.

Modern chemical weapons in the stocks of the major powers can be delivered by artillery shells, aircraft bombs and sprays, or short-range missiles. If a chemical war were to break out, "nonpersistent agents" (which disperse within minutes after their release) would typically be used over short ranges where one's own troops might move in after the attack; "persistent agents" (which last for hours or days) might be used for longer-range attacks.

Despite the high casualty figures against unprepared troops in the trench warfare of World War I, chemical weapons are thought to have only limited military utility against a sophisticated opponent. The effects, which depend on wind, weather, and surprise, are difficult for military planners to predict. Moreover, gas masks and protective clothing provide an effective defense against even advanced chemical agents. Against

Halabja

The most serious recent violations of the Geneva Protocol, which prohibits the use of chemical weapons and other agents, are believed to have been committed by Iraq. According to Iran, after Iranian forces occupied the Iraqi town of Halabja in March 1988 during the Iraq-Iran war, Iraqi aircraft bombarded the city with chemical weapons, killing more than 4,000 civilians, most of whom were members of the Kurdish ethnic minority and reportedly rebellious toward Iraq.

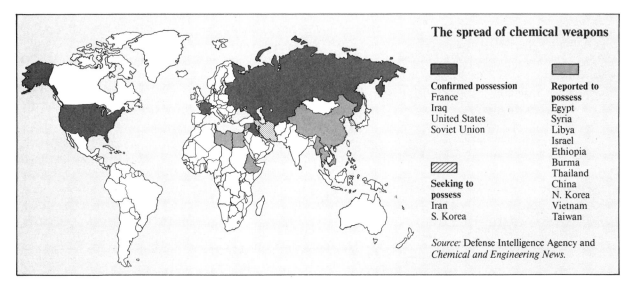

The spread of chemical weapons

Confirmed possession
France
Iraq
United States
Soviet Union

Seeking to possess
Iran
S. Korea

Reported to possess
Egypt
Syria
Libya
Israel
Ethiopia
Burma
Thailand
China
N. Korea
Vietnam
Taiwan

Source: Defense Intelligence Agency and *Chemical and Engineering News.*

an army equipped with modern protective gear, chemical attacks are considerably less effective, shell for shell, than attacks with conventional explosives. The main effect of using chemicals in a war between two well-prepared adversaries would be to force both sides to wear cumbersome protective clothing, thus reducing their combat effectiveness. Chemical weapons could, however, be devastating against unprotected troops and civilians.

Biological weapons are bacteria, viruses, or other living organisms, spread intentionally to cause disease. Development of biological weapons has focused on the limited class of organisms that can survive being dispersed by a weapon, quickly produce a high percentage of fatalities, and yet not lead to uncontrollable epidemics. Examples of such diseases are anthrax, rabbit fever (tularemia), parrot fever, and plague.

"Toxins" are highly poisonous chemicals produced by living organisms which might be used in the same manner as chemical weapons. Some toxins, such as the botulin toxin responsible for botulism and certain shellfish toxins, are deadly in extremely small quantities.

Despite their terrifying nature, biological weapons are probably even less militarily effective than chemical agents. Most diseases that might be used for biological warfare require days to have any effect, and their spread is unpredictable and extremely difficult to control. These features make them undesirable for most battlefield operations. Moreover, some or all of the opposing forces may have been immunized against the agent used against them. Biological warfare, however, could have catastrophic consequences if used against unprotected civilian populations.

It is possible that recently developed techniques in genetic engineering might be used to create new and more deadly organisms which are more suitable for combat use and against which there might be no available medical response. There is considerable scientific controversy over the dimensions of this new threat. Some experts believe that genetic engineering will result in a revolution in biological warfare with potentially disastrous consequences, while others feel that the unpredictability of the effects of biological weapons will always limit their military utility.

Stockpiles

Today, the United States and the Soviet Union have the world's largest chemical arsenals. In 1987, the Soviet Union acknowledged its possession of chemical weapons for the first time, and declared that it had "no more than 50,000 tons of chemical warfare agents." The United States and some NATO countries have questioned the Soviet statement, as previous NATO intelligence estimates of the Soviet stockpile were higher. In 1989 the Soviet Union said it would unilaterally destroy its stockpile of chemical weapons.

The United States has not declared the size of its stockpile, but some independent experts estimate it to be approximately 30,000 tons. According to the Soviet declaration, the US stockpile "roughly corresponds" to Soviet supplies. Much of the US stockpile, however, is either very old or simply stored in bulk containers and not available for immediate use. Both countries have declared that they will not be the first to use chemical weapons, and that their chemical arsenals are intended purely to deter the use of chemical weapons against them.

The United States unilaterally ceased production of chemical weapons in 1969 at the direction of President Nixon. However, the United States is now beginning a controversial production program of new "binary" nerve gas weapons, starting with new artillery shells. An air-delivered chemical bomb called the Bigeye is in limited production but remains mired in political controversy and technical difficulties, and chemical rockets for the Multiple Launch Rocket System are in development. These new weapons are called "binary," since they are composed of two chemicals that are comparatively harmless by themselves, but which create a deadly nerve gas when mixed together at the time the weapon is used. For this reason, binary weapons are safer to handle and store than ordinary chemical munitions.

Some experts question whether the new weapons are really needed to deter Soviet chemical attacks, especially since the political agreement worked out with the NATO allies does not allow their deployment to Europe to replace existing US chemical weapons being removed from Europe. Consequently, in the event of a European war, there would be only limited US chemical weapons immediately in place to deter Soviet use of chemical weapons or to be used in retaliation.

Controlling CBW

The United States has followed two main paths to control chemical and biological weapons. First, the United States has sought arms control agreements to ban the use and ultimately even the possession of such weapons. Second, the United States has maintained defenses against chemical weapons and an offensive chemical warfare capability to deter the use of chemical warfare against the United States or its allies.

The two primary international agreements on chemical and biological warfare are the Geneva Protocol of 1925 and the Biological and Toxin Weapons Convention of 1972. The Geneva Protocol banned the use in war of asphyxiating, poisonous, or other gases and of bacteriological methods of warfare. All major nations are now parties to the Geneva Protocol, though many have reserved the right to use chemical warfare in retaliation to chemical attacks or against nations which are not parties to the Protocol. After 50 years, the United States finally ratified the Protocol in 1975. Although the United States claimed that it had abided by the Protocol throughout this period, some countries have argued that the United States' use of herbicides and tear gases in combat in Vietnam was a violation of the international standards represented by the Protocol. The United States, however, has maintained that the use of such nonlethal chemicals is not forbidden.

International limitations on biological and toxin weapons are much more comprehensive than the control of chemical weapons. In 1969, President Nixon unilaterally ended the US biological weapons program, terminating all offensive research and destroying existing stocks of weapons. The Biological and Toxin Weapons Convention was signed in 1972 and ratified by the United States in 1975. Today, most countries are parties to the Convention. Unlike the Geneva Protocol, which bans only the *use* of chemical and biological weapons, the Biological and Toxin Weapons Convention outlaws the development, production, and stockpiling of all biological or toxin weapons, and requires the destruction of existing stocks.

The Geneva Protocol, the Biological and Toxin Weapons Convention, and other international agreements create an international "norm" discouraging the use of chemical warfare, and the possession or use of biological weapons. Neither treaty, however, includes any specific verification provisions. Nevertheless, the United States has charged the Soviet Union with violations of the Biological Convention in connection with an anthrax epidemic in Sverdlovsk in 1979 and of the Biological Convention and the Geneva Protocol in connection with the alleged use of toxins in Southeast Asia by the Vietnamese and in Afghanistan. The Soviet Union has denied the charges and the US position has been seriously questioned by US experts. (See Chapter 15.)

In the fall of 1986, a step forward was made in openness and verification of the Biological Weapons Convention when the five-year review conference reached agreement on exchanges of information about all high-containment biological research facilities and all unusual outbreaks of disease or toxin-related illness. The United States and the Soviet Union released their biological facility declarations in October 1987.

In the area of chemical warfare, work is now under way to reinforce the Geneva Protocol's ban on wartime use with a global agreement to ban production and stockpiling of all chemical weapons. This work has received renewed impetus in recent years, partly as a result of increas-

Increased US-Soviet Cooperation

In 1987 the Soviet Union accepted the principle of on-site inspection to verify a chemical weapons ban, thus removing a serious obstacle to agreement on a future multilateral treaty. That year, US and Soviet delegations exchanged informal visits to both sides' chemical weapon facilities. In this photo, a Soviet delegation pays a visit to the Tooele Army Depot in Utah, where US chemical munitions are stored in protected shelters.

ing concern over the proliferation of chemical weapons, stimulated particularly by the repeated Iraqi use of chemical warfare in the Iran-Iraq war.

Chemical weapons are relatively cheap and do not require exceptional technological expertise to produce or maintain. For this reason, it has been suggested that they may provide the equivalent of a "poor man's atom bomb" for some Third World countries. As of 1988, the US Defense Department estimated that ten countries worldwide already possessed chemical warfare capabilities. The United States, the Soviet Union, and some other major industrialized nations have informally attempted to stem the flow of chemical technology to countries believed to be seeking chemical weapons. In late December 1988, the Reagan administration charged that Libya was building a chemical plant for the production of chemical warfare agents with the assistance of private West German and other European and Asian contractors.

However, efforts to limit chemical proliferation through technical controls are complicated by the fact that many nations already have the capability to produce chemical weapons. Consequently, efforts to reduce interest in acquiring chemical weapons, by reinforcing international norms against their possession and use, may significantly enhance the effectiveness of non-proliferation measures.

Currently, negotiations for a general ban on the production and stockpiling of chemical weapons are taking place under the auspices of the United Nations-sponsored Conference on Disarmament. For several years, there has been general agreement that a global chemical weapon convention would ban development, production,

possession, transfer, and use of chemical weapons, and require the destruction of all existing weapons and facilities. In 1987, the talks made considerable headway toward a final accord, partly as a result of Soviet acceptance of the basic principles of a 1984 US proposal for mandatory on-site inspections to verify the convention. At the suggestion of President Reagan, an international conference of more than 140 nations met in Paris in early 1989 to address the chemical weapons issue. Although the conference took no binding action, the nations by consensus condemned the use of chemical weapons, reaffirmed the Geneva Protocol, and called for rapid completion of a global chemical disarmament accord.

An agreement banning all chemical weapons now appears within reach despite the fact that considerable work remains to be done on details of verification. Verification is complicated by the ability of ordinary chemical and pharmaceutical plants to produce chemical agents and uncertainties as to the size and composition of current stocks. While such an agreement cannot be perfectly verifiable and a few Third World countries may refuse to sign, a chemical weapons ban, including agreement to dismantle all chemical weapons and chemical weapons plants, combined with strict international inspections, could make a major contribution to reducing the risk of chemical warfare in the future.

President Bush has been closely associated with chemical weapons arms control efforts. In 1984 he presented the draft US treaty to the UN Committee on Disarmament, and during his presidential campaign he pledged to pursue efforts to ban chemical weapons from the face of the earth.

Soviet tanks on maneuvers.

14

Conventional Forces in Europe

Background

Since the end of World War II, massive armies have faced each other across a dividing line running through the middle of Europe. In the relatively small area of West Germany, Belgium, the Netherlands, and Luxembourg, the North Atlantic Treaty Organization (NATO) has stationed close to one million troops. Opposite these are over one million Warsaw Pact troops deployed in East Germany, Poland, and Czechoslovakia. Together, these forces amount to the largest peacetime military confrontation in history.

The potential threat of conflict in the area has for some time been of concern to the West. In particular, NATO has focused on three Warsaw Pact advantages in Central Europe: the number of ground troops, the number of tanks and artillery pieces, and the proximity of the region to large reserve forces in the Soviet Union. Some Western analysts argue that NATO qualitative advantages (more anti-tank weapons, more modern and capable tanks and aircraft, and more

airlift capacity) and the better training and greater reliability of its troops, compensate for the numerical and geographic disparities. In particular, these analysts point out that East European troops, which make up half of the Warsaw Pact's troops in the Central European region, could prove ineffective or unreliable in wartime.

Although increasingly questioned, conventional wisdom has held that the Warsaw Pact could readily defeat NATO in a conventional conflict in Central Europe. To deter such a conflict, NATO in 1967 adopted a strategy of "flexible response," which includes the option to initiate the use of nuclear weapons to counter any Warsaw Pact incursion. (See Chapter 2.) In addition, in the mid-1960s, Western leaders agreed that negotiated reductions to equal levels of conventional forces would help to minimize Warsaw Pact advantages and that lower numbers of conventional forces could make a "standing-start" surprise attack militarily more difficult and thus less likely. (A "standing-start" attack is one that could be launched suddenly using only those forces normally located near the West German border in the initial phase.) In contrast, a more general attack scenario would involve the large scale mobilization of forces, particularly in the Soviet Union, which could be detected easily by NATO intelligence and provide the United States and its NATO allies with significant advance warning to mobilize reserves and prepare defenses.

In view of declining manpower pools and the high expense of keeping personnel on active duty, there was (and still is) some question as to whether all NATO countries will be willing or able to maintain current levels of forces. Even the United States, which has led its allies in defense spending, has felt the strain of defending Western Europe. Periodically, this has led to pressure in Congress for unilateral reductions of US troops in Europe. The most notable of such pressures was the attempt by Senator Mike Mansfield in 1973 to cut US forces by 50 percent.

MBFR

As part of the effort to overcome the NATO-Warsaw Pact conventional imbalance and to alleviate congressional pressure to reduce US troops in Europe, negotiations on Mutual and Balanced Force Reductions (MBFR) in Europe began in October 1973. The initial goal of the Western participants (which included the United States, Canada, Great Britain, Belgium, the Netherlands, Luxembourg, and West Germany) was to reduce the ground force personnel in Central Europe to a common ceiling of 700,000 men on each side. This would have required a larger reduction for the Warsaw Pact, which NATO claimed had around 200,000 more personnel in the area. The Western proposal also included verification measures, such as on-site inspections and pre-notification of force movements in the reduction area. Besides verifying compliance, these measures would have an important confidence-building effect by giving each side greater warning of mobilization.

The Eastern participants (which included the Soviet Union, East Germany, Poland, and Czechoslovakia) held that "approximate parity" existed between the forces of the opposing alliances and that reductions should be equal on both sides. They originally proposed cutting by approximately 17 percent each national component of NATO and the Warsaw Pact. NATO rejected this approach because proportional reductions would have codified existing Warsaw Pact advantages and not allowed for internal adjustment of manpower contributions within the alliances.

In the course of the negotiations, the Warsaw Pact gradually moved toward NATO's proposed common ground forces ceiling. In 1978, both alliances agreed on the ultimate goal of reducing manpower levels for each side to a total of 900,000 combined air and ground force personnel, with a subceiling of 700,000 on ground force personnel. Despite years of discussion, however, the alliances failed to achieve the 1978 goal of a common ceiling, primarily as a result of the inability to establish agreed data on forces before any reductions took place.

In 1985, NATO tabled a proposal which would have postponed clarification of the force data before initiating reductions. It called for phased reductions, with the United States and the Soviet Union making an initial small cut of 5,000 and 11,500 respectively, followed by a three-year period during which the levels of all other forces would be frozen. Although the East responded favorably to this offer, their actual counterproposal fell short of NATO's expectations, particularly in the area of verification.

The CFE Talks

The persistent inability of the sides to negotiate the resolution of the most basic issues, together with the belief that the restricted forum of MBFR had outlived its usefulness, led experts to conclude some time ago that the MBFR negotiations were not likely to lead to an agreement. Since at least 1986, it has appeared likely that MBFR would be discontinued and absorbed into a larger European forum related to, but independent of the 35-nation Conference on Security and Cooperation in Europe (CSCE).

The likelihood of a new set of arms control talks on conventional forces increased with the change of Soviet leadership, which stimulated a number of proposals from the Warsaw Pact for conventional arms reductions and military disengagement in Europe. In April and then again in June of 1986, Soviet General Secretary Gorbachev and the Warsaw Pact Consultative Committee called for an expanded zone of conventional force limitations in Europe and the reduction of 100,000-150,000 troops on each side within one to two years. This would be followed by a reduction of 500,000 troops, or up to 25 percent of the land forces in Central Europe, including associated

equipment such as tactical nuclear weapons and aircraft.

Responding to the Warsaw Pact's June initiative, in December 1986 the NATO foreign ministers issued a declaration on conventional arms control expressing NATO's readiness to open talks with the Warsaw Pact on establishing a new mandate for conventional arms negotiations covering the whole of Europe from the Atlantic Ocean to the Ural Mountains in the western USSR. The declaration proposed two distinct sets of negotiations, one involving all 35 CSCE participants and intended to expand the confidence- and security-building measures adopted in 1986 at the Conference on Disarmament in Europe (see below), and another involving all 16 members of NATO and seven members of the Warsaw Pact. This second forum, initially dubbed the Conventional Stability Talks (CST), but later changed to negotiations on Conventional Armed Forces in Europe (CFE), would address the reduction of both personnel and material in an area stretching from the Atlantic to the Urals.

In February 1987, the 23 NATO and Warsaw Pact countries convened in Vienna to begin discussions on a mandate for the new CFE forum. In May of 1987, the Polish government put forward

Participants in CFE

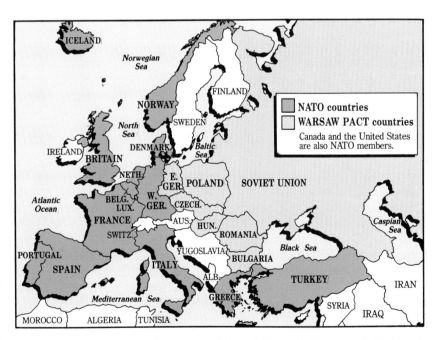

Participants in the talks on Conventional Armed Forces in Europe include the 16 NATO nations and seven Warsaw Pact nations. Twelve other neutral and nonaligned nations, as members of the CSCE process, take part as observers in the CFE talks. All 35 nations participate in separate talks on confidence- and security-building measures.

The Sky's the Limit

US F-15 fighter aircraft fly in formation. Limitations on aircraft have long been a source of dispute between East and West. At NATO's 40th anniversary celebration in May 1989, President Bush broke with NATO's previous position and offered to include combat aircraft in the CFE negotiations. The Soviet Union is particularly interested in limiting NATO's ground-attack aircraft. Among the many issues left to be resolved to complete a treaty, the two sides will have to agree on the types and numbers of aircraft that will be permitted.

a proposal for military disengagement in Central Europe through the gradual withdrawal of "operational, tactical and battlefield nuclear weapons" as well as conventional weapons from nine European countries—the seven MBFR nations plus Denmark and Hungary. The purpose of the Polish plan was "to scale down the level of armaments on both sides so that sudden attack would be impossible." Later that month, the Warsaw Pact Consultative Committee proposed that the two blocs engage in joint consultations on military strategy to help dispel "distrust and suspicion" and to ensure that military concepts and doctrines are geared for defense rather than attack. The Warsaw Pact also offered to address existing imbalances in force structures through "appropriate cutbacks."

By December 1987, the 23 NATO and Warsaw Pact nations had agreed that the objectives of the new conventional force negotiations should be the establishment of a stable and secure balance of forces at lower levels, the elimination of disparities threatening this stability and security, and the elimination of the capability for surprise attacks and large-scale offensive action.

In March 1988, a NATO summit produced an outline for alliance negotiating strategy in the CFE. The strategy called for "highly asymmetrical reductions" by the Warsaw Pact that would "entail the elimination from Europe of tens of thousands of Warsaw Pact weapons relevant to surprise attack." The NATO leaders specifically mentioned tanks and artillery as "among the most decisive components" of forward-deployed, offensively postured forces.

At the June 1988 summit in Moscow, the Soviet Union put forward its proposal for a three-stage reduction in conventional forces. It called

in the first stage for a data exchange on "the numerical strength of the armed forces and armaments of the alliances and each country individually" followed by on-site inspection to verify the data and then reductions to rectify any destabilizing asymmetries in existing force levels. In the second stage, each side could reduce its troops by approximately 500,000, and in the third stage, "further reductions could be made which would leave both sides with such numbers of armed forces . . . as would be sufficient for defense but insufficient for offensive purposes."

On December 7, 1988, in a speech before the UN, Soviet General Secretary Gorbachev announced a unilateral Soviet reduction of 500,000 troops and 10,000 tanks. Of this total, 50,000 men, 5,000 tanks, and six tank divisions would come from its forces based in Eastern Europe. Gorbachev also indicated that the Soviet Union would remove assault bridging and airborne assault units from Eastern Europe and reconfigure its remaining divisions into a "defensive" posture. Two days later, NATO revealed the outline of its opening position for the CFE negotiations. NATO called for parity in tanks, artillery pieces, and armored troop carriers at about 90-95 percent of current NATO levels, limits on any one country's share of the total equipment holdings in Europe, and limits on armed forces stationed on the territory of other countries.

The CFE negotiations, which began in March 1989, made a good start toward reconciling these contrasting approaches. The Soviet Union and its allies seem prepared to agree to deep cuts in the number of tanks, artillery, and armored troop carriers, but they are also anxious to reduce elements of Western forces which they find most threatening: ground attack aircraft and helicopters, and dual-capable (nuclear and conventional) delivery systems. The Warsaw Pact also seeks reductions (up to 40 percent) in troops on both sides and a thinning out of forces in a zone along the inner-German border. The West, for its part, is seeking asymmetric reductions by the Warsaw Pact in its tanks, artillery, and armored troop carriers down to parity slightly beneath current NATO levels. President Bush, at NATO's 40th anniversary summit in May 1989, proposed limits at 15 percent below NATO levels on combat aircraft and helicopters as well as on US and Soviet air and ground forces stationed outside their borders at 10 percent below US levels. These more modest manpower reductions reflect the widespread concern in NATO that Western forces are presently at a minimum for defensive purposes. While the remaining issues may take time to resolve, the two sides now seem close to an agreement in principle, and political, economic, demographic, and public pressure seem to be strongly arrayed in favor of some meaningful reduction of forces in Central Europe.

Whether the CFE negotiations eventually result in a separate MBFR-type agreement, or become part of a larger CDE settlement, the creation of a more stable and less costly conventional balance in Central Europe would ease the fear of conflict and reduce some of the tensions which fuel the nuclear competition. If the sides can build on the more forthcoming Soviet approach to force data and verification issues as demonstrated in the INF Treaty and in the separate statements and unilateral gestures by the Soviet leadership on conventional forces, the prospects for negotiations on conventional forces may be brighter than they have been for years.

Confidence-Building Measures

Confidence-building measures (CBMs) are designed to reduce tensions and the possibility of misperception by making the military environment more predictable through the imposition of operational constraints on military movements and exercises. These measures have received the most attention. Most notable are the set of CBMs contained in the Helsinki Final Act, which was adopted by the 35-nation Conference on Security and Cooperation in Europe (CSCE) forum (33 European countries, the US, and Canada) in 1975. Those CBMs were expanded in 1986 at the Conference on Disarmament in Europe (CDE) in Stockholm, Sweden.

The Helsinki Final Act covers only Central Europe, the region where NATO and Warsaw Pact military forces face each other most directly. It calls for advance notification of all maneuvers involving over 25,000 troops, and for inspections of these exercises by observers from the opposing alliance. The aim of providing such exchanges of information is to reduce the risk that military exercises and practices could increase suspicion, particularly in a crisis, that the other side was preparing for war. Though the agreement was officially "nonbinding," the participating states have generally fulfilled its requirements.

In 1983, the CSCE participants, at their second review meeting in Madrid, agreed to go beyond the Helsinki Final Act by mandating a conference in Stockholm to adopt CBMs that would cover all of Europe and be militarily significant, politically binding, and verifiable. In September 1986 the Stockholm Conference on Disarmament in Europe (CDE) successfully concluded an agreement on several additional confidence-building measures, including:

• forty-two days advance notification of all military exercises and movements exceeding 13,000 troops or 300 tanks;

• one year advance notification of military maneuvers involving more than 40,000 troops;

• mandatory invitations to all other states to observe military exercises involving more than 17,000 troops; and

• verification of compliance with the agreement through three aerial and/or ground "on-site inspections on demand" of military exercises and troop movements.

By 1987, the CDE agreement was being implemented, with both NATO and Warsaw Pact countries cooperating in the conduct of permitted inspections. The fact that the Stockholm confidence-building measures got off to a successful start seems to have improved the likelihood that an expanded CBM regime will be adopted at the follow-on CDE conference which began in 1989. A treaty reducing conventional forces in Europe, will also require CBMs.

There are a variety of approaches to increasing "transparency," enhancing predictability, and building confidence. However, such measures are only as useful as the commitment of the participants. Therefore, CBMs should not be considered unrelated to overall arms control efforts. But by facilitating a higher level of communication and cooperation between the nations most likely to be involved, CBMs could help prevent a war from being provoked by inadvertence, misunderstanding, or miscalculation.

A US nuclear ballistic missile submarine being dismantled prior to decommissioning, September 1985. To remain within SALT Limits, both the United States and the Soviet Union have dismantled or removed a substantial number of missiles and submarines as new strategic systems have come on line.

15

Verification and Compliance

Verification

The acceptability of an arms control agreement depends to a large extent on the confidence of the parties to the agreement that its provisions will be obeyed. Among potential adversaries, this confidence cannot depend on trust or presumed mutual interests. However, while there is general agreement that each side must be able to verify the other side's compliance with an agreement, there is considerable disagreement as to the degree of precision and confidence necessary for the verification of specific treaties.

Ideally, one can argue that even the possibility of any undetected cheating is unacceptable since it brings into question the intentions of the other side. Such a strict standard, however, usually cannot be met with technically practical and politically acceptable arrangements. There are limits on the type and precision of information that existing national technical intelligence systems can collect. Additional information can be collected by on-site inspection, but sovereign

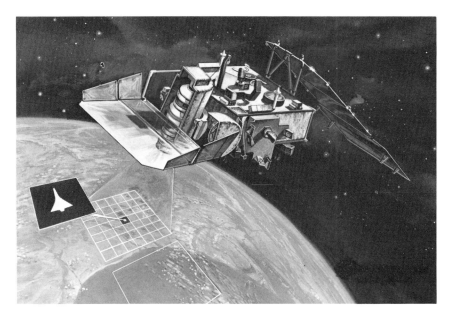

Satellite Surveillance

Reconnaisance satellites are the backbone of US verification methods. The Teal Ruby low-altitude surveillance system in this artist's concept is a recent example of US space-based monitoring technology.

nations are reluctant to allow representatives of their potential adversary unlimited access to sensitive installations and activities. Even if such unlimited access were mutually acceptable to the parties to a treaty, the question would remain whether sufficient information was available from other means of national intelligence collection to target on-site inspections on suspect facilities or activities.

Requirements for absolute verification constitute a barrier to progress in arms control. As Secretary of State George Shultz told the Senate during the ratification hearings on the INF Treaty, "There is no such thing as absolute or 100-percent verification. That would essentially be a case of proving a negative which is difficult if not impossible." Fortunately, absolute verification is not necessary for most arms control agreements.

The approach to verification which has received widespread acceptance is to determine the level of risk a country is prepared to accept in an arms control agreement and then structure the agreement to meet that standard. The concept of "adequate" verification, which was set forth at the beginning of the SALT I negotiations under President Nixon and retained through the Ford and Carter administrations, sought to establish practical verification standards consistent with national security. Adequate verification requires that there should be high confidence that any violations of military significance would be detected in time to permit a response if necessary. Under these conditions, there would be little incentive to cheat and little danger to national security if cheating did occur. For example, if there were an agreement limiting

some weapon to 1,000, the illegal deployment of a quantity of weapons small enough to make detection unlikely (e.g., tens) would have no military significance. On the other hand, illegal activity on a scale associated with the deployment of enough weapons to have some military significance (e.g., hundreds) might make identification of the illegal deployment highly likely. Advocates of this approach argue that it is far better to face the unlikely risk that an opponent might successfully build a few weapons clandestinely under a generally favorable and adequately verifiable arms control agreement than a large number of legal weapons in the absence of the agreement.

The Reagan administration initially argued that "adequate" verification was insufficient for nuclear arms control agreements and that a higher standard, which it called "effective" verification, should be established. However, during the course of the INF Treaty negotiations, the administration's position evolved considerably. In defending the INF Treaty to the Senate in early 1988, the administration used much the same arguments as the Nixon and Carter administrations, asserting that the treaty's verification provisions were appropriate because any "militarily significant" Soviet cheating could be detected in time to develop effective responses. At the same time, the verification procedures adopted by the INF Treaty—on-site inspections and cooperative measures—permit higher confidence that the treaty will be honored than would otherwise be the case and set a precedent for the use of such techniques in treaties where the consequences of Soviet cheating to US security could be more significant.

Compliance with arms control treaties is verified primarily by "national technical means" (NTM), a term which covers all technical intelligence collection systems operated by the U.S. and the Soviet Union outside the territory of the other side. National technical means include space-based systems such as reconnaissance satellites, using photography and other sensors, and land-based sensors such as radars. (See NTM Box.) In reality, NTM means the total resources of the US intelligence community which combines and analyzes data from many different sources. Above all, conclusions can be drawn from the totality of knowledge of Soviet military programs developed since World War II. The Soviet Union has similar intelligence capabilities facilitated by the more open nature of US society. The NTM approach to treaty monitoring differs fundamentally from monitoring by jointly or internationally operated technical systems and from "on-site inspection" (see below) involving observers.

To assist verification by national technical means, "cooperative measures" can be built into arms control accords. For example, under the SALT agreements, the United States and Soviet Union agreed not to conceal activities related to strategic forces or to interfere with the other side's NTM. Since efforts at concealment are usually quite obvious to photo-reconnaissance and other sensors, a ban on concealment can be

NTM at Air and Sea

National technical means (NTM) of verification encompass the total resources of the US intelligence community, including satellites, surveillance aircraft (such as the world's fastest jet, the SR-71, above) and land- and sea-based radars. The USNS Observation Island, below, carries an advanced phased-array radar system (the box structure on the rear deck), used to monitor Soviet ballistic missile tests and reentry vehicle flight trajectories.

National Technical Means of Verification

The United States employs a variety of technical means, which are part of its regular intelligence operations, to verify compliance with arms control agreements. The principal "National Technical Means" (NTM) used for verification are reconnaissance satellite systems using photographic, infrared, radar, and electronic sensors, ground-based radars, seismographs and communications collection stations, and under-water acoustic systems. These technical systems supplement each other and provide a vast amount of information on Soviet military activities. The overlap between these systems also makes it possible to cross-check data for accuracy. The information obtained from these systems can be analyzed against the mass of accumulated information on Soviet military forces that has been developed since the end of World War II.

Photo-Reconnaissance

One of the most important US surveillance techniques is the use of "photo-reconnaissance" cameras, carried aboard satellites which continuously orbit the earth. Some are designed for "area surveillance"; other satellites carry higher resolution cameras which can detect small, technical details but cannot rapidly cover large areas. Infrared photography can penetrate the dark of night, though with less resolution. Infrared sensors can also detect the launch of operational or test missiles at all times. The images collected by these sensors are then either electronically transmitted to earth so that the information is received in near real time or recorded on film and dropped to earth in special recoverable canisters.

Photo-reconnaissance allows US intelligence analysts to monitor regularly a large number of militarily significant areas, such as missile silo fields, production facilities, and submarine bases. Soviet strategic force developments can thereby be closely followed, allowing the United States to judge Soviet compliance with many arms control provisions, such as the SALT II limits on strategic missile launchers and ABM Treaty restraints on ABM launchers and large radars.

Radar Surveillance

Radar is another key surveillance technology. A radar emits electromagnetic impulses that reflect off of distant objects and return to an antenna. The return signals are then processed by computer to measure, identify, and track individual objects.

The United States employs radars based on land, at sea, and on aircraft to provide intelligence of Soviet missile flight tests. Ground-based, over-the-horizon radars can "see" over thousands of miles by reflecting waves off of the upper atmosphere, following the earth's curvature. US "over-the-horizon" radars, deployed around the periphery of the Soviet Union, monitor Soviet missile launches. Phased-array radars, which are composed of large numbers of small radar antennas, each controlled and coordinated by a central computer, can monitor a missile's course and velocity. The reentry of the missile's warheads is observed by ship- and aircraft-based radars, as well as cameras and infrared sensors.

US surveillance radars were able to verify Soviet compliance with a number of SALT II Treaty provisions that control the qualitative improvement of ballistic missiles. These include limits on missile throw-weight, missile dimensions, and the number of reentry vehicles carried.

Radars based in space can be used as a supplement to photo-reconnaissance systems in monitoring Soviet ground activities. Satellite-based radars have lower resolutions than optical systems but can penetrate cloud-cover and operate at all times, unlike their optical counterparts which are dependent on daylight illumination and clear weather.

Electronic Surveillance

A vast amount of information can be obtained through interception of various Soviet electronic transmissions by passive receivers based on aircraft patrolling Soviet border areas, on orbiting satellites, and at ground stations. These systems intercept transmissions from various radiating sources, including Soviet military and civilian communications, test telemetry, and radars.

Artist's concept of a US Rhyolite electronic surveillance satellite.

It is no secret that such information is collected by both sides. Consequently, both sides endeavor to protect their communications through *encryption* (random scrambling of the data) so that transmissions are unintelligible to the other side despite highly sophisticated code breaking techniques. For example, US receivers regularly intercept the radio transmissions from Soviet missiles undergoing flight testing. These transmissions, known as *telemetry*, normally would include such operational data as missile fuel consumption, accelerations, and reentry vehicle performance. By themselves, the data are not particularly meaningful; collectively, they can reveal much of the performance and design characteristics of the missile. Although the SALT II Treaty permitted the encryption of telemetry transmissions, it prohibited the practice when it impeded verification. The precise meaning of this treaty provision has been a contentious issue between the two countries.

Seismic Surveillance

The United States can easily identify aboveground and underwater nuclear explosions, which are prohibited by the 1963 Limited Test Ban Treaty, with satellite infrared and x-ray sensors, world-wide collection of radioactive fallout and hydrophone acoustic arrays in the world's oceans. Underground nuclear tests, limited to explosive yields of 150 kiloton by the unratified (but observed) 1974 Threshold Test Ban Treaty, can be identified and measured by a network of seismic monitors around the periphery of the Soviet Union and at other key geological points around the world.

Each seismic monitor is capable of detecting at great distances the extremely small vibrations in the earth's crust caused by an underground nuclear explosion. Data collected by many seismic monitors is transmitted to a centralized computer where it is analyzed and the location and yield of the event determined.

The principal problem is to distinguish nuclear tests from the large background of natural earthquakes. The point source of a nuclear explosion is sufficiently different from an earthquake that the distinction can be made down to very low yields. Nevertheless, there will always be a low threshold below which a nuclear explosion cannot be identified with confidence and a still lower threshold below which it cannot be detected at all.

Using this worldwide system, US scientists regularly monitor Soviet nuclear tests with yields as small as one kiloton or less and can determine the yields of nuclear explosions to within +/- 50 percent. New seismic arrays have recently been constructed that allow still more accurate calculations. Sophisticated analytical techniques have also been devised to overcome efforts to hide small nuclear explosions within the seismic noise of a large natural earthquake or by detonating it within a large cave to attenuate or "decouple" the seismic signal. In addition, satellite photography can also be used to detect preparations for nuclear tests and to locate the visible subsidence craters left by many underground nuclear explosions.

On-Site Inspection

On-site inspections, previously unacceptable to the Soviet Union as a means of inspecting military forces because of the Soviet obsession with secrecy, are now being conducted routinely to verify compliance with the INF Treaty and the Stockholm CDE accord. A future strategic arms or chemical weapons treaty would also carry provisions for on-site inspections. This photo shows US military inspectors meeting Warsaw pact troops during an inspection conducted under the Stockholm agreement.

effectively verified. If not prohibited, concealment could be effective at preventing the precise counting or exact identification of the concealed systems or activities.

The INF Treaty includes cooperative measures that go far beyond those of previous agreements. The treaty requires the parties to exchange extensive data, covering the number, location and technical characteristics of all deployed and stored INF missiles, as well as detailed plans of sites where the missiles are located. These comprehensive and detailed data exchanges cover hundreds of pages. By comparison, the data exchange in SALT II covered one page. In addition, the INF Treaty includes the unprecedented requirement that the Soviet Union cooperate in allowing satellite inspection of deployed mobile SS-25 missiles (which are themselves not covered by the treaty but have operational and physical similarities to the SS-20 INF missiles). This provision provides that the Soviet Union must on request remove SS-25 missiles from the garages in which they are housed and display the missiles and their launchers for twelve hours.

There are, however, some situations or constraints that cannot be satisfactorily monitored by national technical means alone even when assisted by cooperative measures. In these cases, intrusive on-site inspection (OSI) may be the only technique available to provide adequate confidence, or any information at all, on certain activities. One long-standing example of on-site inspection assisted by cooperative measures is the worldwide safeguarding of civilian nuclear power facilities by the International Atomic Energy Agency to prevent illegal diversion of fissionable materials to nuclear weapons production.

In a dramatic relaxation of its historic obsession with military secrecy, the Soviet Union agreed in the INF Treaty to the following on-site inspection procedures: (1) inspections of missile operating bases and storage facilities to verify the baseline from which the reductions will occur; (2) inspections to confirm the closing of a facility; (3) inspections to observe elimination of missiles and launchers; (4) inspections on short notice of declared facilities; and (5) maintaining inspectors at certain designated production facilities for up to 13 years to verify that banned missiles are not being produced there. (See Chapter 10.) These extensive inspection rights will help ensure that the INF Treaty's provisions on eliminating existing missiles are carried out and greatly complicate potential noncompliance. However, even this comprehensive inspection regime does not contribute to the detection of covert production and deployment of INF missiles at facilities where on-site inspections are not specifically permitted. Ultimately, therefore, detection of treaty violations at such sites will depend upon the ability of NTM to detect prohibited flight-testing and training with INF missiles, and clandestine activities relating to the deployment and production of the missiles.

Although on-site inspections can be a powerful verification tool, there are limits to the effectiveness of on-site inspection. Since on-site inspections did not appear to be acceptable to the Soviet Union when SALT II was negotiated, the United States decided to construct the treaty in a manner that did not require on-site inspections. In fact, it was concluded that on-site inspections would not be particularly effective in determining the number of warheads on missiles in land-based silos and submarine launchers, because the Soviet Union could easily delay an inspection until it had time to change the number of warheads on a particular missile. Consequently, the SALT II Treaty contained certain "counting rules" that permitted verification by NTM alone of the number of deployed MIRVed missiles and the maximum number of warheads on those MIRVed missiles. This procedure depended on the fact that ICBM silos and submarines, which take many years to build, are easy to detect and count by NTM, as opposed to missiles which are relatively easy to conceal. Similarly, NTM can easily detect missile tests, which are necessary for new missiles or increases in the number of warheads on a MIRVed missile. Consequently, the SALT II counting rules provided that any silo or submarine launcher would be assumed to contain a MIRVed missile, if a MIRVed missile had ever been associated (e.g., in testing) with that type of silo, and that any missile that had ever been tested with a MIRV was assumed to be a MIRVed missile. In addition, any MIRVed missile was assumed to have the maximum number of warheads ever tested with that type of MIRVed missile.

In the START negotiations, there has been a move away from these counting rules to declarations as to the number of warheads on MIRVed missiles followed by some as yet unagreed on-site inspection regime. On-site inspections would be necessary because the United States insisted that the two sides declare actual missile MIRV loadings rather than the number of warheads tested. This "declaratory" approach to determining the number of warheads in the arsenal will place severe demands on the rapidity and intrusiveness of the on-site inspection regime associated with a future agreement.

The INF Treaty's inspection regime will undoubtedly prove to be an important precedent as the verification provisions are worked out for the emerging START agreement. Indeed, the United States and the Soviet Union have already agreed to incorporate into START many of the same on-site inspection provisions that are contained in the INF Treaty. However, in the INF Treaty, the value of the on-site inspections is limited because the inspections are permitted only at declared facilities. One reason the treaty did not incorporate the right to inspect any suspect facility at any time (so-called "anywhere, anytime" inspections), is that neither the Soviet Union nor the United States wanted to run the risk that extremely sensitive facilities might become the target of on-site inspections.

In the case of a START agreement with its much greater security implications, some argue that so-called "anywhere, anytime" inspections must be a necessary component even though they might involve Soviet inspectors examining sensitive US facilities. Others believe that such inspections would not improve the chance of detecting treaty violations because neither country would ever allow itself to be caught cheating and would prevent the inspection from occurring or delay it long enough to conceal the illegal activity. However, deliberate denial of inspection rights would in itself be a significant act if the country requesting the inspection had serious reason to believe that a violation was in fact occurring at the suspect site.

The issue of "anywhere, anytime" inspections of suspect sites is only one of many verification issues that must be resolved in the negotiation of a START agreement. Other issues include how to verify sea-launched cruise missiles, which can be concealed relatively easily and can be armed with either conventional or nuclear weapons; how to count the number of air-launched cruise missiles carried by heavy bombers; and how to verify the number of mobile ICBMs. While these are all difficult problems, many believe that they can be adequately verified with imaginative use of cooperative measures and on-site inspections.

The INF Treaty in action. In compliance with the missile destruction provisions of the INF Treaty, Soviet shorter-range missiles arrive at a base in Kazahkstan (top), where engineers tie cakes of explosives to the rockets (center). US on-site inspectors then observe the destruction (bottom).

Compliance

Charges that a country is violating an agreement are very difficult for the public to assess independently because the charges usually involve classified intelligence information on highly specialized technical questions and the interpretation of complex, and sometimes ambiguous, treaty provisions. In fact, US experts often have honest differences of opinion on whether specific situations or activities are in compliance with treaty provisions.

An arms control agreement must be detailed enough for the commitments to be clear, yet general enough to cover future developments and avoid the creation of technical loopholes that might permit legal circumvention of the intent of the treaty. Moreover, in the process of negotiating controversial provisions, ambiguous language that is subject to different interpretations may be adopted to reach agreement. Given the complex technical nature of these issues and the imprecision of language, there will probably always be some "gray areas" as to permitted or prohibited activities in a major arms control treaty. In addition, the information from NTM monitoring systems may not lead to unambiguous conclusions and in the case of quantitative information (such as underground test yields) may involve significant statistical uncertainties as well.

In anticipation of disputes arising from potential problems, the United States and the Soviet Union established the Standing Consultative Commission (SCC) in the ABM Treaty. The Nixon, Ford and Carter administrations all discussed compliance issues with the Soviet Union in the SCC forum, and were able to resolve all contentious issues then outstanding.

During the Senate debate on the SALT II treaty, the Carter administration held that the Soviet Union had a good compliance record on SALT I. To document this conclusion, extensive information was presented in public and classified Senate hearings. The government reported that "[the US] raised a number of issues with the Soviets in SALT I—as they did with us—but in every case the activity in question either ceased or subsequent information clarified the situation and allayed our concern."

The Reagan administration made Soviet compliance with arms control treaties a major public issue in the early 1980s. In January 1984, it released the first of a series of reports that formally charged the Soviet Union with violating several arms control agreements, including SALT II, the ABM Treaty, the Threshold Test Ban Treaty, and the chemical weapons and biological weapons agreements. The report acknowledged that the evidence on some of the alleged violations was ambiguous, but the overall tone of the report was extremely alarmist and painted a picture of wholesale Soviet cheating. The Soviet Union vigorously denied these allegations, and responded with its own list of alleged US treaty violations. The sides have exchanged charges of violations regularly since that time.

US analysts, differ widely in their assessment of the significance of these compliance issues. Some argue that the existing compliance issues demonstrate the futility and danger of the arms control process in dealing with an adversary such as the Soviet Union. Others argue that, on the contrary, the record shows the overall compliance record of both sides has been remarkably good and that most of the charges are either based on questionable data or ambiguous treaty language or are technical points that can easily be resolved.

The charges with perhaps the most potential significance relate to the ABM Treaty. Article I of the ABM Treaty laid out its basic object and purpose: "not to deploy ABM systems for a defense of the territory of its country and not to provide a base for such a defense." The United States has charged the Soviet Union with possibly breaching this central obligation by "preparing an ABM defense of its national territory." Similarly, the Soviet Union has charged that the US strategic defense program violates this basic objective since the program is directed toward the illegal development, testing, and deployment of a comprehensive nationwide defense. These are extremely serious charges which if correct would constitute a "material breach" of the ABM Treaty's objective and would justify under international law the other side withdrawing from or suspending the ABM Treaty.

Specific Compliance Issues

The current US and Soviet charges and countercharges on compliance can only be appreciated by examining in detail some of the more important issues. Understanding of these issues also points up both the power and the problems associated with the arms control process in general, and the monitoring and verification of agreements in particular.

US compliance with the INF Treaty. In West Germany, American soldiers are careful to go "by the book" as they dismantle a Pershing II missile (top). Back in the United States, the Pershing rocket stages are fired (center) and crushed (bottom). Soviet inspectors were on-site to observe the static firing and crushing.

Krasnoyarsk

US and Soviet delegations walk in front of the 11-story-high radar transmitter near Krasnoyarsk, Siberia, in September 1987. By inviting the group of US congressmen and technical experts to visit the radar, which is widely believed to be a violation of the ABM Treaty, the Soviet government signaled a new openness to on-site verification.

The ABM Treaty and the Krasnoyarsk Radar

The most important US charge of Soviet non-compliance concerns the so-called Krasnoyarsk radar which the United States has charged is a "significant" violation of the ABM Treaty. At the ABM Treaty Review Conference in August 1988, the United States announced that it would have to consider whether this violation constituted a "material breach" of the treaty. Such a finding would permit, but not require, the United States to abrogate or suspend all or part of the ABM Treaty.

In mid-1983, US reconnaissance satellites discovered a new large phased-array radar (LPAR) under construction in central Siberia, north of the city of Krasnoyarsk. The radar is located 750 kilometers from the Chinese border and is oriented toward the northeast, looking across several thousand kilometers of Soviet territory. Such large phased-array radars are prohibited by the ABM Treaty, except as early warning radars deployed along the national periphery and oriented outward, or within the one permitted ABM deployment site, or within permitted ABM test ranges, or for space-tracking or national technical means of verification.

The United States has concluded that the radar's siting, orientation, and apparent capabilities indicate that it is primarily designed for ballistic missile detection and tracking. Consequently, the United States has charged that the Krasnoyarsk radar is a clear violation of the ABM Treaty since it is either an early-warning radar which is neither on the periphery of the Soviet Union nor oriented outward, or an ABM battle-management radar outside permitted ABM deployment areas or test ranges. The Soviet Union originally rejected these charges and claims that the Krasnoyarsk radar was intended for space-tracking and therefore allowed by the ABM Treaty. More recently, Soviet willingness to consider measures to resolve the problem suggest tacit acceptance of the fact that it is at least a technical violation of the treaty.

There is general agreement among Western experts that the Krasnoyarsk radar is a violation of the ABM Treaty. The location and orientation of this radar, the elevation of its transmitting and receiving faces, and its similarity to other Soviet early warning radars demonstrate that it would perform a permitted early warning function at a prohibited location since it is clearly not on the national periphery oriented outward. While the radar could well have some space-tracking capabilities, most experts agree that the Soviet claim that the radar is primarily intended for space tracking is not credible.

Most independent experts also agree that the Krasnoyarsk radar is not a battle management radar, as is sometimes charged. The radar appears to have been placed in its illegal inland location primarily to provide cost-efficient early warning and not to serve a battle management function in connection with a nationwide ABM system. The radar is an undefended, soft target which would be extremely vulnerable to attack; and by virtue of its location and orientation, it would be of very little value as part of a nationwide defense.

The Soviet Union has clearly been anxious to find a way to remove the Krasnoyarsk radar as a contentious issue in US-Soviet relations blocking progress on arms control. In 1987 Gorbachev invited a delegation of US congressmen and technical staff to visit the site. The delegation found the radar to be several years from completion, and the following month Gorbachev announced that construction at Krasnoyarsk would be suspended. At the Five-Year ABM Treaty Review Conference in August 1988, the Soviet delegation offered to dismantle the equipment at the site. Subsequently, the site was given to the Soviet Academy of sciences for unspecified scientific purposes, and in his speech to the UN General Assembly in December 1988, President Gorbachev offered to turn the facility over to the international scientific community for environmental or other scientific purposes. In these circumstances, President Bush will probably find it difficult to carry out earlier threats to declare the illegal Krasnoyarsk radar a "material breach" of the ABM Treaty.

SALT II

In 1984 the United States charged the Soviet Union with a number of violations of its political commitment not to undercut the unratified SALT II Treaty. The two principal charges alleged the Soviet Union had deployed a prohibited second "new type" of ICBM and had engaged in prohibited encryption of missile telemetry. On the basis of these charges, the United States in May 1986 repudiated its own political commitment to the SALT II agreement and in November 1986 exceeded the sublimit on MIRVs and ALCMs in the agreement.

In the first compliance issue, the United States charged that a new Soviet land-based, mobile missile with a single warhead (the SS-25) violated the SALT II provisions permitting each side to flight test and deploy only one "new type" of light ICBM. The Soviet Union had already declared that another new system, a land-based missile with 10 warheads (the SS-24) was its allowed one "new type." "New type" is defined in the treaty as one that *differs from an existing type by more than five percent* in certain technical parameters—length, diameter, launch-weight, and throw-weight. This provision was not intended to preclude either side from testing and deploying new ICBMs, but only to ensure that any such new ICBMs did not significantly increase the ability to deliver warheads. It was believed that changes smaller than five percent could not be monitored and would not be militarily significant.

The United States claimed that the SS-25 was an illegal second "new type" of ICBM because its throw-weight (lifting power) was estimated to be 92 percent greater than that of an existing missile, the SS-13, which the Soviet Union had set as the standard of comparison for the SS-25. The Soviet Union rejected this allegation, claiming that the SS-25 was a permitted variation of the SS-13. Specifically, the Soviet Union has asserted that the United States had *overestimated* the throw-weight of the SS-25 by including equipment (an instrumentation package) used during testing that was not on the deployed missile, and *underestimated* the throw-weight of the SS-13 by excluding its penetration aids package and the guidance system for the final stage which was carried on the third stage of the booster rocket. If the throw-weight of the SS-13 were to include these additional devices and the throw-weight of the SS-25 were to exclude the testing package, the Soviet Union claimed the SS-25 would be within the permitted five percent variation.

This compliance dispute hinged on the SALT II Treaty's formal definition of "throw-weight." The treaty's definition of throw-weight clearly states that penetration aids and guidance devices should be included but does not mention instrumentation packages used during testing, presumably because they are not included in an operational missile. The United States has not explained on what basis it excludes these additional devices from its calculation of the SS-13's throw-weight, and on what basis it includes the instrumentation package on the SS-25 in the missile's throw-weight. Whether the SS-25 would in fact fit within the five percent limit on throw-weight using the Soviet reading of the treaty language depends upon the actual weights of the various elements of the throw-weight. This information, which is not public and the United States may not know in detail, has apparently not been volunteered by the Soviet Union.

Secretary of State George Shultz acknowledged problems with the government's case when he stated, "There are questions about whether in a purely technical sense it [the SS-25] fits within treaty language as might be interpreted by a lawyer." Indeed, Congressman Lee Hamilton (D-IN), Chairman of the House Permanent Select Committee on Intelligence, argued that the SS-25 "does not reasonably add up to an unequivocal violation."

In the second SALT II compliance issue, the United States charged that "extensive encryption of telemetry" on Soviet missile flights violated the SALT II prohibition on "impeding" verification through the deliberate denial of missile test information. During flight-tests, the performance data of ballistic missiles is normally radioed to ground-based receiving stations. These radio signals, known as "telemetry," can be monitored by the other side and analyzed to retrieve technical data. The country testing a missile can randomly scramble or "encrypt" these radio signals so that it is impossible for the eavesdropping country to understand the technical information being communicated. In the SALT II Treaty, each party was prohibited from using "deliberate concealment measures which impede verification." In a common understanding, both parties agreed that the encryption of telemetry would be permitted, except when the practice "impedes verification of compliance with the provisions of the treaty."

The administration argued that the Soviet Union had encrypted their missile telemetry extensively for several years, in a manner that impeded US ability to verify the performance characteristics governed by SALT II of such missiles as the SS-25, SS-24 and the SS-18. Soviet negotiators argued that its encryption practices did not impede verification of the relevant provisions of SALT II and asked the United States to identify the specific telemetry information it needed for verification. US negotiators refused to specify this information on the grounds that it would endanger sensitive intelligence sources and methods.

This compliance issue hinged on the interpretation of the word "impede." It is apparently not clear in the negotiating record whether "impede" means "to prevent" or whether it means "to make more difficult." Soviet encryption practices have certainly made verification more difficult, but given the specificity of the administration's

charge that the throw-weight of the SS-25 is 92 percent greater than that of the SS-13, encryption has obviously not prevented monitoring of very detailed qualitative provisions. Many experts believe that, while the Soviet Union has exploited inherently ambiguous language, the lack of an agreed interpretation makes it difficult to sustain an actual violation charge. They point to the conclusion of Representative Hamilton: "What we have is not an open and shut case of Soviet noncompliance. Instead, it is a case where treaty language is not as precise as it should be."

Threshold Test Ban Treaty

The United States has charged that a number of Soviet underground nuclear tests constitute "likely" violations of the 1974 Threshold Test Ban Treaty, which prohibits underground nuclear weapon tests having yields exceeding 150 kilotons. The treaty, which was signed by President Nixon in 1974, has never been ratified by the United States or the Soviet Union, but both have stated that they are adhering to the treaty.

The US Government has charged that it is "likely" that a number (10-20) of Soviet tests have exceeded the 150-kiloton threshold since the signing of the treaty. The Soviet Union has rejected these charges. Moreover, there is a substantial controversy within the US scientific community over the interpretation of the seismic data from the Soviet tests. A growing number of seismologists have concluded that the available data does not support a conclusion that the Soviet Union has been testing above the 150-kiloton threshold.

The US charge is based on US government estimates of the yields of Soviet nuclear tests derived from the measurement of the seismic magnitudes of the events at stations outside the Soviet Union. The validity of this charge depends on two separate factors, "regional bias" and "statistical uncertainty," which are critical to the interpretation of the data. "Regional bias" defines the systematic differences in the propagation of seismic signals from various geographical regions caused by differences in the underlying geologies. Such a "regional bias" is known to exist between the Semipalatinsk region, site of most Soviet nuclear tests, and the Nevada Test Site, site of US nuclear tests. As a result, a Soviet nuclear test sends stronger seismic signals through the earth than a test of the same yield would at the US test site. If based on US test data, Soviet tests would therefore appear larger than they actually were. Many US seismologists, both in and out of government, believe the United

States has been consistently overestimating the yields of Soviet tests by not properly accounting for this "regional bias" factor.

In addition, yield estimates based on the measurement of seismic waves inherently involve substantial statistical uncertainty. The administration argues that this uncertainty is as large as a factor of two. Thus, a test that has a true value of 150 kilotons may be measured as having a value as low as 75 kilotons or as high as 300 kilotons. Looked at another way, in a group of tests with true yields of 150 kilotons, half the tests would appear to be above the threshold and half below. Therefore, while the "measured" yields of some Soviet tests since 1974 may have been more than 150 kilotons, the actual yield of the tests could very well be at or below 150 kilotons.

For these technical reasons, this compliance charge has been widely questioned in the scientific community. For example, Dr. Roger Batzel, then director of the Lawrence Livermore Laboratory, testified in 1987 that "the Soviets appear to be observing some yield limit. Livermore's best estimate of this yield limit, based on a probabilistic assessment, is that it is consistent with TTBT compliance." This conclusion has been affirmed by the director of the Los Alamos National Laboratory and by many other scientists.

The Reagan administration has made the long-delayed ratification of the TTBT contingent upon Soviet agreement to direct on-site determination of the yields of all tests above 50 kilotons. After extended negotiations, the Soviet Union agreed at the 1988 Moscow Summit to the US proposal for a Joint Verification Experiment (JVE) to test US and Soviet technical approaches to this problem using a US underground nuclear test at the Nevada Test Site and a Soviet underground nuclear test at Semipalatinsk. The US approach (CORRTEX) is based on the use of an electric cable lowered into a bore-hole directly over or several meters away from the nuclear device to measure the rate of expansion of the hydrodynamic shock wave from the explosion; the preferred Soviet approach is based on the use of seismic measurements. Although either of these techniques should reduce the statistical uncertainty of yield measurements, the basic problem will remain since there will still be uncertainty (reportedly + or - 30 percent) in yield measurements. The new calibration data should, however, help to resolve the "regional bias" issue.

The experiments were performed at the two test sites in the summer of 1988 with large contingents of US and Soviet scientists and technicians present to emplace the measuring equipment and observe the tests. However, the delegation of experts that met in Geneva to consider the results were unable before the end of 1988 to complete work on the additional verification procedures to reinforce the TTB, thereby leaving future steps on nuclear testing negotiations to the Bush administration.

CBW Treaty Issues

The United States has charged the Soviet Union with violating both the Geneva Protocol, which bans the use of chemical and biological weapons in war, and the Biological and Toxin Weapons Convention, which bans the production and stockpiling of biological and toxin weapons.

As early as 1978, refugee reports led the United States government to raise questions concerning the possibility that chemical warfare was being used in Southeast Asia. In 1981, the United States charged the Soviet Union with supplying toxins to Vietnam for use as "yellow rain" in Southeast Asia and with using chemical warfare in Afghanistan. The toxic ingredient in yellow rain was said to be trichothecene mycotoxins—poisonous toxins produced by molds, which were said not to occur naturally in Southeast Asia.

Since then, there has been a major controversy over the evidence offered by the Reagan administration to support its charges. All of the available samples of "yellow rain" have been found to consist mostly of pollen and to be identical to samples of the excrement of Southeast Asian honeybees. While two private laboratories initially found traces of trichothecenes in a few samples, these results have never been confirmed by other laboratories, and the US Army chemical warfare laboratory has not found trichothecenes in any of its hundreds of samples from Southeast Asia. Moreover, recent studies indicate that trichothecenes occur naturally in Southeast Asia. In addition to the disputed samples, there are numerous refugee reports alleging attacks with chemical warfare. But recently declassified documents show that a US government interview team cast serious doubt on the refugee evidence, finding the reports self-contradictory and impossible to verify.

The other major issue relating to compliance with the Biological and Toxin Weapons Convention relates to a serious outbreak of anthrax in the Soviet city of Sverdlovsk in 1979. The United States has charged that the epidemic resulted from an explosion at a nearby facility which had previously been suspected as a possible biological warfare installation. A report on the incident by an individual who claimed to have seen the victims included the information that many suffered from the rare pulmonary form of anthrax, indicating they were caused by inhalation of anthrax spores as would be the case after an explosion.

From the beginning, the Soviet Union stated that the epidemic was caused by contaminated meat and therefore did not relate to the convention. The fact that the epidemic continued for several weeks gave some credence to the Soviet explanation since an epidemic caused by a single release of spores would presumably cause infections only over a brief period. It was also known that anthrax had long been endemic to the Sverdlovsk region.

Until recently, Soviet refusal to discuss the issue, formally or informally, raised further suspicions. In several recent forums, however, including the 1986 Review Conference for the Convention, Soviet representatives have provided more information in support of their version of the event to show that the victims did not suffer from pulmonary anthrax but intestinal anthrax, as would be the case from infected meat. In 1988, a team of senior Soviet medical doctors who had been involved in treating Soviet victims of the Sverdlovsk anthrax outbreak visited the United States and gave a detailed account of the event, including photographs of autopsies of alleged victims to demonstrate they had died of intestinal anthrax.

Compliance vs. Noncompliance

This discussion has focused, as has the public debate, on charges of treaty violations. It should be recognized, however, that both superpowers have operated for the most part in strict compliance with almost all of the provisions of the many arms control agreements they have signed over the last 25 years. Consequently, the agreements have served the US national security pur-

poses for which they were intended. This fact must be borne in mind when assessing the significance of various alleged violations of various treaties and the appropriate reactions to the violations.

None of the alleged violations presents a significant threat to the security of the United States. Moreover, with the exception of the Krasnoyarsk radar, none of the noncompliance issues appear to involve a clear-cut treaty violation. And the Krasnoyarsk radar does not in itself affect the central objective of the ABM Treaty or pose a military threat to the United States. The other US and Soviet charges of noncompliance are all at least debatable either because they involve or exploit ambiguous treaty language or are based on uncertain or incomplete information.

There is probably general agreement that even marginally important and debatable compliance issues should be pursued and resolved since they might indicate an intent to undercut or eventually repudiate a treaty. To ignore such actions could erode the treaty environment and public confidence in arms control. The issue is not whether possible violations should be challenged but rather the standards of evidence required to justify formal charges which inevitably undercut public confidence in arms control and potentially have serious consequences in international relations.

During the Reagan administration, charges of violations were made publicly in a much more confrontational manner than in any previous administrations. Supporters of this approach would argue that it has helped resolve these issues by focusing world opinion on them and has deterred the Soviet Union from more extensive violations in the future. Critics would argue that this approach created a false impression of Soviet noncompliance with international agreements and has undercut public support for arms control. Moreover, critics would argue that such a confrontational public approach makes resolution of the issues more difficult, since great powers will not easily acknowledge that they have acted, even accidentally, in violation of their international obligations.

APPENDICES

Appendix I: Strategic Nuclear Forces of the United States and the Soviet Union

United States

TOTAL LAUNCHERS*

ICBMs	1,000
SLBMs	608
BOMBERS	291
	1,899

TOTAL WARHEADS**

On ICBMs	2,450
On SLBMs	5,312
On BOMBERS	4,808
	12,570

US SLBM totals exclude two 16-tube POLARIS submarines whose missile tubes have not been dismantled but are no longer operational and one 24-tube TRIDENT submarine which has begun sea trials but has not yet been outfitted with TRIDENT D-5 missiles.

**Weapons totals are based on the ICBM and SLBM counting rules agreed to at the U.S.-Soviet summit in Washington, D.C., December 7-10, 1987. Warhead numbers do not include US long-range SLCMs or weapons aboard U.S. FB-111 aircraft. Bomber loadings are based on aircraft carriage capability and weapons availability. Actual operational loadings are likely to be lower.*

	Launchers	Warheads
ICBMs		
MINUTEMAN II	450 x 1	450
MINUTEMAN III	500 x 3	1,500
MX (PEACEKEEPER)	50 x 10	500
Totals:	1,000	2,450
SLBMs		
C-3	224 x 10	2,240
C-4	384 x 8	3,072
Totals:	608	5,312
BOMBERS		
B-52G (ALCM)	98 x 16	1,568
B-52H (ALCM)	78 x 20	1,560
B-52H	18 x 8	144
B-1B	95 x 16	1,520
B-1B (ALCM)	2 x 8	16
Totals:	291	4,808

Breakdown of US Forces:

ICBM warhead levels assume 450 MINUTEMAN II, 1,500 (500 X 3 MIRV) MINUTEMAN III, and 500 (50 X 10 MIRV) MX (PEACEKEEPER) warheads. **SLBM levels** include 14 POSEIDON submarines carrying 16 C-3 missiles each with 10 warheads per missile; 12 POSEIDON submarines carrying 16 C-4 missiles each with eight warheads per missile; and eight TRIDENT submarines carrying 24 C-4 missiles each with eight warheads per missile. **Bomber levels** include 194 B-52 and 93 B-1B bombers in the active inventory. Four additional B-1Bs are considered test aircraft, two of which have been equipped with ALCMs. Bomber loadings assume 4,808 weapons (1,736 spaces for ALCMs and 3,072 bombs and SRAMs. In actuality, only 1,614 ALCMs will be available for deployment until 1990, when the Advanced Cruise Missile (ACM) comes on line.) Excluded are 61 FB-111 aircraft under the Strategic Air Command, about 250 B-52s in storage at Davis Montham airbase and on display, and 69 B-52Gs recently converted and reassigned to conventional missions. The United States generally maintains its strategic force at a high state of readiness, with 30 percent of its bomber force on 24-hour alert, over 50 percent of its missile-carrying submarines on station or in transit, and more than 90 percent of its ICBMs ready for immediate launch.

Recent US Changes:

All 50 MX (or PEACEKEEPER) ICBMs, each with 10 warheads, are now in silos at F.E. Warren Air Force Base near Cheyenne, Wyoming. Five B-52G squadrons (98) are now equipped with ALCMs. Each aircraft is assumed to be carrying up to eight ALCMs externally and up to eight SRAMs and/or gravity bombs internally. Seventy-eight B-52H aircraft have been converted to carry ALCMs, with the entire force of 96 to be converted by the end of 1989. Each B-52H is assumed to carry up to 12 wing-mounted ALCMs and up to eight SRAMs and/or gravity bombs in its bomb bay. Ninety-three (of the 100 delivered) B-1B bombers, each assumed to be carrying up to 16 SRAMs and/or gravity bombs, are now operational. In September 1987 and November 1988, three B-1B bombers crashed during routine training flights. A POSEIDON submarine carrying 16 C-3 missiles recently returned to port for deactivation, leaving 14 POSEIDONs operational. The ninth TRIDENT submarine began sea trials but will not be outfitted with 24 TRIDENT D-5 missiles until March 1990, when the new missile reaches its initial operational capability. (Excluded are about 340 nuclear long-range SLCMs which are now available for deployment on 67 attack subs and surface ships.)

Soviet Union

TOTAL LAUNCHERS*

ICBMs	1,376
SLBMs	942
BOMBERS	170
	2,488

TOTAL WARHEADS**

On ICBMs	6,572
On SLBMs	3,426
On BOMBERS	1,000
	10,998

Soviet SLBM totals do not include 36 non-SALT-account-able SS-N-5 missiles on 12 non-nuclear-powered GOLF-II submarines. Soviet bomber totals exclude about 15 MYA-4 BISON bombers which are under dispute. The United States believes the bombers remain SALT-accountable; the Soviet Union claims they have been converted to refueling tankers and should not be counted.

**Weapons totals are based on the US-Soviet summit in Washington, D.C., December 7-10, 1987. Warhead numbers do not include Soviet long-range SLCMs or weapons aboard Soviet BACKFIRE aircraft. Bomber loadings are based on aircraft carriage capability. Actual operational loadings are likely to be lower.*

	Launcher	Warheads
ICBMs		
SS-11	376 x 1	376
SS-13	60 x 1	60
SS-17	108 x 4	432
SS-18	308 x 10	3,080
SS-19	330 x 6	1,980
SS-24	50 x 10	500
SS-25	144 x 1	144
	Total: 1,376	Total: 6,572
SLBMs		
SS-N-6	240 x 1	240
SS-N-8	286 x 1	286
SS-N-17	12 x 1	12
SS-N-18	224 x 7	1,568
SS-N-20	100 x 10	1,000
SS-N-23	80 x 4	320
	Total: 942	Total: 3,426
BOMBERS		
BEAR-H(ALCM)	75 x 6	450
BEAR-A	15 x 2	30
BEAR-B/C/G	70 x 4	280
BLACKJACK	10 x 24	240
	Total: 170	Total: 1,000

Breakdown of Soviet Forces:

ICBM and SLBM warhead levels are based on counting rules established at the December 1987 US-Soviet summit in Washington, D.C. **SLBM levels** include missiles aboard 62 submarines: 15 YANKEE I, one YANKEE II, 18 DELTA I, four DELTA II, 14 DELTA III, five DELTA IV, and five TYPHOON submarines. Sixty of these submarines are operational and two have begun sea trials. Also included are six SS-N-8 missiles on one Hotel-class submarine. **Bomber levels** include 160 TU-95 BEAR bombers and 10 TU-160 BLACKJACK bombers. Eighty-five Bear bombers carry between two and four weapons per aircraft, either bombs or air-to-surface missiles. Seventy-five BEAR-H bombers are assumed to carry six AS-15 ALCMs each. Ten BLACKJACK bombers are each assumed to carry up to 24 bombs or air-to-surface missiles. Excluded are 15 MYA-4 BISON bombers and 321 non-SALT-accountable TU-26 BACKFIRE aircraft, over 160 of which are assigned to Soviet Air Armies and the remainder to Soviet Naval Aviation. The Soviet Union maintains its strategic forces at a relatively low level of readiness, with no bombers on alert, a relatively small percentage of its ICBMs ready for immediate launch, and only about 20 percent of its missile-carrying submarines on station or in transit.

Recent Soviet Changes:

Approximately 75 BEAR-H bombers with AS-15 ALCMs are now operational. More than 30 BISON bombers were dismantled as BEAR-Hs were deployed. The status of the remaining 15 BISONs is in dispute. About 144 mobile SS-25s are now deployed and an equal number of SS-11 launchers have been dismantled in compensation. Twenty 10-warhead SS-24 ICBMs have been fielded on rail-mobile launchers and 30 have been deployed in modified SS-19 silos. A number of SS-17 launchers are being dismantled in order to compensate for the mobile SS-24s. Four DELTA IV submarines are considered operational and a fifth has begun sea trials. Each DELTA IV carries 16 SS-N-23 SLBMs with up to four warheads per missile. Four TYPHOON-class submarines are currently operational and a fifth sub is undergoing sea trials. Each TYPHOON carries 20 SS-N-20 SLBMs with up to 10 warheads per missile. The TU-160 BLACKJACK bomber recently became operational. At least 11 BLACKJACKS have been produced, but one was lost in an accident in May 1987. Seventeen YANKEE-class subs have been removed from service as new subs entered sea trials. On October 6, 1986, a YANKEE-class sub carrying 16 SS-N-6 SLBMs burned and sank off the U.S. Atlantic coast. (Excluded are SS-N-21 SLCMs which are now available for deployment on reconfigured YANKEE, SIERRA, and AKULA submarines.)

US and Soviet force charts current as of June 1989.

Appendix II: British, French and Chinese Nuclear Weapons

System	Range(km)	Launchers	Warheads/Launcher	Total Warheads
Great Britain				
Polaris SLBM	4,600	64	2-3 MRVs	64
Bombs[1]				80
				144
France				
M-4 SLBM	4,500	16	6 RVs	96
S-3	3,500	18	1 RV	18
M-20 SLBM	2,900	80	1 RV	80
				194
Bombs[1]				95
Pluton	120	32		32
ASMP[2]	250+[3]	31		31
				158
People's Republic of China				
DF-3 (CSS-2) IRBM	2,600	85-125	85-125	85-125
DF-5 (CSS-4) ICBM	12,000	~10	~10	~10
DF-4 (CSS-3) ICBM	7,000	~10	~10	~10
HY-2 (CSS-NX-4) SLBM	3,300	24	24	24
DF-2 (CSS-1) MRBM	1,100	40-60	40-60	40-60
Bombs[4]				~400

[1] *Bombs are carried by British Tornados and French Mirage IIIs and IVAs.*
[2] *ASMP is carried by Mirage IVPs and Mirage 2000N.*
[3] *The operational range of the ASMP, including the range of the Mirage IVP or Mirage 2000N, is more than 4,000 km.*
[4] *Bombs carried by B-4 Bull, B-5 Beagle, and B-6 Badger aircraft.*

Appendix III: Abbreviations and Acronyms

ABM	Antiballistic missile
ACDA	Arms Control and Disarmament Agency
ALCM	Air-launched cruise missile
ALPS	Accidental Launch Protection System
AOA	Airborne Optical Adjunct
ASAT	Antisatellite weapon
ASW	Antisubmarine warfare
ATBM	Antitactical ballistic missile
BMD	Ballistic missile defense
CAT	Conventional Arms Transfers Talks
CBM	Confidence-building measure
CBW	Chemical and biological warfare
CDE	Conference on Disarmament in Europe
CEP	Circular error probable (measurement of missile accuracy)
CFE	Conventional Armed Forces in Europe talks
C³I	Command, control, communications, and intelligence
CIA	Central Intelligence Agency
CSCE	Conference on Security and Cooperation in Europe
CTBT	Comprehensive Test Ban Treaty
DOD	Department of Defense
DST	Defense and Space Talks
ELF	Extremely low frequency
EMP	Electromagnetic pulse
ERIS	Exoatmospheric reentry vehicle interception system
FBS	Forward-based systems
GLCM	Ground-launched cruise missile
HEDI	High endoatmospheric defense interceptor
HOE	Homing Overlay Experiment
IAEA	International Atomic Energy Agency
ICBM	Intercontinental ballistic missile
INF	Intermediate-range nuclear forces
IRBM	Intermediate-range ballistic missile
JCS	Joint Chiefs of Staff
LOW	Launch on warning
LPAR	Large phased-array radar
LTBT	Limited Test Ban Treaty
LUA	Launch under attack

MAD	Mutual assured destruction
MaRV	Maneuvering reentry vehicle
MBFR	Mutual and Balanced Force Reductions
MHV	Miniature Homing Vehicle
MIRV	Multiple independently targetable reentry vehicle
MOU	Memorandum of Understanding
MPS	Multiple protective shelter
MX	Missile experimental
NATO	North Atlantic Treaty Organization
NEACAP	National Emergency Airborne Command Post
NORAD	North American Aerospace Defense Command
NPT	Nonproliferation Treaty
NRRC	Nuclear Risk Reduction Center
NSC	National Security Council
NST	Nuclear and Space Arms Talks
NTM	National technical means (of verification)
OSI	On-site inspection
OTA	Office of Technology Assessment
PAL	Permissive action link
PNE	Peaceful nuclear explosion
PNET	Peaceful Nuclear Explosions Treaty
psi	Pounds per square inch (measurement of blast overpressure)
RV	Reentry vehicle (of a ballistic missile)
SAC	Strategic Air Command
SALT	Strategic Arms Limitation Talks
SAM	Surface-to-air missile
SBI	Space-based interceptor
SCC	Standing Consultative Commission
SDI	Strategic Defense Initiative
SDIO	Strategic Defense Initiative Organization
SICBM	Small Intercontinental ballistic missile
SIOP	Single integrated operational plan
SLBM	Submarine-launched ballistic missile
SLCM	Sea-launched cruise missile
SNDV	Strategic nuclear delivery vehicle
SRAM	Short-range attack missile
START	Strategic Arms Reduction Talks
SVC	Special Verification Commission
TACAMO	Take charge and move out (command and control aircraft)
TTBT	Threshold Test Ban Treaty
WTO	Warsaw Treaty Organization

Appendix IV:
Glossary of Arms Control Terms

accidental launch protection system (ALPS) Limited ABM system designed to protect against the accidental or unauthorized launch of nuclear missiles.

active defense The protection of civil and military targets through the use of defensive weapons, such as anti-ballistic missile systems and anti-aircraft artillery. (See passive defense)

aggregate ceiling A ceiling or limit on two or more different categories of weapons, such as the SALT II limit on the total number of ICBM launchers, SLBM launchers and heavy bombers.

air defense The protection of civil or military targets from enemy bombers.

air-to-surface ballistic missile (ASBM) A ballistic missile carried by and launched from a bomber. For the purposes of SALT II, ASBMs are any such missiles capable of a range greater than 600 kilometers. Although ASBMs were included in the overall SALT II aggregates, to date neither superpower has deployed them.

airborne warning and control system (AWACS) A flying command post. AWACS has the capacity to detect hostile radar systems and aircraft and to control friendly air forces in offensive and defensive missions.

air-launched cruise missile (ALCM) See cruise missile.

anti-ballistic missile (ABM) system A defense system to intercept strategic ballistic missiles in flight.

anti-satellite weapon (ASAT) A system designed to destroy or disable enemy satellites in orbit.

anti-submarine warfare (ASW) The detection, identification, tracking, and destruction of enemy submarines. ASW can be either strategic (aimed at neutralizing an opponent's ballistic missile submarines), or tactical aimed at defending convoys, aircraft carriers, or other naval targets from an opponent's attack submarines.

anti-tactical ballistic missile (ATBM) A defense system designed to intercept short-range or "tactical" ballistic missiles. (See anti-ballistic missile (ABM) system)

area defense Defense of a large geographic area against missiles or aircraft.

Arms Control and Disarmament Agency The independent US agency that deals with arms control matters.

arms transfer The sale or grant of arms from one nation to another.

Atoms for Peace 1953 proposal by President Eisenhower, which called on the United States and the Soviet Union to reduce their nuclear arsenals and focus on exploring the peaceful uses of nuclear energy. The proposal also shifted the emphasis of US nuclear proliferation policy from the denial of nuclear technology to the cooperative development of civilian nuclear power, provided a country agreed not to develop nuclear weapons.

ballistic missile A missile that is lifted into space by a booster rocket and then descends toward its target in a free-falling ballistic trajectory.

ballistic missile defense (BMD) See anti-ballistic missile (ABM) system.

Baruch Plan 1946 proposal by the Truman administration to eliminate all nuclear weapons and place the development and use of atomic energy under the control of an independent international authority accountable to the UN Security Council. The new agency would ensure that nuclear materials and technology would not be used to make nuclear weapons.

battlefield nuclear weapons Relatively small, short-range nuclear weapons (missiles, bombs, artillery shells, or land mines) designed to be used on the battlefield.

binary chemical weapon A weapon containing two relatively harmless chemicals, which when mixed combine to form a highly toxic chemical agent.

"bolt from the blue" attack An all-out surprise attack during a period of low tension. The goal of such an attack would presumably be to destroy enough of the opponent's military capability to ensure victory.

bomber An aircraft capable of delivering nuclear and/or non-nuclear ordnance. Long-range bombers are those capable of traveling 6,000 or more miles on one load of fuel; medium-range bombers can travel between 3,500 and 6,000 miles without refueling.

boost phase The first phase of a ballistic missile flight, lasting from launch to burnout of its final stage engines (currently 3-5 minutes).

breakout A sudden abrogation or massive violation of an arms control treaty through the extensive deployment of weapons designed to alter the military balance.

breeder reactor A reactor that produces more nuclear fuel than it consumes while generating power.

bus See post-boost vehicle.

catalytic war Type of nuclear war in which a third country deliberately triggers war between the superpowers.

circular error probable (CEP) A measure of missile accuracy. A missile's CEP is the radius of a circle around the target in which 50 percent of the warheads aimed at that target will land.

civil defense The protection of civilian populations from attack, usually by means of fallout or blast shelters or evacuation of major population centers.

cold launch A technique for launching a ballistic missile which leaves the silo undamaged and thus allows for its reloading. The missile is ejected from the silo by a gas generator and the rocket engines ignite only after the missile has cleared the silo.

command, control, communication, and intelligence (C^3I) The information-processing systems used to detect, assess and respond to actual and potential military and political crises or conflicts. C3I includes systems which transmit commands and manage material and manpower during crises or conflicts, as well as in peacetime.

compliance Adherence to the terms and limitations of an arms control agreement or treaty.

Comprehensive Test Ban Treaty (CTBT) A proposed agreement to ban all nuclear testing.

Conference on Disarmament in Europe (CDE) A multilateral negotiating forum among the US, the USSR, Canada, and 33 European nations reached in September 1986, which provides for a series of confidence building measures relating to advance notification of large military exercises.

Conference on Security and Cooperation in Europe (CSCE) A 35-nation conference which produced a 1975 agreement on human rights, economics, and security. The security agreement provides for confidence building measures such as notification of major military maneuvers in Europe.

Conventional Armed Forces in Europe (CFE) Multilateral negotiations among the US, the USSR, and the European nations concerning conventional forces in Europe.

cooperative measures Measures taken by one side in order to enhance the other side's ability to verify compliance with the provisions of an agreement.

confidence-building measures (CBMs) Negotiated or unilateral measures taken to increase "transparency" and demonstrate a nation's lack of belligerent or hostile intent, as distinguished from measures which actually reduce military capabilities.

Conventional Arms Transfer (CAT) Talks Negotiations between the US and the USSR in 1977-78, which sought to constrain arms transfers.

counterforce Military strategies, attacks, or weapons directed against an opponent's military forces, command posts, and other war-fighting targets.

countervailing strategy Nuclear strategy, adopted under the Carter administration, which stressed counterforce targeting, greater flexibility in a protracted nuclear war, and survivable command and control centers to conduct such a war.

countervalue Military strategies, attacks, or weapons directed against an opponent's population, society and economy.

counting rules Procedures established to facilitate the counting of weapons for arms control purposes.

crisis stability A situation in which incentives are minimal to launch a strategic nuclear attack first during a crisis.

cruise missile A pilotless, jet-propelled guided missile. Cruise missiles may be armed with conventional or nuclear warheads and launched from an aircraft (air-launched cruise missiles), a submarine or ship (sea-launched cruise missiles), or a land-based platform (ground-launched cruise missiles). [ALCM, SLCM and GLCM]

damage limitation The capacity to reduce the damage from a nuclear attack. Damage limitation strategies include passive defense (such as the hardening of missile silos), active defense (such as anti-ballistic missile (ABM) systems), and pre-emptive strikes designed to reduce an adversary's offensive forces.

data base A jointly agreed description of the forces of each side, sometimes exchanged as part of an arms control agreement.

decapitation The destruction of an opponent's leadership or the disruption of communication between the leadership and commanders and weapons in the field.

declaratory policy The stated nuclear weapons policy of a country, as distinguished from "targeting" policy, how the weapons would actually be used, or "procurement policy" determining the actual structure of nuclear forces.

decoy A facsimile of a weapon system or component (such as a missile warhead) designed to complicate attempts to destroy or disable the actual weapon. The decoy need only resemble its counterpart from the perspective of the attacking weapon. (Flares, for example, are fired by a jet aircraft as decoys to confuse heat-seeking missiles homing in on the engine's exhaust.)

Defense and Space Talks Negotiations between the US and USSR, intitiated in 1985, which focus on strategic defense issues and the ABM Treaty.

deliberate concealment Intentional measures taken to deny national technical means the ability to verify an arms control agreement.

delivery vehicle A device, whether a ballistic or cruise missile or bomber, which carries one or more warheads through its flight.

deployment The placement of a weapon into a combat-ready position.

depressed trajectory The flight path of a missile which is fired at a lower than usual angle to the ground and thus travels at a lower than normal altitude. Missiles fired with a depressed trajectory have reduced flight time and would increase the vulnerability of those targets such as bombers on the ground, which depend on warning time for their survivability.

deterrence Dissuasion of a potential adversary from initiating an attack or conflict by the threat of retaliation.

development The stage of work on a new weapon system after laboratory research, but before full-scale testing and deployment.

directed-energy weapons Weapons which employ beams of energy, such as lasers or particle beams, to destroy or disable targets.

discrimination The ability of a surveillance system to distinguish targets from decoys and other penetration aids.

dismantlement Taking apart weapon systems in order to remain in compliance with an arms control agreement.

dual-capable system A weapon system capable of carrying nuclear or conventional warheads.

dual-track decision The 1979 NATO decision to deploy intermediate range forces (INF) on NATO soil and at the same time attempt to obtain an arms control agreement on intermediate range nuclear forces with the Soviet Union.

early deployment A proposed plan of the Reagan administration to deploy a limited ballistic missile defense in the mid- to late-1990s.

early warning Early detection of an enemy attack, usually by means of surveillance satellites and long-range radar.

electromagnetic pulse (EMP) A sharp burst of electromagnetic energy produced by a nuclear explosion. The resulting electric and magnetic fields may cause damage to unprotected electrical and electronic equipment at great distances.

electronic countermeasures Countermeasures utilizing sophisticated defense electronics which attempt to confuse an adversary's analysis of radar data, including saturating airwaves with electronic noise and creating false electronic images or spoofing.

Emergency Action Message Presidential command authorizing the use of nuclear weapons. This message would direct the execution of a preplanned option from the Single Integrated Operational Plan (SIOP) through the Secretary of Defense and the Joint Chiefs of Staff to nuclear force commanders, who would in turn pass the orders to operations officers.

encryption Encoding transmitted information in a manner to prevent others from understanding it.

enhanced radiation warhead An atomic warhead designed to release more of its energy as neutron radiation than an ordinary nuclear weapon. Commonly referred to as a 'neutron bomb,' this device would be lethal to troops at distances at which it would inflict less damage on structures than an ordinary nuclear weapon.

enrichment Processing natural uranium to increase the concentration of the fissile isotope, Uranium 235.

equivalent megatonnage (EMT) A common measure of the destructive effect of nuclear weapons to take into account the fact that the area effect of a nuclear weapon does not increase directly as the yield, but as the yield to the two-thirds power.

escalation A shift in a conflict to an increased level of violence or a broader geographic area. In discussions of nuclear weapons, escalation implies an increase in the strategic significance of the weapons employed, for example, from conventional forces to tactical nuclear weapons to strategic missiles and bombers.

extremely low frequency (ELF) Communication system which is capable of transmitting messages underwater to submerged submarines worldwide.

fallout The spread of radioactive particles from clouds of debris produced by nuclear blasts. "Local fallout" falls to the earth's surface within twenty-four hours of the blast. "Delayed fallout" may take years to return to earth.

first strike A surprise attack on an opponent's strategic nuclear forces in an attempt to destroy his retaliatory capability.

first use The introduction of nuclear weapons into a conflict at any level. A "no-first-use" pledge by a nation obliges it not to be the first to use nuclear weapons.

fission The process of splitting atomic nuclei, stimulated by the bombardment of the nuclei with neutrons. The process yields vast amounts of energy and more neutrons capable of splitting other atoms.

flexible response A NATO strategy of responding to a Warsaw Pact attack with a similar or higher level of force, beginning with conventional forces and escalating to tactical or strategic nuclear forces if necessary.

flight test A missile launch conducted typically for missile development, reliability, or troop training.

forward-based systems (FBS) Forces based on allied territory or on US aircraft carriers which are capable of reaching an adversary's territory.

fractional orbital bombardment system (FOBS) A weapon system with a semi-orbital trajectory which could potentially attack with less warning time from an unexpected direction.

fractionation The division of a missile payload into separate re-entry vehicles, or the degree of such a division. Another term for MIRVing.

fratricide The destruction of an attacking nuclear weapon by the detonation of other attacking weapons. This phenomenon could decrease the effectiveness of a large-scale attack on closely spaced targets such as missile silos.

functionally related observable differences (FRODs) Differences in those features of a weapon system related to its mission which can be monitored by national technical means of verification. SALT II used FRODs to deal with verification difficulties posed by weapon systems that have similar characteristics to but different missions from other weapon systems.

fusion The process of combining atomic nuclei with the release of large amounts of energy.

general and complete disarmament (GCD) The total abandonment of military forces and weapons (other than internal police forces) usually foreseen as occurring through an agreed schedule of force reduction. In 1961, in the so-called McCloy-Zorin Principles, the United States and the USSR agreed to GCD as the ultimate objective of their negotiations.

geosynchronous orbit An orbit around the earth at such an altitude that a satellite will circle the earth once a day, thereby appearing to hover over exactly the same point at all times. Because their position in relation to earth is fixed, such satellites are used for communications and early warning.

ground launched cruise missile (GLCM) See cruise missile.

hardened target A target protected against the blast, heat, and radiation effects of nuclear weapons of specific yields. Hardening is usually measured by the number of pounds per square inch (psi) of blast overpressure which a target can withstand.

hard target kill capability The capacity of a weapons system, related to its accuracy and yield, to destroy a hardened target such as a missile silo.

heavy bomber The term used in SALT II to describe those aircraft included in the aggregate limitations of the agreement. Under the Treaty, heavy bombers include the US B-52 and B-1, the Soviet TU-95 Bear and Mya-4 Bison, future bombers capable of carrying out intercontinental missions as well as or better than those systems, bombers equipped to carry cruise missiles with ranges greater than 600 kilometers and bombers equipped for air-to-surface ballistic missiles (ASBMs).

heavy missile A category of missile with a large payload. In the SALT II negotiations a heavy missile was defined as any missile heavier than the Soviet SS-19 ICBM.

homing device A device, mounted on a missile, that uses sensors to detect a target and guide the missile toward it.

hotline Direct communications link between the United States and the Soviet Union, which allows quick communication between leaders or their representatives in time of crisis.

hydrogen bomb See thermonuclear bomb.

inertial guidance The guidance system used in a ballistic missile which detects and corrects deviations from the intended trajectory by measuring acceleration, allowing the missile to steer itself without sensing any outside information.

intercontinental ballistic missile (ICBM) A ballistic missile with a range of 5,500 kilometers or more. Conventionally, the term ICBM is used only for land-based systems, in order to differentiate them from submarine-launched ballistic missiles (SLBMs), which can also be of intercontinental range.

intermediate-range nuclear forces (INF) A category of weapons which encompasses ballistic and cruise missiles (such as the US Pershing II and GLCMs and the Soviet SS-20), with ranges between 500 and 5,500 kilometers.

International Atomic Energy Agency (IAEA) A United Nations organization, founded in 1956, whose purpose is to promote peaceful uses of nuclear technology, prevent the diversion of safeguarded nuclear materials, and maintain health and safety standards for the nuclear industry and the environment.

kiloton (kt) A measure of the yield of a nuclear weapon, equivalent to 1,000 tons of TNT. (See megaton)

kinetic energy weapon A weapon whose destructive force derives from a collision with its target, as opposed to the detonation of a nuclear or conventional warhead.

large phased-array radar (LPAR) See phased-array radar

launch-on-warning (LOW) The act of launching retaliatory strategic missiles and/or bombers on receipt of warning that an opponent had launched an attack.

launch under attack (LUA) The act of launching retaliatory strategic missiles and/or bombers on confirmation that a nuclear attack has occured. Confirmation involves the determination that at least one nuclear weapon has detonated on the nation's territory.

launcher A platform from which a weapon is fired. For land-based missles, this is a silo or an above-ground platform; for submarine-launched missiles, this is a launch tube; for a gravity bomb or air-launched cruise missile, this is a bomber.

light-water reactor The most common type of nuclear power reactor which uses enriched uranium as fuel. The spent fuel of a light-water reactor contains significant amounts of plutonium which can be used to make nuclear explosives.

limited nuclear options A strategic doctrine, developed in 1974 under Secretary of Defense James Schlesinger, that involved controlled, limited nuclear strikes against specific military, command and control centers, or economic targets.

linkage The coupling of arms control negotiations with non-arms control issues, such as human rights or international behavior. Also, in a European context, the coupling of American and European security.

maneuvering reentry vehicle (MaRV) A ballistic missile reentry vehicle that can alter its trajectory during flight.

massive retaliation Nuclear doctrine formulated in the Eisenhower administration which emphasized countering any type of aggression with a massive nuclear response.

megaton (mt) A measure of the yield of a nuclear weapon, equivalent to 1,000,000 tons of TNT.

memorandum of understanding Document attached to an international agreement which clarifies the understanding and interpretation of the agreement, or provides additional information necessary to the implementation of the accord.

mid-course phase The flight of ballistic missile warheads through space after the boost phase but before re-entry (lasting 20-25 minutes for a typical ICBM.)

missile experimental (MX) A US ICBM, now called the Peacekeeper, which has 10 highly accurate MIRVed warheads. It is now deployed in silos and may be deployed on railroad cars.

mobile ICBM launcher Launching platform for an ICBM that can move or be moved from one location to another. Two common types of mobile ICBM launchers are "rail mobile" and "road mobile" systems.

multiple independently targetable reentry vehicle (MIRV) A package of two or more warheads which can be carried by a single ballistic missile but are deliverable to separate targets. (See fractionation)

Mutual and Balanced Force Reductions (MBFR) Multilateral negotiations (1973-1989) among the US, the USSR, and European nations which sought to limit NATO and Warsaw Pact conventional forces.

mutual assured destruction (MAD) The present situation in which the superpowers have the ability to inflict an unacceptable degree of damage upon each other even after absorbing a first strike; a condition which deters both sides from initiating hostilities.

National Command Authority (NCA) The President and the Secretary of Defense or their duly deputized alternates; the only entity which can authorize the use of nuclear weapons.

National Emergency Airborne Command Post (NEACAP) Plane stationed at Grissom Air Force Base, Indiana, which stands ready to rendezvous with a White House helicopter and evacuate the President in the event of a nuclear war, and from which the President or his successor could command a nuclear strike. Also called the doomsday plane.

national technical means (NTM) Intelligence gathering systems under national control, such as photo-reconnaissance satellites and ground based radars, used to monitor compliance with agreed arms limitations.

no-first-use doctrine A doctrine which commits a nation not to use nuclear weapons first in a war. (See first use)

North American Aerospace Defense Command (NORAD) US-Canadian headquarters responsible for global aerospace surveillance and the defense of North America against aircraft and missile attack.

North Atlantic Treaty Organization A security alliance formed in 1949 to defend against possible Soviet aggression. Members include the US, Belgium, Britain, Canada, Denmark, France, Greece, Iceland, Italy, Luxembourg, Netherlands, Norway, Portugal, Spain, Turkey, and West Germany.

nuclear freeze The generic term for proposals calling for a halt to the testing, production and deployment of some or all nuclear weapons and delivery systems.

Nuclear Risk Reduction Centers (NRRCs) Centers in the US and USSR, agreed to in 1987, to facilitate information exchange relating to current and future arms control treaties and to missile tests, naval maneuvers, and other military activities.

Nuclear and Space Arms Talks (NST) Negotiations between the US and USSR initiated in 1985, which encompass three sets of talks on defense and space, INF, and START.

nuclear weapons-free zone An area in which the production, deployment, and possibly passage of nuclear weapons is prohibited.

nuclear winter A potential consequence of nuclear war, where smoke from burning urban areas would cause a severe worldwide drop in temperature, lasting for weeks or months with large scale ecological impacts.

on-site inspection (OSI) A means of verification which involves visits to actual or suspect weapon production or deployment sites by representatives of the other party or parties to an agreement, or by an international authority.

Open Skies Proposal Eisenhower administration plan which would have permitted each superpower to conduct aerial inspection of the other to build confidence and to prevent suspicion or miscalculation.

parity A balance of forces where the overall capabilities of opposing nations are roughly equivalent.

passive defense The protection of civil or military targets by changes made to the targets themselves, as opposed to "active" measures taken to intercept incoming weapons. Passive defense measures for civilian targets include fallout shelters and other forms of civil defense. Military targets can be passively defended by hardening, camouflage, dispersal, and other techniques.

payload The weapons and penetration aids carried by a delivery vehicle (i.e., ballistic missile or aircraft). Sometimes refers to the carrying capacity of the delivery vehicle.

peaceful nuclear explosion (PNE) The non-military use of nuclear detonations for purposes such as stimulating natural gas, diverting rivers, or canal excavation.

penetrability The ability of a nuclear missile or bomber to pass through active defenses.

penetration aids Techniques and/or devices employed to overcome an opponent's defenses.

Permissive Action Link (PAL) Locks which prevent a nuclear weapon from being used without proper authorization.

phase one deployment Projected first stage of deployment for the Strategic Defense Intiative, consisting of ground-based and space-based interceptors, providing only a partial defense against Soviet attack.

phased-array radar A radar which electronically points its beam in different directions without mechanically moving an antenna. Phased-array radars have the speed and accuracy needed for advanced defenses, such as anti-ballistic missile (ABM) systems, and are specifically limited by the ABM Treaty.

plutonium An extremely toxic chemical element which is radioactive, and is capable of releasing tremendous quantities of energy by undergoing nuclear fission. Plutonium is not found in nature, but is created as a waste product of nuclear reactors.

point defense Defense of an individual target.

post-boost phase The period of ballistic missile flight between the final burnout of the booster and the deployment of re-entry vehicles.

post-boost vehicle (PBV) Also known as the "bus." A small rocket carrying one or more nuclear warheads which maneuvers after the boost phase to release each warhead at a specific point with a specific velocity to assure that it is on the trajectory to its separate target. All MIRVed missiles and some single-warhead missiles are equipped with PBVs.

pounds per square inch (psi) A measure of nuclear blast overpressure or dynamic pressure, used to cal-culate the effects of a nuclear detonation or the ability of a structure to withstand a nuclear blast.

precision-guided munition (PGM) Also known as a "smart weapon." PGMs contain sensors and guidance systems which allow them to home in on individual targets.

preemptive strike A damage-limiting attack launched against an opponent's forces in anticipation of an attack.

proliferation The spread of nuclear weapons to states not previously possessing them. Sometimes refered to as "horizontal" proliferation to distinguish it from "vertical" proliferation in an existing nuclear weapons state.

qualitative limitations Restrictions on the type or capability of a weapon system as distinct from limits on the number of warheads or strategic delivery vehicles. In SALT II, such qualitative limitations include a prohibition on more than one new type of ICBM for each side, restrictions on missile launch-weight and throw-weight, and limitations on the number of re-entry vehicles a missile may carry.

quantitative limitations Limits on the number of weapon systems in certain categories.

radar A technique or system for detecting objects by transmitting radio waves (e.g., microwaves) and sensing the waves reflected by the target. The reflected waves provide information on the distance and direction, and sometimes the velocity, size, and shape of the target.

rational sufficiency Alternative nuclear policy discussed in the Carter administration. Proponents of rational sufficiency argued that the US nuclear arsenal was sufficiently large and diverse to inflict unacceptable damage on the Soviet Union even after a Soviet first strike, and that this capability served as an effective deterrent.

reentry vehicle (RV) That part of a ballistic missile which contains a nuclear warhead and is designed to re-enter the earth's atmosphere in the terminal portion of the missile's trajectory.

reload capability The capacity of a missile launcher to receive and fire a new weapon within a reasonable period after initial launch. If the period is quite short, the launcher is said to have rapid reload capability.

reprocessing plant A facility required to separate the uranium and plutonium present in spent reactor fuel. The plutonium recovered through reprocessing can be reused as reactor fuel or for nuclear explosives.

salvage fuzing A fuzing system whereby a weapon detonates when attacked or threatened with destruction. Salvage fuzing is a commonly proposed counter-measure to ABM systems, since the detonation of a warhead when intercepted might still cause some damage, or could make subsequent interceptions difficult.

sea-launched cruise missile (SLCM) See cruise missile.

second strike A strategic nuclear retaliation to an opponent's first strike.

short-range attack missile (SRAM) A nuclear air-to-surface missile, such as those deployed on B-52s, designed to attack ground targets and particularly to suppress enemy air defenses.

single integrated operational plan (SIOP) United States targeting and strike plan for waging nuclear war with the Soviet Union.

site defense See point defense.

space mine A satellite carrying an explosive charge that would serve as an ASAT system by tracking or maneuvering into the vicinity of a hostile satellite and exploding on command to destroy the satellite.

Special Verification Commission (SVC) Commission established by the INF Treaty, where U.S. and Soviet representatives will resolve questions relating to implementation of and compliance with the obligations assumed under the treaty and will agree upon measures needed to improve the viability and effectiveness of the treaty. The SVC is separate and distinct from the Standing Consultative Commission, which performed similar duties under previous arms control agreements.

Standing Consultative Commission (SCC) A US-Soviet committee established in accordance with the provisions of the SALT I agreements and incorporated into SALT II. The SCC must meet at least twice a year to address questions of compliance with the provisions of the treaties and establishment of procedures to implement the treaties.

Star Wars See Strategic Defense Initiative.

stealth technology A combination of structural design and utilization of special materials to shield aircraft and missiles from detection by an adversary's radar detection systems.

stockpile The total supply of weapons, including those currently deployed and those in storage.

strategic Relating to the war-making capabilities of a nation, strategic forces are those designed to attack the homeland of an adversary and destroy his war-making potential. (See tactical and theater.)

Strategic Air Command (SAC) Branch of the US Air Force that oversees land-based nuclear missiles and long-range bombers.

Strategic Arms Limitation Talks (SALT) Negotiations between the United States and the USSR between 1969 and 1979 which sought to limit the strategic nuclear forces of both sides, and resulted in the 1972 SALT I Agreement, the 1972 ABM Treaty, and 1979 SALT II Treaty.

Strategic Arms Reduction Talks (START) Negotiations between the US and the USSR, initiated in June 1982, to seek reductions in the strategic offensive arsenals of both sides.

Strategic Defense Intiative (SDI) Program, initiated by President Reagan in 1983, to develop an advanced ballistic missile defense.

strategic nuclear delivery vehicle (SNDV) Delivery vehicle designed to carry nuclear warheads over intercontinental range. Refers to ICBMs, SLBMs, and strategic bombers.

submarine-launched ballistic missile (SLBM) A ballistic missile deployed on a submarine.

surface-to-air missile (SAM) A ground-launched missile designed for use against incoming enemy bombers.

tactical Relating to battlefield operations as distinguished from theater or strategic operations. Tactical weapons or forces are those designed for combat with opposing military forces rather than for striking an opponent's homeland. (See strategic and theater.)

tactical nuclear weapon See battlefield nuclear weapon

telemetry Electronic signals transmitted from a missile during a flight test to provide information about the missile's performance.

terminal phase The final phase of a ballistic missile trajectory, lasting about a minute or less, in which the RVs reenter the atmosphere and fall toward their targets.

theater Relating to the specific geographic area of battle and the land, sea and air activities within that zone.

thermonuclear bomb A nuclear weapon that derives a significant fraction of energy from a fusion reaction.

throw-weight The maximum weight of the warheads, dispensing and guidance units, and penetration aids which can be delivered by a missile over a particular range in a stated trajectory.

triad The traditional nomenclature for the three components of US and Soviet strategic nuclear forces—land-based intercontinental ballistic missiles; submarine-launched ballistic missiles; and strategic bombers.

verification Monitoring the party to a treaty's compliance with treaty provisions, either by national technical means and/or on-site inspection and other cooperative measures.

Vladivostok Agreement Joint statement outlining a framework for SALT II, signed by US President Ford and Soviet General Secretary Brezhnev, in Vladivostok on November 24, 1974.

war-fighting strategy A nuclear strategy focused on fighting wars with nuclear weapons rather than on preventing their occurrence.

warhead That part of a missile, torpedo, rocket, or other munition which contains the nuclear, conventional, chemical or other component intended to damage or destroy a target.

Warsaw Treaty Organization (WTO) An Eastern European security alliance formed in 1955. Members include the USSR, Bulgaria, Cszechoslovakia, East Germany, Hungary, Poland, and Romania.

yield The force of a nuclear explosion, frequently expressed as the equivalent of energy produced by tons of TNT. (See kiloton and megaton.)

Appendix V: Major Post-War Arms Control Agreements, 1959-1988

1959 Antarctic Treaty: Twelve nation agreement to protect the peaceful status of the Antarctic Continent. Bans the following from Antarctica:
- establishment of military bases or fortifications;
- military maneuvers;
- stationing or testing of any type of weapon;
- nuclear explosions; and
- radioactive waste disposal.

The Treaty provides each party with the right to full on-site and aerial inspections of all Antarctic installations in order to verify these provisions.

1963 Hot Line Agreement: Bilateral agreement establishing a direct communications link between US and Soviet heads of state for use in "time of emergency." Seeks to reduce the risk of a nuclear exchange stemming from accident, miscalculation, or surprise attack. Both sides connected by transatlantic cable and radio telegraph circuits for continuous direct communications. Updated by a 1971 agreement to include two US-USSR satellite communications circuits, along with multiple terminals in each country.

1963 Limited Test Ban Treaty (LTBT): Trilateral Agreement negotiated by the US, USSR, and UK prohibiting tests of nuclear devices in the atmosphere, in outer space, and under water. Allows nuclear testing to continue underground, so long as radioactive debris is not allowed "outside the territorial limits" of the state conducting the test. The three original signatories also pledged to seek "the discontinuance of all test explosions of nuclear weapons for all time." The Treaty has since been signed by a total of 116 countries, including potential nuclear states Argentina, Brazil, India, Israel, Pakistan, and South Africa. Though two major nuclear powers, France and the People's Republic of China, have not signed, they are now abiding by its provisions.

1967 Outer Space Treaty: Trilateral agreement between the US, USSR, and UK banning:
- placement of nuclear weapons or "weapons of mass destruction" in orbit around the Earth;
- installation of nuclear weapons or "weapons of mass destruction" on the moon, on any other celestial body, or in outer space itself; and
- use of moon or any other celestial body for military purposes, including weapons testing of any kind, military maneuvers, and the construction of military installations.

The Treaty guarantees the right of any party to inspect installations and equipment of other signatories based on any celestial body to ensure compliance with these provisions. Eighty-six other countries have since signed the agreement.

1967 Latin American Nuclear Weapon Free Zone or "Tlatelolco" Treaty: Multilateral agreement signed by 24 Latin American countries banning the manufacture, acquisition, testing, deployment, or use of nuclear weapons in Latin America. Argentina has not yet ratified the treaty and Cuba is the only country that has neither signed nor ratified the treaty. Two protocols are attached: The first protocol, which calls upon nations outside of the treaty zone to apply these provisions to their territories within the zone has been signed by all four countries with such territories (the US, UK, the Netherlands, and France), although France has not yet ratified it; the second protocol which pledges adherence to the denuclearization of Latin America and renouncing the use or threatened use of nuclear weapons against any of the 24 Contracting Parties has been signed and ratified by all five nuclear powers—the US, USSR, France, UK, and the People's Republic of China.

1968 Nuclear Non-Proliferation Treaty (NPT): Multilateral agreement signed and ratified by the US, USSR, UK, and 133 non-nuclear-weapon states to prevent the spread of nuclear weapons and to assure that the peaceful nuclear programs of non-nuclear-weapon states are not diverted to weapons production. Non-nuclear-weapons signatories specifically pledged not to develop, manufacture, or acquire nuclear weapons. In turn, the nuclear-weapon powers agreed to share "the applications of nuclear energy for peaceful purposes" with non-nuclear-weapon signatories on a "nondiscriminatory basis." The parties agreed to prohibit the exportation of nuclear weapons and to regulate peaceful nuclear exports and programs through international safeguards, carried out by the International Atomic Energy Agency (IAEA). The three nuclear weapons parties also agreed to pursue negotiations "in good faith on effective measures relating to cessation of the nuclear arms race at an early date."

1971 Seabed Treaty: Multilateral agreement between the US, USSR, UK, and 84 other countries banning the emplacement of nuclear weapons or "weapons of mass destruction" on the ocean floor beyond a 12-mile coastal zone. Allows signatories to observe all seabed "activities" of any other signatory beyond the 12-mile zone in order to ensure compliance.

1971 "Accidents Measures" Agreement: Bilateral agreement between the US and USSR obligating both sides to improve "existing organizational and technical arrangements to guard against the accidental or unauthorized use of nuclear weapons." Each party pledged to notify the other in case of any accidental or unintentional use of nuclear weapons or any other occurrence which could risk the outbreak of nuclear war and to warn the other in advance of any planned missile flight tests extending beyond its national territory and aimed to land in international waters.

1972 Biological Weapons Convention: Multilateral agreement between the US, USSR, UK, and 108 other countries banning the development, production, stockpiling or acquistion of biological agents or toxins capable of being used in weapons and of the equipment associated with their use. The parties also pledged to destroy or divert to peaceful purposes all such agents or equipment within nine months.

1972 SALT I ABM Treaty (Amended in 1974): Bilateral ratified treaty of "unlimited duration" between the US and USSR limiting each side's anti-ballistic missile (ABM) systems in order to prevent the deployment of nationwide ABM defenses, or a base for such a system. Each country is restricted to a single deployment area of 100 ABM launchers and missiles. The Treaty prohibits the development, testing and deployment of space-based, sea-based, air-based and mobile land-based systems and components. Precise qualitative and quantitative limits regulate these deployments and restrain future improvements of ABM technologies. Specific provisions also restrain the upgrading of air-defense systems and early-warning radars for anti-ballistic missile defense. Compliance is monitored by national technical means of verification and overseen by a Standing Consultative Commission, which is to be used to promote the objectives and implementation of the agreement.

1972 SALT I Interim Agreement: Bilateral agreement between the US and USSR of five-year duration which froze the number of strategic ballistic missile launchers at 1972 levels. Construction of additional land-based ICBM silos is prohibited, while SLBM launcher levels can be increased if corresponding reductions are made in older ICBM or SLBM launchers. Modernization of launchers is allowed, however, if kept within specific dimensions. As under the ABM Treaty, both parties pledge not to impede or interfere

with national technical means of verification used to monitor compliance and to use the Standing Consultative Commission to solve compliance problems.

1973 Prevention of Nuclear War Agreement: Bilateral agreement between the US and USSR obligating them to make the prevention of nuclear war an "objective of their policies." Both sides also pledged not to use or threaten to use force in any way which may "endanger international peace and security" and to conduct "urgent negotiations" at any time in which there is a risk of nuclear war.

1974 Threshold Test Ban Treaty (TTBT): Bilateral, unratified agreement between the US and USSR prohibiting underground nuclear weapon tests with yields above 150 kilotons. Compliance is monitored through the use of national technical means (e.g. seismic stations outside the testing country). A protocol to the agreement specified that tests take place at strictly defined testing sites and that upon ratification technical information be exchanged to improve verification procedures.

1975 Helsinki Accords: A multilateral agreement among 35 nations, including the US, USSR, and most European countries, reached at the Conference on Security and Cooperation in Europe, providing for cooperation in human rights, economics, and security. Most importantly, the accords codified the postwar European boundaries.

1976 Peaceful Nuclear Explosions Treaty (PNET): Bilateral, unratified agreement between the US and USSR prohibiting peaceful nuclear explosions, which were not covered by the TTBT, with yields exceeding 150 kilotons and group explosions (i.e. a number of individual explosions used for excavation purposes) having an aggregate yield of over 1,500 kilotons, no one of which can be more than 150 kilotons. A companion treaty to the TTBT, the PNET provides for verification through national technical means, data exchanges and visits to sites of explosions in certain instances. It also establishes a Joint Consultative Commission to deal with compliance and implementation concerns.

1977 Environmental Modification Convention: Multilateral agreement with 48 signatories prohibiting the hostile use of "environmental modification techniques" with widespread and long-lasting effects.

1979 SALT II Treaty: Bilateral, unratified agreement between the US and USSR setting equal aggregate ceilings and subceilings on strategic offensive weapon systems and imposing qualitative restraints on existing and future strategic systems. Specifically, the SALT II equal ceilings include:

- 2,400 aggregate limit on strategic nuclear delivery vehicles (ICBMs, SLBMs, and heavy bombers) upon entry into force; to be reduced to 2,250;
- 1,320 subceiling on MIRVed ballistic missile launchers and heavy bombers with long-range cruise missiles;
- 1,200 subceiling on MIRVed ballistic missiles; and
- 820 subceiling on MIRVed, land-based ICBMs.

As under the SALT I agreements, compliance under SALT II is monitored through national technical means of verification, along with provisions covering non-interference with or concealment from verification systems, and use of the Standing Consultative Commission to resolve treaty problems. In 1986 the U.S. repudiated its political commitment to remain within the SALT II limits.

1985 South Pacific Nuclear Free Zone Treaty: Multilateral agreement among the nations of the South Pacific, which prohibits the testing, manufacture, and stationing of nuclear explosive devices, and the dumping of nuclear waste, within the zone.

1986 Stockholm Agreement: Multilateral agreement by the US, the USSR, and 33 European nations reached in September 1986 at the Conference on Disarmament in Europe (CDE), providing for a series of confidence building measures relating to advance notification of large military exercises in Europe.

1987 Nuclear Risk Reduction Centers Agreement: Bilateral agreement between the US and the USSR, establishing national Risk Reduction Centers in the capital of each country. The centers facilitate government-to-government communication via direct satellite links (facsimile communications) and serve as confidence building measures intended to reduce the risk of accidental war.

1987 INF Treaty: Bilateral ratified treaty between the US and USSR, which requires parties to eliminate all intemediate-range missiles (IRMs), shorter-range missiles (SRMs), and associated launchers, equipment, support facilities, and operating bases worldwide and to ban flight testing and production of these missiles as well as production of their launchers. Compliance is monitored using national technical means, five types of on-site inspection, and cooperative measures. The treaty establishes the Special Verification Commission (SVC) to "resolve questions relating to compliance with the obligations assumed" under the treaty.

1988 Ballistic Missile Launch Notification Agreement: Bilateral agreement between the US and USSR requiring each nation to notify the other party, "no less than twenty-four hours in advance, of the planned date, launch area, and area of impact for any launch of a strategic ballistic missile."

Appendix VI: Select Bibliography

General

Blacker, Coit D., and Gloria Duffy, eds. *International Arms Control: Issues and Agreements*. Palo Alto, CA: Stanford University Press, 2nd Edition, 1984, 502pp.

Bundy, McGeorge. *Danger and Survival: Choices About the Bomb in the First Fifty Years*. New York, NY: Random House, 1988, 735pp.

Carnesale, Albert and Richard N. Haass, eds. *Superpower Arms Control: Setting the Record Straight*. Cambridge, MA: Ballinger, 1987, 392pp.

Chant, Christopher. *Compendium of Armaments and Military Hardware*. New York, NY: Routledge and Kegan Paul, 1987, 568pp.

Dyson, Freeman. *Weapons and Hope*. New York, NY: Harper and Row, l984, 340pp.

Freedman, Lawrence. *The Evolution of Nuclear Strategy*. New York, NY: St. Martin's Press, 1981, 473pp.

Freedman, Lawrence. *The Price of Peace: Living with the Nuclear Dilemma*. New York, NY: Holt, 1986, 288pp.

George, Alexander L., Philip J. Farley, and Alexander Dallin, eds. *US-Soviet Security Cooperation: Achievements, Failures, Lessons*. New York, NY: Oxford University Press, 1988, 746pp.

Halperin, Morton. *Nuclear Fallacy: Dispelling the Myth of Nuclear Strategy*. Cambridge, MA: Ballinger, 1987, 168pp.

Halloran, Bernard F., ed. *Essays on Arms Control and National Security*. Washington, DC: US ACDA, 1986, 395pp.

Krepon, Michael. *Strategic Stalemate: Nuclear Weapons and Arms Control in American Politics*. New York, NY: St. Martin's Press, 1984, 64pp.

Krepon, Michael and Mary Umberger. *Verification and Compliance: A Problem Solving Approach*. New York, NY: McMillian, 1988, 308pp.

Kull, Steven. *Minds At War: Nuclear Reality and the Inner Conflicts of Defense Policymakers*. New York, NY: Basic Books, 1988, 341pp.

McNamara, Robert S. *Blundering Into Disaster: Surviving The First Century of the Nuclear Age*. New York, NY: Pantheon Books, 1986, 212pp.

Morris, Charles R. *Iron Destinies, Lost Opportunities: The Arms Race Between the U.S.A. and the U.S.S.R., 1945-1987*. New York: Harper & Row, 1988, 544pp.

National Academy of Sciences. *Nuclear Arms Control: Background & Issues*. Washington, DC: National Academy Press, 1985, 378pp.

Newhouse, John. *War and Peace in the Nuclear Age*. New York, NY: Alfred A. Knopf, 1989, 486pp.

Nye, Joseph S., Jr., Graham T. Allison, and Albert Carnesale. *Fateful Visions: Avoiding Nuclear Catastrophe*. Cambridge, MA: Ballinger, 1988, 299pp.

Osgood, Robert E. *The Nuclear Dilemma in American Strategic Thought*. Boulder, Co: Westview Press, 1988, 138pp.

Rhodes, Richard. *The Making of the Atomic Bomb*. New York, NY: Simon and Schuster, 1986, 886pp.

Scott, Robert Travis, ed. *The Race for Security: Arms and Arms Control in the Reagan Years*. Lexington, MA: Lexington Books, 1986, 292pp. Selections from *Arms Control Today*, 1981-1986.

Seaborg, Glenn T., and Robert Martson, eds. *Stemming the Tide: Arms Control in the Johnson Years*. Lexington, MA: Lexington Books, 1987, 495pp.

Segal, Gerald, ed. *Arms Control in Asia*. New York, NY: St. Martin's Press, 1987, 182pp.

Smoke, Richard. *National Security and the Nuclear Dilemma: An Introduction to the American Experience*. New York, NY: Random House, 1987, 336pp.

Talbott, Strobe. *The Master of the Game: Paul Nitze and the Nuclear Peace*. New York, NY: Alfred A. Knopf, 1988, 416pp.

Tsipis, Kosta. *Arsenal: Understanding Weapons in the Nuclear Age*. New York, NY: Simon and Schuster, 1983, 342pp.

US Congress. House. Committee on Foreign Affairs. Subcommittee on Arms Control and International Security and Science. *Fundamentals of Nuclear Arms Control*. Washington, DC: US GPO, 1986, 424pp.

York, Herbert F. *Making Weapons, Talking Peace: A Physicist's Odyssey From Hiroshima to Geneva*. New York, NY: Basic Books, 1987, 389pp.

Effects of Nuclear Weapons

Katz, Arthur M. *Life After Nuclear War: The Economic and Social Impacts of Nuclear Attacks on the United States*. Cambridge, MA: Ballinger, 1981, 464pp.

National Research Council. *The Effects on the Atmosphere of a Major Nuclear Exchange*. Washington, DC: National Academy Press, l985, 193pp.

Solomon, Frederic and Robert Martson, eds. *The Medical Implications of Nuclear War*. Washington, DC: National Academy Press, 1986, 619pp.

U.S. Office of Technology Assessment. *The Effects of Nuclear War*. Washington, DC: US GPO, l980, 283pp. The results of this study are reprinted in Michael Riordan, ed. *The Day After Midnight: The Effects of Nuclear War*. Palo Alto, CA: Cheshire Books, 1982, 144pp.

The Soviet Union and Arms Control

Berman, J., and John C. Baker. *Soviet Strategic Forces: Requirements and Responses*. Washington, DC: Brookings Institution, 1982, 171pp.

English, Robert D., and John J. Halperin. *The Other Side: How Soviets and Americans Perceive Each Other*. New Brunswick, NJ: Transaction Books, 1987, 155pp.

Garthoff, Raymond L. *Detente and Confrontation: American-Soviet Relations from Nixon to Reagan*. Washington, DC: The Brookings Institution, 1985, 1147pp.

Holloway, David. *The Soviet Union and the Arms Race*. New Haven, CT: Yale University Press, 1983, 211pp.

Sherr, Alan B. *The Other Side of Arms Control: Soviet Objectives in the Arms Control Era*. Winchester, MA: Unwin Hyman, 1988, 325pp.

SALT

Arms Control Association. *Countdown on SALT II*. Washington, DC: ACA and the Ploughshares Fund, 1985, 68pp.

Newhouse, John. *Cold Dawn: The Story of SALT*. New York, NY: Holt, Rinehart & Winston, 1973, 302pp.

Smith, Gerard. *Doubletalk: The Story of SALT I*. Lanham, MD: University Press of America, 1985, 566pp.

Talbott, Strobe. *Endgame: The Inside Story of SALT II*. New York, NY: Harper and Row, 1979, 319pp.

Willrich, Mason, and John B. Rhinelander. *SALT: The Moscow Agreements and Beyond*. London, UK: The Free Press, 1974, 361pp.

Wolfe, Thomas. *The SALT Experience*. Cambridge, MA: Ballinger, 1979, 405pp.

ABMs and ASATS

Boffey, Philip M., et.al. *Claiming the Heavens: The New York Times Complete Guide to the Star Wars Debate*. New York, NY: Times Books, 1988, 299pp.

Boutwell, Jeffrey, Donald Hafner, and Franklin Long, eds. *Weapons in Space: The Politics and Technology of BMD and ASAT Weapons*. New York, NY: W.W. Norton, 1985, 386pp.

Bruce, James T., Bruce W. MacDonald, and Ronald L. Tammen. *Star Wars at the Crossroads: The Strategic Defense Initiative Organization after Five Years*. Washington, DC: Office of Senator Bennett Johnson, June 12, 1988, 108pp.

Carter, Ashton and David Schwartz. *Ballistic Missile Defense*. Washington, DC: Brookings Institution, 1984, 455pp.

Durch, William J. *The ABM Treaty and Western Security*. Cambridge, MA: Ballinger, 1989, 161pp.

Garthoff, Raymond L. *Policy vs. Law: The Reinterpretation of the ABM Treaty*. Washington, DC: Brookings Institution, 1987, 117pp.

National Campaign to Save the ABM Treaty. *Briefing Book on the ABM Treaty and Related Issues*. Washington, DC: 1986, 50pp.

Nye, Joseph, Jr. and James A. Schear. *On The Defensive?: The Future of Strategic Defense Initiative*. Lanham, MD: The University Press of America for the Aspen Strategy Group, 1988, 205pp.

Nye, Joseph S. and James A. Schear, eds. *Seeking Stability in Space: Anti-Satellite Weapons and The Evolving Space Regime*. Lanham, MD: Aspen Strategy Group and University Press of America, 1987, 167pp.

Stares, Paul. *The Militarization of Space*. Ithaca, NY: Cornell University Press, 1985, 334pp.

Stares, Paul B. *Space and National Security*. Washington, DC: The Brookings Institution, May 1987, 210pp.

Union of Concerned Scientists, John Tirman. ed. *Empty Promise: The Growing Case Against Star Wars*. Boston, MA: Beacon Press, 1986, 238pp.

US Congress, Office of Technology Assessment. *Ballistic Missile Defense Technologies, Anti-Satellite Weapons, Countermeasures, and Arms Control*. Princeton, NJ: Princeton University Press, 1986, 460pp.

Command and Control

Bracken, Paul. *The Command and Control of Nuclear Forces*. New Haven, CT: Yale University Press, 1983, 252pp.

Carter, Ashton B., John D. Steinbruner, and Charles A. Zraket, eds. *Managing Nuclear Operations*. Washington, DC: Brookings Institution, 1987, 751pp.

Ford, Daniel. *The Button: The Pentagon's Strategic Command and Control*. New York, NY: Simon and Schuster, 1985, 270pp.

Lebow, Richard Ned. *Nuclear Crisis Management: A Dangerous Illusion*. Ithaca, NY: Cornell University Press, 1987, 232pp.

Pringle, Peter, and William Arkin. *S.I.O.P.: The Secret U.S. Plan for Nuclear War*. New York, NY: W.W. Norton & Co., 1983, 287pp.

Ury, William L. *Beyond the Hotline: How Crisis Control Can Prevent Nuclear War*. New York, NY: Penguin Books, 1986, 187pp.

Nuclear Weapons in Europe

Kelleher, Catherine M. and Gale A. Mattox. *Evolving European Defense Policies*. Lexington, MA: Lexington Books, 1987, 340pp.

Rudney, Robert and Luc Reychler, eds. *European Security Beyond the Year 2000*. New York, NY: Praeger, 1988, 317pp.

Schwartz, David N. *NATO's Nuclear Dilemmas*. Washington, DC: The Brookings Institution, 1983, 270pp.

Nuclear Weapons Testing

Fetter, Steve. *Toward A Comprehensive Test Ban.* Cambridge, MA: Ballinger, 1988, 205pp.

Joeck, Neil, and Herbert York. *Countdown on the Comprehensive Test Ban.* University of California Institute on Global Conflict and Cooperation and Ploughshares Fund, 1986, 20pp.

Miller, Richard L. *Under the Cloud: The Decades of Nuclear Testing.* New York, NY: The Free Press, 1986, 547pp.

Natural Resources Defense Council. *Known Soviet Nuclear Explosions, 1949-1985 Preliminary List.* Washington, DC: NRDC, 1989.

Natural Resources Defense Council. *Known US Nuclear Tests July 1945 to 31 December 1985.* Washington, DC: NRDC, 1988.

Seaborg, Glenn T. *Kennedy, Khrushchev, and the Test Ban.* Berkeley, CA: University of California, 1981, 320pp.

Nuclear Proliferation

Congressional Research Service. Joint Committee Print. House Committee on Foreign Affairs and Senate Committee on Governmental Affairs. *Nuclear Proliferation Factbook.* Washington, DC: US GPO, 1985, 591pp.

Council on Foreign Relations. *Blocking the Spread of Nuclear Weapons: American and European Perspectives.* New York, NY: Council on Foreign Relations, 1986, 183pp.

Dewitt, David, ed. *Nuclear Non-Proliferation and Global Security.* Beckenham, UK: Croom Helm for the Research Programme in Strategic Studies, York University, Ontario, 1986, 304pp.

Goldblat, Jozef, ed. *Nonproliferation: The Why and the Wherefore.* London, UK: Taylor and Francis, 1985, 343pp.

Jones, Rodney, Cesare Merlini, Joseph Pilak, and William Potter, eds. *The Nuclear Suppliers and Non-Proliferation.* Center For Strategic and International Studies. Washington, DC: Lexington Books, 1985, 253pp.

Lewis, John Wilson, and Xue Litai. *China Builds the Bomb.* Stanford, CA: Stanford University, 1988, 329pp.

Reiss, Mitchell. *Without The Bomb: The Politics of Nuclear Nonproliferation.* New York, NY: Columbia University Press, 1988, 337pp.

Simpson, John. *Nuclear Non-Proliferation: An Agenda for the 1990's.* Cambridge, UK: Cambridge University Press, 1987, 237pp.

Spector, Leonard S. *Going Nuclear.* Cambridge, MA: Ballinger, 1987, 370pp.

Spector, Leonard S. *The New Nuclear Nations: The Spread of Nuclear Weapons.* Cambridge, MA: Vintage, 1985, 367pp.

Spector, Leonard S. *The Undeclared Bomb: The Spread of Nuclear Weapons 1987-1988.* Cambridge, MA: Ballinger, 1988, 499pp.

CBW

Aspen Strategy Group. *Chemical Weapons and Western Security Policy.* Lanham, MD: The University Press of America for the Aspen Strategy Group and European Strategy Group in cooperation with the Aspen Institute Berlin, 1986, 55pp.

Sims, Nicholas A. *The Diplomacy of Biological Disarmamnent: Vicissitudes of a Treaty in Force, 1975-1985.* New York: St. Martin's, 1988, 356pp.

Stringer, Hugh. *Deterring Chemical Warfare: US Policy Options for the l990s.* Washington, DC: Pergamon Brassey, l986, 76pp.

Conventional Forces

Boutwell, Jeffrey, William Ayres, John P. Holdren, and Catherine McArdle Kelleher. *Countdown on Conventional Forces in Europe: A Briefing Book.* Cambridge, MA: American Academy of Arts and Sciences and Ploughshares Fund, 1988, 24pp.

Borawski, John, ed. *Avoiding War in the Nuclear Age: Confidence-Building Measures for Crisis Stability.* Boulder, CO: Westview Press, 1986.

Borawski, John. *From the Atlantic to the Urals: Negotiating Arms Control at the Stockholm Conference.* Washington, DC: Pergamon-Brassey's, 1988, 261pp.

Dean, Jonathan. *Watershed in Europe: Dismantling the East-West Military Confrontation.* Lexington, MA: Lexington Books, l987, 304pp.

Ferrari, Paul L., Raul L. Madrid, and Jeff Knopf. *U.S. Arms Exports: Policies & Contractors, 1988 edition.* Cambridge, MA: Ballinger, 1988, 476pp.

Verification and Compliance

Arms Control Association. *Analysis of the President's Report on Soviet Noncompliance with Arms Control Agreements.* Washington, DC: The Arms Control Association, March 12, 1987, 20pp.

Duffy, Gloria. *Compliance and the Future of Arms Control.* Cambridge, MA: Ballinger, 1988, 258pp.

Krass, Allan S. *Verification: How Much is Enough?* Philadelphia, PA: Taylor & Francis, 1985, 300pp.

Scribner, Richard A, Theodore J. Ralston, William D. Metz. *The Verification Challenge: Problems of Strategic Nuclear Arms Control Verification.* Boston, MA: Birkhauser, 1985, 249pp.

Tsipis, Kosta, David W. Hafemeister, and Penny Janeway, eds. *Arms Control Verification: The Technologies that Make it Possible.* Washington, DC: Pergamon-Brassey's, 1986, 419pp.

Reference Works

Arkin, William, Thomas Cochran, and Milton M. Hoenig. *Nuclear Weapons Databook: U.S. Nuclear Forces and Capabilities.* Cambridge, MA: Ballinger, 1984, 342pp.

Arkin, William M., Robert S. Norris and Thomas B. Cochran. *The Bomb Book: The Nuclear Arms Race In Facts And Figures.* Washington, DC: Natural Resources Defense Council, December 1987, 59pp.

Cochran, Thomas B., William M. Arkin, Milton M. Hoenig, and Robert S. Norris. *Nuclear Weapons DataBook Volume II: U.S. Nuclear Warhead Production.* Cambridge, MA: Ballinger, 1987, 223pp.

Collins, John. *U.S.-Soviet Military Balance: 1980-1985.* Washington, DC: Pergamon-Brassey's, 1985, 400pp.

Institute for Defense and Disarmament Studies. *Peace Resource Book: A Comprehensive Guide to Issues, Groups, and Literature.* Cambridge, MA: Ballinger, 1986.

Kincade, William H. and Priscilla B. Hayner, eds. *The ACCESS Resource Guide: An International Directory Of Information On War, Peace, And Security 1988 Edition.* Cambridge, MA: Ballinger, 238pp.

US Arms Control and Disarmament Agency. *Arms Control and Disarmament Agreements: Texts and Histories of Negotiations.* Washington, DC: US GPO, 1982, 239pp.

Annual Private Publications

Center for the Study of Armament & Disarmament/Arms Control Association. *Arms Control, Disarmament, and International Security: An Annual Bibliography.* Claremont, CA: Regina Books.

International Institute for Strategic Studies. *The Military Balance* and *Strategic Survey.* London, UK: International Institute for Strategic Studies.

Kruzel, Joseph, ed. *American Defense Annual.* Lexington, MA: Lexington Books.

Royal United Services Institute (RUSI) and Brassey's *Defense Yearbook.* London, UK: Brassey's Defense Publishers.

Stockholm International Peace Research Institute. *World Armaments and Disarmament: The SIPRI Yearbook.* Oxford, UK: Oxford University Press.

United Nations Department of Disarmament Affairs. *The United Nations Disarmament Yearbook.* New York, NY: UN Department of Disarmament Affairs.

Official US Annual Publications

Strategic Defense Initiative Organization. *Report to Congress on the Strategic Defense Initiative.* Washington, DC: US Department of Defense.

US Arms Control and Disarmament Agency. *Annual Report to Congress.* Washington, DC: ACDA.

US Arms Control and Disarmament Agency. *Documents on Disarmament.* Washington, DC: US GPO.

US Arms Control And Disarmament Agency. Joint Committee Print. *Fiscal Year Arms Control Impact Statements.* Washington, DC: US GPO.

US Department of Defense. *Soviet Military Power.* Washington, DC: US GPO.

US Joint Chiefs of Staff. *Military Posture Statement.* Washington, DC: US GPO.

US Secretary of Defense. *Department of Defense Annual Report.* Washington, DC: US GPO.

Periodicals

Arms Control Today (Arms Control Association)

Arms Control: The Journal of Arms Control and Disarmament

Arms Control Reporter (Institute for Defense and Disarmament Studies)

Bulletin of Atomic Scientists (Educational Foundation for Nuclear Scientist, Inc.)

Chemical Weapons Convention Bulletin (Federation of American Scientists)

Defense Monitor (Center for Defense Information)

Defense News

Foreign Affairs (Council on Foreign Relations)

Foreign Policy (Carnegie Endowment for International Peace)

International Security (Harvard Center for Science & International Affairs)

Orbis (Foreign Policy Research Institute)

Science (American Association for the Advancement of Science)

Scientific American

Strategic Review (United States Strategic Institute)

Survival (International Institute for Strategic Studies)

World Policy Journal (World Policy Institute)

Illustration Credits

Chapter 1

Page 4: Associated Press. Page 6: Bill Fitzpatrick, The White House. Page 8: US Air Force. Page 10: Grzegorz Stanczyk.

Chapter 2

Pp. 16-17: 1. Soviet Premier Nikita Khruschev at the United Nations, September 18, 1959 (U.N.); 2. US Titan II ICBM in its silo (US Air Force); 3. Hiroshima devastation (No credit); 4. Model of the Sputnik satellite (Novosti); 5. *Enola Gay* B-29, the aircraft that delivered the Hiroshima bomb (Los Alamos National Laboratory); 6. Prime Minister Aleksei Kosygin and President Lyndon Johnson at the Glassboro summit, 1967 (Lyndon Baines Johnson Library); 7. The Berlin Wall, 1963 (Department of Defense); 8. Polaris missile launch, 1960 (Department of Defense); 9. President John F. Kennedy and Premier Nikita Khruschev at Vienna in 1961 (Black Star); 10. Mushroom cloud from Hiroshima (Department of Defense); 11. Lyndon Johnson (far right) looks on as Secretary of State Dean Rusk signs the Nuclear Proliferation Treaty, 1968. Page 18 (top): Los Alamos National Laboratory; (bottom): Los Alamos National Laboratory. Page 19 (Upper Right): Harry S. Truman Library; (Lower Right): Arms Control and Disarmament Agency. Page 20: US Air Force. Page 21: Dwight David Eisenhower Library. Page 22 (Right): US Air Force; (Upper Left): National Atomic Museum; (Lower Left): US Air Force. Page 23: John F. Kennedy Library. Page 24: US Air Force. Page 25: Lyndon Baines Johnson Library.

Chapter 3

Pp. 26-27: 1. President Reagan with Secretary of State George Shultz (standing) and advisers at the Rekjavik summit, 1986 (Pete Souza, The White House); 2. Three exposed MIRV warheads of a Minuteman III missile (Los Alamos National Laboratory); 3. President Nixon and Henry Kissinger; 4. B-52H bomber refueling, 1979 (US Air Force); 5. Test launch of a Trident I SLBM (US Navy); 6. Soviet Scud missile on parade (US Air Force); 7. (From left) Henry Kissinger, President Gerald Ford, and Soviet General Secretary Leonid Brezhnev at Vladivostok, 1974 (Gerald Ford Library); 8. Missile tubes open on the (Trident) US ballistic missile submarine Ohio (US Navy); 9. Pershing II missile during test launch (US Army); 10. President Reagan and Soviet leader Mikhail Gorbachev at the Washington summit, Dec. 1987 (Pete Souza, The White House). Page 28 (Upper Left): US Air Force; (Right): Nuclear Weapons Graphics Project. Page 29 (Lower Left and Lower Right): Nuclear Weapons Graphics Project; (Top): US Air Force. Page 30: The White House. Page 31 (Left): Gerald Ford Library; (Right): Jimmy Carter Library. Page 32 (Top Right): US Air Force; (Left): US Air Force; (Bottom Right): US Navy. Page 33: The White House. Page 34 (Top): *Soviet Military Power*; (Middle): Department of Defense; (Bottom): Department of Defense. Page 35: The White House. Page 36: David Valdez, The White House.

Chapter 4

Page 46: US Air Force. Page 48: *Soviet Military Power 1984*. Page 49: US Navy. Page 50: *Worldview*, Council on Religion and International Affairs.

Chapter 5

Page 52: Jimmy Carter Library. Page 54: Gerald Ford Library. Page 55: Arms Control Association. Page 56: Department of Defense. Page 57: US Air Force.

Chapter 6

Page 58: Robert Del Tredici. Page 61: Arms Control Association. Page 62 (Top): *Soviet Military Power 1987*; (Middle): US Navy; (Bottom): General Dynamics. Page 64: Terry Arthur, The White House.

Chapter 7

Page 66: Department of Defense. Page 68 (Left): US Army; (Top Left): US Army. Page 69 (Top Left): *Soviet Military Power 1985*; (Bottom): Department of Defense. Page 70: Arms Control and Disarmament Agency. Page 71: Raytheon. Page 72: No credit. Page 74: Department of Defense. Page 75: IEEE Spectrum, Sept. 1985. Page 76 (Top Left): Department of Defense; (Top Right): US Army; (Bottom): US Navy. Page 77 (Top): Lockheed Missiles and Space Company, Inc. Page 79 (Middle): McDonnell Douglas; (Bottom): Department of Defense. Page 80 (Top): Department of Defense; (Bottom): McDonnell Douglas Co. Page 81 (Top): Lockheed Missiles and Space Company, Inc; (Bottom): General Dynamics. Page 82 (Top): Department of Defense; (Bottom): TRW Inc. Page 83: Department of Defense. Page 85: *Soviet Military Power 1987*.

Chapter 8

Page 86: US Air Force. Page 88 (Upper left): Jim Ludtke illustrations; (Lower right): US Air Force. Page 89 (Upper right): US Air Force; (Lower left): US Air Force. Page 90: Paul B. Stares, *Space and National Security*, Brookings Institution, 1987.

Chapter 9

Page 92: Strategic Air Command. Page 94 (Left): TRW, Inc. Page 94: US Air Force. Page 95: US Air Force. Page 96: Robert Del Tredici. Page 97: Robert Del Tredici. Page 99: Pete Souza, The White House.

Chapter 10

Page 100: US Army. Page 102: Paul Valerry. Page 103 (Top right): US Army; (Bottom right): Novosti Press Agency. Page 105: US Army. Page 106: Arms Control Association. Page 107 (Top Right): Novosti; (Bottom left): Novosti. Page 108: Pete Souza, The White House.

Chapter 11

Page 110: US Department of Energy. Page 112,113,116,117: NRDC. Page 114 (Left): US Army; (Upper Right): ERDA Photo; (Lower Right): Los Alamos Scientific Laboratory. Page 115: Arms Control Association.

Chapter 12

Page 118: Indian Atomic Energy Commission. Page 120: Norsk Telegrambyra. Page 121: Carnegie Endowment for International Peace. Page 124 (Top): South America map by Arms Control Association; (Bottom): Brad Wye and the Arms Control Association.

Chapter 13

Page 126: Arms Control Association. Page 128: International Iran Times. Page 129: *Issues in Science and Technology*, Spring 1986. Page 131: Lynn R. Johnson, *Salt Lake Tribune*.

Chapter 14

Page 132: SovFoto. Page 134: 155mm Howitzer, US Army. Page 135: Brad Wye and the Arms Control Association. Page 136: US Air Force.

Chapter 15

Page 138: US Navy. Page 140: Department of Defense. Page 141 (Top): US Air Force; (Bottom): US Air Force. Page 143: *Science '85*. Page 144: US Army. Page 146 (Top): Tass; (Middle): Tass; (Bottom): Tass. Page 147 (Top): Associated Press/Worldwide Photo; (Middle): Tomayasu, US Air Force; (Bottom): Tomayasu, US Air Force. Page 148: US Congressional Delegation.

Index

The ARMS CONTROL ASSOCIATION

11 Dupont Circle, N.W., Washington, D.C. 20036 (202) 797-6450

OFFICERS

GERARD C. SMITH . . . . Chairman
SPURGEON M. KEENY, JR. . . . . President and Executive Director
BARRY E. CARTER . . . . Vice President and Treasurer
BETTY G. LALL . . . . Secretary
JOHN B. RHINELANDER . . . . General Counsel

BOARD OF DIRECTORS

JOSEPH CARDINAL BERNARDIN
Archbishop of Chicago

McGEORGE BUNDY
Professor of History, New York University
Former Special Assistant for National
   Security Affairs to President Kennedy
   and President Johnson

BARRY E. CARTER
Georgetown University Law Center
Former National Security Council Staff
   Member

WILLIAM T. COLEMAN, JR.
O'Melveny & Meyers
Former Secretary of Transportation

LLOYD CUTLER
Wilmer, Cutler & Pickering
Former Counsel to the President

SIDNEY D. DRELL
Deputy Director, Stanford Linear
   Accelerator

RALPH EARLE II
Former Chief SALT II Negotiator and
   Director, ACDA

RANDALL FORSBERG
Executive Director, Institute for
   Defense and Disarmament Studies

ADMIRAL NOEL GAYLER (USN, Ret.)
Former Commander-in-Chief, US
   Forces Pacific
Former Director, National Security
   Agency

MARVIN L. GOLDBERGER
Director, Institute for Advanced Study
Former Member of the President's
   Scientific Advisory Committee

BENJAMIN HUBERMAN
President, The Consultants International
   Group
Former Deputy Science Adviser to the
   President and Senior Staff Member,
   National Security Council

THOMAS L. HUGHES
President, Carnegie Endowment for
   International Peace

ROBERT JOHANSEN
Director of Graduate Studies,
   Institute of International Peace Studies,
   University of Notre Dame
Senior Fellow, World Policy Institute

SPURGEON M. KEENY, JR.
President and Executive Director, ACA
Former Deputy Director of ACDA

HENRY KENDALL
Professor, M.I.T.
Chairman, Union of Concerned Scientists

ARTHUR B. KRIM
Chairman of the Board, Orion Pictures
Former Member of General Advisory
   Committee on Arms Control and
   Disarmament

BETTY G. LALL
Senior Fellow and Director, Arms Control
   Verification Project, Council on Economic
   Priorities
Adjunct Professor, New York University
Former Staff Director, Senate
   Subcommittee on Disarmament

ROBERT S. McNAMARA
Former President, The World Bank
Former Secretary of Defense

WILLIAM F. McSWEENY
President, Occidental International
   Corporation
Executive Vice President, Occidental
   Petroleum

SAUL H. MENDLOVITZ
Professor, International Law,
   Rutgers University
Senior Fellow, World Policy Institute

EDWARD P. MORGAN
Author and News Commentator,
   "In the Public Interest"

**LT. GEN. ROBERT E. PURSLEY
(USAF, Ret.)**
President, Logistics Management Institute
Former Commander, US Forces, Japan
   and 5th Air Force

STANLEY R. RESOR
Debevoise and Plimpton
Former Undersecretary of Defense and
   Secretary of the Army

JOHN B. RHINELANDER
Shaw, Pittman, Potts, Trowbridge &
   Rhinelander
Former Undersecretary, HUD
Former Legal Adviser, SALT I

SARGENT SHRIVER
President, Special Olympics International
Of Counsel, Fried, Frank, Harris, Shriver
   & Jacobson
Former Ambassador to France
Former Special Assistant to the President
   and Director of the Peace Corps

MARSHALL SHULMAN
Professor Emeritus and Former Director
   of the Harriman Institute,
   Columbia University
Former Soviet Affairs Special Adviser to
   the Secretary of State

GERARD C. SMITH
Former Ambassador at Large and
   US Special Representative for
   Non-Proliferation Matters
Former Chief SALT I Negotiator and
   Director, ACDA

PAUL C. WARNKE
Clifford & Warnke
Former Chief SALT II Negotiator and
   Director, ACDA

DANIEL YANKELOVICH
Daniel Yankelovich Group, Inc.
President, The Public Agenda Foundation

Join the Arms Control Association

The Arms Control Association plays a leading role in promoting public understanding of effective arms control policies through its highly regarded press and public education programs and its service as the central clearinghouse for arms control information. ACA focuses these efforts on international agreements to control and reduce nuclear and conventional arms and to prevent the proliferation of nuclear weapons.

As an ACA member, you will receive *Arms Control Today*, the monthly journal that gives the latest, most informed view of developments in this vital field. ACA members also receive special Association publications.

We invite you to join our organization, to use our resources, and to share in the challenge of reducing the nuclear threat.

To join, simply clip out the order form and mail to the Arms Control Association. If you are already one of our valued members, please continue your support by renewing your membership.

❏ I would like an annual membership in the Arms Control Association. ($12.50 of my annual membership dues is for a one-year subscription to *Arms Control Today*.) Dues and contributions in excess of $12.50 are tax-deductible.

    ❏ $50 or more $_____ Contributing
    ❏ $25 Individual (US)
    ❏ $12.50 Student
    ❏ $40 International Associate

❏ I would like a one-year subscription to *Arms Control Today*. I do not wish to join the Association at this time.

    ❏ $25 Individual (US)
    ❏ $30 Institutional
    ❏ $40 International

❏ This is a renewal.

❏ Please send me _____ additional copies of *Arms Control and National Security: An Introduction* for $14.95 each, including postage and handling. Discounts are available for quantity orders. For information call ACA at (202) 797-6450.

❏ I am enclosing a check for $_____ payable to the Arms Control Association. (US funds only.)

Name _____

Organization _____

Address _____

City/State/ZIP_____

Mail to:
The ARMS CONTROL ASSOCIATION
11 Dupont Circle, N.W., Washington, D.C. 20036
(202) 797-6450